TWO ROADS
TO SUMTER

TWO
ROADS
TO
SUMTER

*by William and
Bruce Catton*

McGraw-Hill Book Company, Inc.

NEW YORK   TORONTO   LONDON

To David Bruce

[C O N T E N T S]

INTRODUCTION

The two cabins were less than one hundred miles apart, in what was then the half-settled wilderness of west-central Kentucky. There are monuments on both sites now, and historical markers, and museum-piece restorations of the frontier setting in which the two boys were born. The region still carries its indefinable air of history once in the making, and thoughtful tourists who make the pilgrimage to either spot will find much to contemplate. An ironic coincidence, surely—nothing more—that the two men who opposed each other as chief executives of a divided nation in 1861 should have their origins less than a year apart in the backwoods of Kentucky. Yet in the lives of Jefferson Davis and Abraham Lincoln, as in the fateful controversy that led their country into war, much that gave meaning was present in the rugged land from which they sprung.

The American Civil War is far too big to be explained solely in the lives of two men. The size of the struggle was greater than the size of any of the participants—except possibly for the hundreds of thousands of nameless Americans of both sections who carried most of the load and paid the ultimate price. Yet when one tries to see just how this war came about, why the people on both sides fought so hard and what the whole of it finally means, one does come back to the two protagonists, the two American presidents who faced one another in the most terrible war America has fought.

They were of their respective peoples, and they spoke for them; they were wholly representative, in their hopes, their achievements and their failures; and they came from the same place. They were two Kentuckians who at last came to speak for (and to demand much of) the two sections which began as one and which came to be so tragically hostile and in the blood and smoke of unlimited war laid the foundation for a new unity and a new definition of the meaning of American freedom.

Abraham Lincoln and Jefferson Davis did not bring the war about. They were, as the word went then, moderates, sharing a common vision of the ultimate value of an undivided country, hoping that the country could compose its differences without loss of blood. But the war came, partly in spite of these men and partly because of them, and when it came they fought one another, and led others to fight, so tenaciously that the nation had its most fearful trial by combat. Lincoln and Davis were both the leaders of their peoples and the victims of their times. Most men in the North and most men in the South unquestionably wanted to find some peaceful solution to the controversy that was splitting the country; beyond any doubt these two leaders wanted the same thing. The tragedy was that in the end the moderate way collapsed. The nation had stumbled into a situation where it was no longer possible to be moderate.

So the country tried to work out a solution by violence. The solution it finally got was imperfect and is today incomplete, and we still have problems. As we grapple with these problems we are driven to go back and try to see how the whole thing happened —to explore the terrible drift toward war, to try to understand why Americans a little more than a century ago defined freedom in ways so different that they had to fight. One thing we can see clearly; at least the business came from the heart. Somehow, in the very center of America, radically diverse understandings of the meaning of the American experiment took shape. These diverse understandings were built-in; they came out of what Americans were and hoped for; and when the showdown came no one quite knew how to reconcile them and work out a synthesis.

So these two moderate men, Abraham Lincoln and Jefferson Davis, became leaders in a war which was fought altogether without moderation. Perhaps one way to gain a comprehension of what happened then is to trace the parallel careers of these two men whose origins were so close and whose backgrounds were so similar. What follows here is an attempt to show how and why their paths went so far apart and at last met so tragically; an effort to see where and how their stars became so crossed.

Two Kentuckians: one went this way, the other went that way, and of the men who followed them 600,000 lost their lives. This book tries to examine what those separate ways were, why they were taken, and what they led toward.

[ONE]

LIKE A CROUCHING LION

Always America looked westward. The nation was built on hope, ambition, and a contradictory bundle of dreams, and the pattern seldom varied. Whether they came to worship God in a fresh atmosphere, or to find security and fortune from a continental supply of cheap land, or merely, as one sardonic New Englander put it, to catch fish, the men who first crossed the ocean and the men who followed or went beyond them in later years had their eyes on a spot real or imagined, but always somewhere over the western horizon. First it was the fringe of settlements along the Atlantic coast. Then it was the uncharted back country a few miles inland. By the middle of the eighteenth century the restless vanguard which always drew the nation westward in its wake was crossing the wooded Appalachians into the vast, rich basin of the Mississippi. Once this region took shape in men's imagination as the new American West, the country's future was assured.

For several generations—from the expulsion of Bourbon France as a New World power till the age of Andrew Jackson—the core of this new West was Kentucky. Kentucky in its heyday was both symbol and target of national growth, a vital focus and crossroad of American empire. Strung out along the south bank of the Ohio from the western Appalachians to the Mississippi, its dense forests and varied soil irregularly furrowed by a succession of rivers that coiled northward and westward into the Ohio, Kentucky was always a sought-after prize. It long was the "dark and bloody ground" of tribal struggle, and it remained a strategic bastion in a sequence of later contests: Briton and Frenchman, Indian and pioneer, rebel and redcoat, Whig and Democrat, and ultimately Northerner and Southerner vied for the region. Kentucky was always conscious of its importance. "Right here," one enthusiastic citizen proclaimed shortly after the Civil War, "in the very center of the Mississippi Valley, lying like a crouching lion, stretched east and west, is Kentucky, the thoroughfare of the continent."

Thoroughfare it was and had been, since before the Revolution. And in the characters and attitudes embraced by the widening human stream that flowed into and beyond Kentucky could be found all the tangled components of the American dream—what the new nation was and what it hoped to become, what it wanted and what it feared and what it ultimately got, the varied drives and cross-purposes that impelled the scattered population of thirteen seaboard commonwealths to straddle a continent in less than seventy-five years.

Every issue that the young republic would have to solve or compromise or learn to live with was paraded through Kentucky's early years. Fertile acres and overweening land hunger drew the speculator and the farmer westward through the Cumberland Gap, brought the lawyer after them to litigate happily through the maze of clouded titles, and made government land policy a matter of paramount concern. It was the promise of good land that brought Jefferson Davis's father and Abraham Lincoln's grandfather to Kentucky in the years following the Revolution—two more unwitting volunteers in the straggling procession of self-seeking individuals who took America with them as they moved. When little Jefferson was a mere toddler, and again when Abraham was a small boy, talk of even better land and better terms somewhere else—always land, always better terms, so often somewhere else—sent the Davis family out of Kentucky on its way South, and a few years later sent the Lincoln family out of

Kentucky on its way North. The Davises and the Lincolns had come, settled unknown to each other a few miles apart, and then moved on, repeating the familiar pattern of the westward movement. And within the same twelvemonth, during their sojourn in Kentucky, to each a son was born; from this obscure starting point the long trails to Richmond and Washington began.

Land hunger, a built-in hostility toward Englishmen and Indians, and rambunctious frontier nationalism inspired Kentucky's representatives in Congress to press America's maritime demands against Britain and chant "On to Canada!" until the desired war came in 1812. Davis and Lincoln were too young to remember such talk at the time, but in later years they heard older members of the family recall the excitement that gripped Kentucky's back settlements as the war fever mounted, and as a youngster in Mississippi Davis took pride in the fact that his three older brothers had gone off to fight. The buoyant nationalism and recurrent land-hunger remained: in 1846, their expansionist zeal having identified itself as the nation's manifest destiny, Kentuckians and other Westerners joyfully filled the ranks that wrested an empire from Mexico. Yet this same hotbed of nationalism, a few decades earlier, had toyed with the idea of quitting the Union in response to European blandishments, and had echoed Thomas Jefferson's hostility to the Sedition Act of 1798 by enunciating the principle of state sovereignty—with overtones of nullification—in the famous Kentucky Resolves.

Commercial growing pains after 1800 introduced the region to fierce battles over banking and currency. The interests of property and "sound money" collided with the impatient, credit-hungry promoters and speculators whose schemes were based on the notion that the supply of specie need have no bearing on the printing of bank notes. The tariff became a recurrent issue in the Bluegrass for decades after the War of 1812, if only because Kentucky's perennial favorite son chose to make it a part of his program. Henry Clay believed in protective tariffs and federal spending and the discernible outlines of a planned economy, and when young Lincoln entered politics in the eighteen-thirties, it was as a disciple of the magnetic Clay. When young Davis took the same step a few years later, be it noted, he did so as a believer in free trade and limited government, a follower of Jefferson, and Clay's opponent.

There was also the problem of transportation. Walled off by the mountains and remote from seaboard markets, Kentuckians quickly saw that the Mississippi River system had to be the major avenue and outlet for their products. The right to use this avenue, without interference, became a cornerstone of their policy as early as the seventeen-eighties. They also demanded the right to deposit goods for transshipment at New Orleans, and while this port and the entire west bank of the river remained in Spanish hands no Kentuckian could draw an easy breath. Whatever happened, Kentucky would follow the river to the sea.

Furthermore, it would withhold full allegiance from any government that failed to support this policy, and would object strenuously to any interference with the river traffic, all of which placed Kentucky at the very vortex of American politics and diplomacy in the post-Revolutionary era. For more than a decade after Yorktown the new nation was unable to bring matters west of the mountains under effective control. Many Kentuckians listened attentively as Spaniards and Frenchmen whispered grandly of new inland empires and unrestricted use of the great river whenever the western settlements chose to detach themselves from the Union and play international politics. Americans back east got the message. Statehood for Kentucky in 1792 and the purchase of Louisiana a decade later were direct outgrowths of this western concern for the vital outlet at New Orleans.

Kentucky's loyalty to the Union was assured from the moment the national government asserted its sovereignty in the West, but her citizens never forgot the river highway. Early in the new century the steamboat began its conquest of the western waters, and each time the busy craft whistled for a landing or nosed against a crowded levee the American interior moved a step closer to the markets of the world. The value of the great inland waterway became more apparent every year, and at midcentury, when a national crisis touched off rumbles of disunion in the angry

Gulf states, the most famous Kentuckian sounded a warning that brought the old Spanish problem up to date.

"My life upon it," said Henry Clay, speaking to the Senate before crowded galleries, "that the vast population which has already concentrated and will concentrate on the headwaters and the tributaries of the Mississippi will never give their consent that the mouth of that river shall be held subject to the power of any foreign State or community whatever. Such, I believe, would be the consequence of a dissolution of the Union . . ." Clay was the voice of Kentucky, and he had made the position clear.

Here was the roster of tangled, overlapping issues that confronted the growing republic: land, territorial expansion, Indians, nationalism, state rights, banking and currency, tariff, transportation. Less than half a century after its first settlement the Bluegrass had sounded nearly every note on the dissonant American scale.

And not least, Kentucky was a dwelling place for the institution of slavery.

There were slaves in Kentucky almost from the start, by virtue of her Virginia parentage. (Kentucky was a portion of the princely trans-Appalachian domain, including also the entire area now contained in the states of Ohio, Indiana, Illinois, Michigan, and Wisconsin, that the old royal charters enabled Virginia to claim.) After much effort, the new government managed to persuade Virginia and other seaboard states to relinquish their various western claims; the concept of the national domain, from which new and equal states would someday be created, was the great legacy that America's first government bequeathed to its successor when the reins were handed over in 1789.

Kentucky duly joined the Union under this concept in 1792, but only after several years as a sprawling, remote county of Virginia. As a result, slaveowners and their chattels were numbered in the tide of immigration from the Old Dominion, and the institution was well transplanted by the time the erstwhile county was ready for statehood. The opposition that existed was not strong enough to prevent the admission of Kentucky as a slave state.

But slavery in Kentucky was destined for a unique existence. Geography and circumstance had decreed that the Bluegrass would never be a western facsimile of the Old Dominion. The land and the way of life were different, and the peculiar institution was not cast in the tidewater mold. (Nor was it cast in the mold of the deep South, where cotton growing became a mania early in the nineteenth century.) As the Civil War would demonstrate, Kentucky was more western than southern.

Kentucky developed neither the single predominant staple nor the large plantation unit that formed the basis for slavery along the Atlantic and Gulf coastal plains. Instead, Kentuckians formed a diversified economy based upon numerous small or middle-sized farms and a variety of products. They raised tobacco, hemp, horses, mules, cattle, hogs, and cereal grains, and for every thousand-acre plantation on the tidewater model there were nearly four hundred farms in the twenty- to five hundred-acre category. Commerce and small industry also thrived; many quit the land to become boatbuilders, rivermen, millers, loggers, distillers, packers, and textile workers. The pattern was typically western, and Kentucky resembled its neighbors north of the Ohio more than its mother Virginia.

Slavery could exist in such a region, but it could never flourish as in central Alabama or coastal South Carolina or southside Virginia. In 1860 only seventy of Kentucky's 39,000 slaveholders owned more than fifty slaves, only seven owned more than a hundred, and the proportion of slaves to total population—about twenty per cent—had been decreasing since 1830. The typical agricultural unit was a small farm worked by free labor, as was the case with Abraham Lincoln's father, or by one or two, or at most a handful of slaves, as was the case with Jefferson Davis's father, who had brought a pair of field hands when he migrated from Georgia. Under these conditions slavery became diffuse and comparatively mild, with relatively few of the harsh trappings—large gangs, overseers, absentee owners—that came to typify it in other areas.

Citizens of Kentucky were never able, first or last, to close
ranks after the fashion of most Southern states and give slavery
their unqualified support. Sizable pockets of antipathy or indifference to slavery existed in several parts of the South—in eastern
Tennessee, for example, and in the western portions of Maryland,
Virginia, and North Carolina, where the number of slaveowners
and Negroes was quite small. But Kentucky's ambivalence on
the subject was distributed throughout the state, as apt to exist
in the rich tobacco, horse, and hemp country around Lexington
as in the isolated mountain districts. Nowhere else in the nation
was the entire, broad spectrum of American attitudes on this
explosive question so clearly reflected—from the violent denunciations of unqualified abolitionists through varying bands of dislike,
indifference, and support to the outright worship of the cotton
belt variety.

(Attitudes elsewhere, of course, did not become hard and fast
until relatively late. They were fluid and uncertain during and
after the Revolution, and they remained so until the thirties and
forties, when an awakening conscience in the North confronted
the waxing power of King Cotton just as Manifest Destiny was
rolling into new territories and forcing men to decide just how
far slavery was going to follow the flag. Then the lines hardened,
fatally. But in Kentucky the uncertainty was fairly constant, almost as marked in the eighteen-fifties as seventy-five years before.)

Kentucky's confusion was understandable. Slaveowners came
from Virginia as a matter of course, but the thought currents that
flowed westward with the early settlers through Cumberland Gap
or down the Ohio were potent and disturbing. Kentucky's early
years coincided with the golden age of Virginia's intellectual and
political pre-eminence, when the enlightened influence of Washington, Jefferson, Patrick Henry, and George Mason was most
deeply felt. Kentucky was founded during one revolution and
achieved statehood during another, and many who followed Daniel
Boone's forest trail to the Bluegrass were keenly aware of the
strivings in the Continental Congress and the French National
Assembly. The Declaration of Independence and the Rights of
Man were more than catchwords to this generation. Beside such

a heritage, slavery was a fundamental anachronism. From the very outset, hostility was transplanted side by side with slavery in Kentucky.

The rich infusion of Virginia blood that flowed through its quondam western county threatened slavery with a second solvent. Kentucky was never the tidewater once removed; it sounded no more than the barest echo of the smiling, languid region where the Old World ideal of a landed aristocracy had perhaps come closest to fulfillment in the less hospitable American atmosphere. Kentucky drew its sustenance instead from the Virginia of Piedmont and Valley and Blue Ridge, the rolling wooded up-country west of tidewater. Here the rivers and the way of life were swifter and more tumultuous, the farm units smaller, the institution of slavery less firmly entrenched. Some of these Virginians had simply moved west from the Bay region at one time or another, in search of fresh soil and elbow room, and several had amassed large estates after the tidewater model. The majority, however, were plain folk of relatively modest origin—yeomen farmers, frontier lawyers, ministers, artisans, tradesmen.

And a great many of them were newcomers, part of the migratory flood of the eighteenth century that had spilled southward out of Pennsylvania into the western valleys of Maryland, Virginia, and the Carolinas. Among these were many Ulster Scots who had emigrated after 1700 and tended to keep moving once they arrived, together with a scattering of Welshmen, Quakers, Irishmen, Swiss, and Germans, and a few uprooted Puritan New Englanders. What these folk tended to have in common, along with a recurrent wanderlust, were ambition, dogged courage, the capacity for hard work, an unalloyed Protestantism of the soul-searching and querulous variety, and an innate, pugnacious irreverence for such Old World trappings as caste, rank, privilege, or authority. They were rugged individualism incarnate, and the stamp of their spirit upon the land was indelible.

In the move to Kentucky these people were both vanguard and vital center. Among them was stern-visaged, redheaded George Rogers Clark, from Charlottesville in the heart of the Jefferson country. Clark reached Kentucky during the early years of the Revolution, led a tatterdemalion band of frontier riflemen into the trackless country north of the Ohio, and in effect took the trans-Appalachian West away from Great Britain after an unbelievable campaign. Among them, also, was a distant kinsman of Abraham Lincoln's named Daniel Boone. Born in eastern Pennsylvania of Quaker parents, Boone accompanied his family in a southwesterly drift that included a twelve-month stay in the Shenandoah Valley and ended in the wild Yadkin River country of frontier North Carolina, whence young Daniel set his eyes on Kentucky.

After the Revolution many of Virginia's war veterans, armed with land warrants or general restlessness, set out confidently for the Bluegrass. Joining this movement were a Major Crittenden and one Colonel Richard Taylor. The Major's son was John Jordan Crittenden, whose eminent career in state and national politics would be capped by the eloquent, vain attempt to compromise away the Civil War in 1861; his own boys, Thomas and George, symbolically took opposite sides in the struggle. Colonel Taylor's son was a strong-willed youngster named Zachary, who would someday leave his calling card in Mexico and ride military fame into the White House amid the crescendo of sectional conflict.

One could never predict just how the Virginia seedlings were going to grow in the rich Kentucky soil. An attorney named John Breckinridge moved to the Bluegrass from the upper Shenandoah Valley in 1793. He soon became a power in Kentucky politics and won the confidence of Thomas Jefferson, with whom he collaborated on an important project. The two drafted a set of resolutions protesting the Federalist-sponsored Sedition Act of 1798, and in the same year, under Breckinridge's expert guidance, the Kentucky legislature passed the entire set: the Kentucky Resolutions were a ringing state-rights manifesto that would eventually become one of the cornerstones in the South's political philosophy.

The Breckinridge family remained strong in Kentucky. One of John's grandsons, John Cabell Breckinridge, who served in both Houses of Congress and as vice president under James Bu-

chanan, ran for President on a Southern-rights ticket in 1860 and
shortly afterward quit his native state to join the Confederacy,
where combat service, the rank of major general, and a cabinet
post awaited him. But a second branch of the family pointed
in a different direction. Robert J. Breckinridge, son of the elder
John and an uncle of John Cabell, was an outspoken, influential
Presbyterian divine who provided the antislavery forces in Kentucky with forthright leadership and later became one of Abraham Lincoln's mainstays in the touch-and-go battle to keep Kentucky in the Union in 1861.

Or there were the Clays, who defy easy analysis. Henry, the
most famous of them, came to Kentucky at the age of twenty
from the ragged Hanover County region a few miles north of
Richmond. In 1797, with a log-cabin-schoolhouse education and
no family connections, "without patrons, without the favors or
countenance of the great or opulent," as Clay himself rather
grandly put it, the youth opened a law practice in Lexington on
the basis of his newly won Virginia license and a brief legal training under two of Richmond's most eminent jurists. Clay also had
an inexhaustible fund of political shrewdness, native wit, oratorical
skill, ambition, and personal charm, and he soon embarked upon
a magnificent career in national politics. Kentuckians worshipped
"Harry of the West," always, and Americans learned to love and
respect him—if they never fully trusted him—and before he re-
tired Henry Clay had achieved much: a plantation in the Bluegrass, fame, honor, high office, power, the nation's undying grati-
tude for his role as compromiser during recurrent sectional crises—
everything, in fact, save his fondest goal. Though he pursued it
avidly and with near success for twenty-five years, the presidency
always eluded his grasp, and Clay's many triumphs were constantly tinged with the one great disappointment.

Another branch of the family also left its mark in Kentucky.
Green Clay, an older cousin of Henry's, left Virginia in 1777, aged
twenty, with a degree of skill at land surveying which quickly
won him power and fortune in the title-clouded scramble for Kentucky homesteads. Within a few years surveyor Clay had become
a man of wealth and influence, a slaveowner and gentleman planter

with a fine estate in Madison County and a voice that commanded respect throughout the Bluegrass.

In 1810 Green Clay had a son. Surely no elaborate psychological interpretation, no lengthy analysis of genes and chromosomes, can altogether explain Cassius Marcellus Clay. Born into Kentucky's new aristocracy, this most bizarre member of the Clay tribe tacked controversy onto his coat of arms and carved a jagged trail through the social and political life of his state. Cash Clay was sheer love of combat and raw frontier courage, a sort of one-man Donnybrook, spendidly equipped and eternally ready to rock the boat.

The antislavery movement gave focus and significance to this turbulent career. At Yale Cassius Clay was exposed to the scorching message of William Lloyd Garrison, and the stocky, firm-jawed young man returned to Kentucky permanently infected with the virus of abolitionism. He immediately began to sound forth about it, verbally and in print—even establishing a small antislavery newspaper—and because tact and soft words and moderation formed no part of his repertoire he made bitter enemies, in which he exulted. The storm center of Kentucky's acrimonious debate over slavery thereafter accompanied Cash Clay. Nothing could silence him, although many attempts were made. His weapons included a sharp pen, a sharper tongue, and an assortment of frontier persuaders that ranged from pearl-handled bowie knives to small cannon. These were not stage props; his labors were constantly punctuated with physical violence, and he bore the scars of frequent murderous assaults—always giving better than he got, and never in the slightest degree intimidated. Neither before, during, nor after the Civil War (he survived until 1903, a defiant and untamed figure to the end), was Kentucky allowed to forget Cassius M. Clay.

Often the trail originated much farther to the eastward. James Guthrie's father came to America from County Cork in 1774, settling near the headwaters of the Potomac River in northwestern Virginia. Fourteen years later he was in Kentucky, where he served in the militia, entered politics, and won a seat in the state leg-

islature. His son, born in 1792, applied his talents to the business
world with marked success. By the eighteen-fifties, the blunt, un-
prepossessing James Guthrie was a power in the land: wealthy
banker and railroad builder, Secretary of the Treasury under Buchanan, mentioned frequently as a possible presidential candidate
on the Democratic ticket in 1860.

Most important, he was the president of the Louisville & Nashville Railroad, a strategic route that became of enormous military
value when the war broke out. As Union sentiment gradually
triumphed in Kentucky in 1861, Guthrie elected to stay with his
railroad and put it to work for the Northern cause (knowing that
the Lincoln government was apt to take it away from him if he
showed any lack of zeal). The association was highly profitable
to all concerned. The Louisville & Nashville made huge profits
from four years of swollen military traffic, and the route remained
indispensable to Federal armies throughout the War in the West.

Also from Ireland, descended from an Englishman who had
gone there to uphold Oliver Cromwell's iron authority a century
before, came James Birney, a runaway still in his teens. Young
Birney acquired a small stake by working in a Philadelphia store,
then made the long trip to Kentucky in 1788, where he opened
a store of his own, established a bagging factory and a rope walk,
and prospered. He married well, bought slaves, built a country
estate, and had a son: James Gillespie Birney, born in 1792. His
father's growing wealth and social standing provided the boy with
a comfortable childhood, a good education, and bright prospects
for a successful career of his own. After a few years of law practice, planting, and politics in Kentucky and northern Alabama
the younger Birney, a slaveowner by inheritance and by purchase,
took a long look at the institution and decided that he had to
fight it. Within two years, beginning in 1832, he liquidated his
holdings in Alabama, emancipated his slaves, and moved steadily
up the antislavery scale. Starting out as an advocate of Negro
colonization—young America's blind, delusive hope that the race
problem could be solved by removing one of the races—Birney
next embraced the idea of gradual emancipation and finally
became an outright abolitionist.

Birney was not cut from the harsh, sharp-edged pattern that a consistently bad press has succeeded in stamping on most workers in the abolition movement. Calm and judicious, he seemed to radiate "the utmost candor, a simple, earnest intent in pursuit of truth, a quick conscience, perfect fairness—the traits of a mind that *could not be partisan*." To be sure, Birney was thenceforth partisan enough in the antislavery cause, but he always avoided the angry covenant-with-death fulminations of William Lloyd Garrison and never laced his zeal with intemperance or hysteria. From Kentucky, where despite a few stalwart supporters his earnest message met with hostility, Birney moved to Ohio and later New York and thence into national politics; twice a presidential candidate and long a leader of the small antislavery party that helped keep the movement alive in its early years, his role in stirring Northern opinion on the slavery question was a large one.

The voice of New England was occasionally heard in Kentucky. Amos Kendall, whose exodus began in Dunstable, Massachusetts, moved from Kentucky's banking and currency struggle into the upper echelons of national politics under the banner of Andrew Jackson. After serving prominently in Jackson's Kitchen Cabinet and contributing much to the creation and early guidance of the Democratic Party machine, the astute Kendall became a successful patent lawyer and survived to give counsel to the Union cause and its President during the Civil War.

The Lincolns also extended back to New England. Abraham Lincoln's grandfather and namesake moved to Kentucky in 1782 from Rockingham County in western Virginia, itself a way station on a family trail that led back northeastward through Pennsylvania and New Jersey to seventeenth-century Massachusetts. Indians killed the elder Abraham within two years of his arrival in the Bluegrass; his infant son Thomas was raised by kinfolk, later took up farming in the half-settled region south of Louisville and drifted unknowingly and aimlessly toward the momentous log-cabin birth-date in 1809.

And, sometimes, the route to Kentucky dipped far to the southward. Around the middle of the eighteenth century Evan Davis, of Welsh descent, journeyed from his native Pennsylvania to the new colony of Georgia. His only son, Samuel Emory Davis, was born there in 1756. When the time came young Samuel joined the War for Independence and fought against the British in South Carolina and Georgia, mustering out as a captain and receiving a two-hundred-acre tract near Augusta in reward for his services. Marrying a Scotch-Irish girl he had met in South Carolina during the war, Samuel Davis settled on his new tract, acquired a couple of field hands, and devoted himself in earnest to farming and child raising.

A decade and five children later, in 1793, Davis took his family and his slaves to Kentucky, whence tales of varied opportunity and fertile acres were circulating on the Atlantic seaboard. The Davises settled on a heavily forested six-hundred-acre tract in the southwestern part of the new state, between the settlements at Hopkinsville and Bowling Green. While Sam Davis, aided by the Negroes and the older boys, cleared land and planted small stands of wheat and corn and began experiments in tobacco culture and horse raising, new Davis children continued to arrive. Four boys and a girl had made the trip from Georgia; four more girls appeared at approximately two-year intervals on the new Kentucky homestead. The tenth and last child, named Jefferson in honor of Samuel Davis's political hero, was born on June 3, 1808.

The fathers of the two Civil War presidents were by all odds the least noteworthy among these new Kentuckians. History does not tell us much about Samuel Emory Davis and Thomas Lincoln, and it would not notice them at all but for their sons; in every other respect these oddly parallel lives were remarkably undistinguished. Restless, vaguely discontented spirits, hard working and reasonably full of thwarted ambition, Sam Davis and Tom Lincoln were thoroughly typical of the unpretentious, unspectacular multitudes that formed the American bedrock.

(Such men are perhaps closer to the mainstream of our existence than we realize. Understandably enough, Americans have always concentrated on the success story. The other side of the coin may be worth looking at—not the resounding failures or the congenital misfits but the unsung, average folk whose lives tell a quiet story

of ambition gently trailing off into obscurity. America is equally
a tale of might-have-beens and used-to-bes, of ghost towns and
shuttered mills, abandoned farms and weed-grown railbeds, and
a thousand other evidences of blunted hopes and dreams gone
sour. Slow heartbreak and continued frustration have gone into
the national fiber along with triumph and achievement, and as
often as not the bright vision simply went to seed before its
ripening.)

Of such, the eminent few and the unknown many, was Kentucky made. The settlers kept coming, and the scattered villages
and isolated farming communities grew and thrived, and Kentucky
mushroomed from remote county to prosperous commonwealth.
Prominent among its higher values was an overriding love of
Union, a conscious and lasting sense of identity with the interests
of the nation. In certain respects Kentuckians came to share the
general Southern outlook: they believed in the principle of state
rights and resented Yankee abolitionism. But they were more
Western than Southern, and because their feelings about slavery
were always ambivalent they never let this or any other institution dilute the highly concentrated frontier patriotism that typified the American West. As sectional conflict loomed, their primary concern was always that the Union be maintained; the
solution to any problem, even that of slavery, must be found
within the national framework, never outside it.

Kentucky thus became and long remained the center of compromise sentiment. For decades her important spokesmen strove to
mediate between North and South. They helped produce the settlements that temporarily resolved the Missouri controversy in
1820, the tariff dispute in 1833, and the territorial conflict in 1850,
and the earnest voice of compromise was still emanating from
the Bluegrass even after the battle lines began to form in the
spring and summer of 1861. Nowhere was the awful tragedy of
civil conflict more apparent, and at first the state would have
none of it. When it finally became clear that neutrality was
impossible there were many who cast their lot with the Confed-

eracy, but the agonized majority gave varying degrees of support to the Federal cause. In the last extremity, the Union was more important than state rights, or slavery, or anything else.

Kentucky's Unionism was an indissoluble blend of material interest and emotional attachment. Her citizens shared the pragmatic American view, born of frontier necessity, that the national government existed to serve the people—in the direct form, if need be, of land grants or aid to transportation projects; the government had on occasion responded to this sentiment. In part, then, loyalty to the nation was an exchange for services rendered or services sought.

Economically, the state was tied to all parts of the country, and disunion was bound to damage the swelling commercial arteries that crisscrossed the rich Ohio Valley. The Mississippi River remained vitally important. Kentucky livestock, whiskey, grain, tobacco, and hempen products were sold in the deep South and the industrial Northeast. After 1850 the railroad pushed beyond the Appalachians and began to reorient the Middle West toward the eastern seaboard. Trade with nearby northern neighbors flowed back and forth across the Ohio, and manufactured goods from the mills in New England and Pennsylvania rolled westward along the new rail lines to stock Kentucky's markets. The true meaning of all this was grasped more widely here than anywhere else. The economy was urgently insisting that the country remain united, and to Kentuckians, at least, the alternative was clear. It meant ruin.

And yet love of Union went far beyond federal aid and commercial profit. The nation had come to symbolize everything that really mattered to these energetic Westerners, and Fourth of July orators evoked an instant and heartfelt response. Responding to all the familiar catchwords—democracy, liberty, opportunity— knowing by personal experience that beneath the verbiage there was substance, they had come forward with a rush whenever the national destiny seemed at stake: in 1775, in 1812, in 1846, against red men and Britishers and Mexicans and any combination of foes that threatened to arise.

These people were part of something important. Tilled acres and town meetings, laden steamboats and small colleges and rural churches were ultimately dependent upon a great experiment in popular government that must at all costs be preserved and extended. Long before he put it into words, Kentuckians had identified themselves with what Lincoln in wartime would call "the last, best hope of earth," and when he closed his first inaugural with an appeal to "the mystic chords of memory, stretching from every battlefield and patriot grave," men in the Bluegrass knew exactly what he meant.

Ardent nationalism had put down roots everywhere, but the distinctive Kentucky brand had spread far beyond her borders by the eighteen-fifties. The state was both way station and final stopping place in the restless march of settlement, and in a real sense the sprawling heartland of midwestern America was simply Kentucky writ large. Hundreds of thousands of her citizens had moved north of the Ohio and west of the Mississippi between 1800 and 1860, and the Kentucky state of mind was pervasive over a broad area. The extended version included Missouri, the southern halves of Ohio, Indiana, and Illinois, and western Virginia (which became a separate state during the Civil War, so far had its people drifted in sentiment and orientation from the parent commonwealth). In 1861 the white population of this area was almost equal to that of the Confederacy. The outcome of the war would depend in large part upon what this self-conscious borderland might do, as Presidents Lincoln and Davis knew.

Significantly, Lincoln remained a citizen of this greater Kentucky all his life, while Davis's associations with his native state and its attitudes were transient and relatively brief. Still a youngster when his family drifted northward from Kentucky into southern Indiana, Lincoln was just approaching manhood when a later move took them to central Illinois. This was the typical pattern of Kentucky emigration, and the people young Abraham knew in all of his later homes were similar in background and outlook to his father's erstwhile neighbors in the Bluegrass. Their attitudes were filtered and processed by the innermost workings of his own restless mind and, with a few twists added, these attitudes were clearly visible in Lincoln the man.

The Davises, on the other hand, left Kentucky much farther behind, and they left as they had entered it—on a trail leading South. Little Jefferson was less than two years old when the family moved to Mississippi. Aside from brief visits, he returned only twice: in 1815, for two years at a boys' school in Springfield (a bare thirty miles east of the Hardin County farm that Thomas Lincoln was even then about to vacate in favor of Indiana), and again in 1821, for three years of college in Lexington. The exposure was relatively brief, but young Davis made some lasting friends during his stay in Lexington, and a recognizable bit of Kentucky seems to have rubbed off on him.

This much, certainly, rubbed off on both of them, and it smacked strongly of the Ohio Valley: Jefferson Davis and Abraham Lincoln were patriots whose devotion to the Union ran deep. Each would serve this country according to his lights, and here, at the very end, the trails parted. For Jefferson Davis's brand of patriotism was inextricably bound up with the principle—by no means alien to Kentucky—of state sovereignty. Both the man and his native commonwealth denied that inherent conflict existed between nationalism and state rights, and both hoped until the last that such conflict might be avoided. When it came, most of Kentucky went one way while Davis went the other, casting his lot with the seceded states because he now felt that the Union he once loved had become a threat to those fundamental liberties it had formerly protected.

There was the point. To Abraham Lincoln, in 1860, the Union still inscribed upon its banners all that was fundamental and worthwhile, and his devotion was only strengthened when state sovereignty became the last refuge for the institution of slavery. On this latter subject Lincoln had gone, albeit far more cautiously, the way of Cassius Clay. Davis had merely gone to Mississippi, where the right to own slaves was first taken for granted, then fiercely defended, and finally enshrined. To Davis, who had, unlike Lincoln, grown up with slaves about the household and saw no reason to question so familiar a relationship, the institution was truly benevolent—a "positive good." He faced the question as forthrightly as Lincoln did, and with equal conviction. Freedom, said the Kentuckian gone south, belongs only to those capable of mastering it—in other words, to the white man—and is none the less precious for that. If freedom means anything, said the Kentuckian gone north, sooner or later it has to go across the board.

Kentucky—and the nation as a whole, in fact—stood closer to the Davis view in 1861. But a majority in Kentucky, as in the nation, would choose to battle for the Union rather than against it, and as wartime leader they had elevated a man who knew exactly why the Union was worth saving. Having contributed patriotic Americans to both the Union and the Confederate White Houses in 1861, the state ended by fighting a little harder for the man whose patriotism could not be separated from the notion that freedom is for everybody. When the test came, most citizens of Kentucky, like the majority of Americans, would shun the implications but accept the principle as truth.

[T W O]

THE SHAPING YEARS

The two trails that originated so close together in frontier Kentucky took off in opposite directions almost immediately, the one southward to Louisiana and Mississippi in 1810, the other northward into Indiana in 1816. Before the sustained, climactic confrontation in 1861 these paths converged—never quite touching—on two occasions, both mildly symbolic. In 1832 young Jefferson Davis, of the United States regulars, trim and correct in his lieutenant's uniform, and young Abraham Lincoln, volunteer captain of militia, familiarly rawboned and lanky in ill-fitting homespun, took part in the campaign against Black Hawk's uprising in the upper Mississippi Valley. This was the last significant Indian campaign east of the Mississippi, inevitable climax of a two-century retreat before the uncompromising advance of white civilization. For the next half century the western tribes would impede and interrupt this advance on the Great Plains and in the Rocky Mountain plateaus, but with the capture of Black Hawk the settled, populous half of the country could rest secure in the knowledge that scalping parties and Indian alarms were part of a chapter that was closed.

Over a decade later, in the middle forties, the disparate careers of Lincoln and Davis angled into proximity once more. War was

[24]

again the occasion, this time with Mexico. Another civilization, far less primitive than Black Hawk's but equally overmatched, had taken alarm at the continental appetite of American expansionists. War between Mexico and the United States broke out in 1846, ostensibly over a strip of disputed boundary along the Rio Grande and more fundamentally over which nation would ultimately lay title to the vast southwestern empire that stretched from Texas to the California coast. On the American side the conflict was attended by a political debate of ominous proportions. The United States entered this war confidently and won it handily, but in the midst of her preparations and her victory celebrations was the slavery question.

The Mexican War brought Lincoln and Davis onto the national scene for the first time. They served in successive Congresses. A Democrat, Davis supported the war in Congress and left Washington to fight in it, emerged a military hero, and came back to the capital in 1847 to serve in the United States Senate. A Whig, Lincoln followed the party line and criticized the war, lost support at home as a result, and did not even seek re-election in 1848. He left Washington to face the dim obscurity of a local law practice in distant Illinois.

The two paths had diverged once again, in more ways than one. The Kentucky cabins were far behind both men, yet by the late forties Jefferson Davis alone had measurably transcended his backwoods origins. For him college had been followed by West Point, military service in a variety of frontier outposts, a plantation in Mississippi, social standing, Congress, military glory, and a Senate seat. Lincoln, drifting with his family from Indiana to Illinois as a young man, could look back upon the barest rudiments of schooling, a succession of humdrum jobs—farm laborer, flatboatman, rail splitter, storekeeper, postmaster, surveyor's assistant—followed by a fitful law practice, four terms in the lower house of the Illinois legislature, and a pointedly brief and undistinguished term in the national Congress. His future looked every bit as uncertain as his past.

But the Mexican War, which had applied so marked a turn to these two oddly assorted careers, had also injected national politics with the fateful controversy that would ultimately rewrite the destiny of both.

From the very outset, the circumstances of environment and fortune that operated on the two Kentucky youths were profoundly different. Samuel Davis was always a cut above Tom Lincoln in terms of social standing, education, and inner fibre; the Davises were not gentry, exactly, but they were of the solid, ambitious, yeoman stock from which second-generation gentry constantly emerged. So, too, in fact, were the Lincolns: perhaps it was the elder Abraham's death that removed the fine cutting edge from Thomas Lincoln, that permeated this vaguely discontented spirit with indecision and an appearance of gears that did not quite mesh. Whatever the cause, Tom Lincoln's repeated moves in search of the better life had a drifting, rootless quality, while Samuel Davis's quest smacked of purpose and resolve.

To both men, in any case, Kentucky eventually lost its appeal. Intrigued by the stories of good land and bright prospects that circulated upward from the Mississippi delta in the early years of the century, Samuel Davis sold his Kentucky homestead in 1810 and packed family and belongings into wagons for an eight-hundred-mile trek to the southward. He first located along the Bayou Teche in eastern Louisiana, a moist, well-watered region where fertile soil was accompanied by a plague of malarial mosquitoes; within a year he transferred northward across the Louisiana border to Wilkinson County in the southwestern corner of Mississippi, about twenty miles east of the great river.

In this wild, luxuriant region, underlaid with rich, alluvial soil and overhung with a profuse, subtropical foliage of cypress, magnolia, live oak, and Spanish moss that gave the ante-bellum South so much of its legendary flavor, Sam Davis had found the comfortable base for his infant son's rise to prominence and fame. Mississippi was still a territory in 1811, six years away from statehood but already undergoing the boom that would carve another rich commonwealth out of the retreating wilderness. In the ultimate sense this may have been, as the poet described it, "tropic empire seeking the warm sea, last foray of aristocracy," but such illusions would come later; the rank and file of newcomers to the Gulf coastal plain were largely motivated by a hardheaded, sharp-eyed, workaday realism that kept its visions at arm's length. If he could, a man simply went where the prospects seemed most inviting and tried his hand at whatever paid the best.

In the America of James Madison and James Monroe, and for several decades thereafter, this was very apt to mean cotton. Cotton: infinitely marketable item in the booming mill towns of Lancashire and New England, soon endowed with regal adjective, at once a business and a necessity and a way of life.

Samuel Davis's share in this rapid frontier expansion was char-acteristically modest; it was an elder brother, not the father, who blocked out the distant upper reaches of young Jefferson's future. In Wilkinson County Sam Davis built his last home, a spacious, one-and-a-half-story frame house with plastered hall and wide veranda, embroidered by orchard and flower garden. For its day this was solid comfort by any standard, and in frontier Missis-sippi it was tantamount to luxury, but Sam Davis's prosperity had reached its peak. His career as cotton planter had begun rela-tively late. Fifty-six when he moved to Wilkinson County, the elder Davis worked his fields and his handful of slaves for thirteen years and watched eminence and wealth come to more fortunate neighbors who had started with no more than he. It rankled. In 1823, about a year before his death, the discontented old pioneer set out on one last venture in the pursuit of fortune, making the arduous journey to Philadelphia in a vain attempt to claim a share in his grandfather's estate. While on this final mission he wrote young Jefferson a confused letter in which despair and agitation of mind were clearly evident. Samuel Davis had gone farther and searched harder than Thomas Lincoln in pursuit of a higher self-imposed goal, but whatever it was had more or less impartially eluded both.

Sam Davis was fully able, however, to provide his youngest son with as good an education as the American West could offer. For Jefferson, two years in a local log school were followed, in 1815, by a trip to Kentucky for enrollment in a Dominican Boys' School —of sufficient repute, apparently, to overcome any scruples that his father, a confirmed Baptist, might have had about sending a boy of seven to a Catholic institution so many miles from home. It was quite an undertaking, and on the seven-hundred-mile jaunt young Davis began gathering his first retainable impressions of the country's scope, variety, and raw energy. He traveled in the keeping of one Major Hinds, family friend and veteran of the War of 1812. The high spot of the trip was a visit in Nashville with Andrew Jackson, under whom Hinds had fought at New Orleans. After two years of learning English, Latin, and general discipline from the diligent friars, Davis returned home by steamboat down the Ohio and Mississippi—this last an adventure in itself, in one of the rickety, smoke-belching, combustible craft that were just beginning to rewrite the history of the American interior.

Mississippi provided a boys' boarding school, then an academy in nearby Woodville, for the next four years of Jefferson's school career, and in 1821, just turned thirteen, the boy prepared to leave home once more. He was now, in the opinion of his local mentors, ready for college, and his father again looked to Kentucky for a suitable institution. He chose Transylvania, in Lexington, already forty years old and easily the finest school west of the mountains, its claim to university status enforced by colleges of medicine, law, and theology, its faculty recruited from Harvard, Yale, the British Isles, and France. Old Sam Davis had always believed, somewhat bitterly, that knowledge was power ("the want of which has brought mischief and misery on your father in his old age," he would write in that last, despairing letter), and he was determined that this deficiency would never impede his son's progress. Three years later, at the end of his junior year at Transylvania and a bare three days after his father's death, Jefferson Davis accepted an appointment to the United States Military Academy at West Point.

The good fortune that had always stayed just out of old Samuel's reach was smiling in earnest upon his youngest son. When Jefferson Davis left Lexington for West Point in the late summer of 1824 he was just sixteen, a handsome, robust, blue-eyed youth with poise, confidence, and an abundance of quiet charm. Although reserved in manner, with a degree of self-control that would achieve stoic quality in later years, the new cadet was by no means the thin-lipped monument of austerity in cold marble that gazes haughtily from the wartime portraits. (This latter-day image of frozen aloofness was always no more than a mask, beneath which were passion and sensitivity of Lincolnesque proportions—unless it can be argued, as one might, that a mask so tightly worn and so uniformly presented to the outside world is a fundamental part of the man, after all.) Young Davis's unimpeachable dignity was tempered by wit and warmth and a lingering fondness for youthful escapades. He had performed creditably at Transylvania. People liked and respected him, impressed not only by charm and good manners but by the obvious intelligence of an alert and active mind. There were, it seemed clear, the makings of a bright future here.

And he was headed for West Point. The Academy on the Hudson was a bare twenty years old, but the quality of instruction and training that it offered, notably in the increasingly important engineering and technical fields, had already given it a high standing among the general run of American colleges. The youth's decision to make West Point the capstone of an already impressive schooling reveals the firm hand of his eldest brother, whose influence on Jefferson's career was of surpassing importance from that time forward.

The first of Samuel's children, twenty-four years older than Jefferson, Joseph Emory Davis had moved rapidly and with quiet competence toward the high station his father had vainly sought. Joseph came of age when the family was in Kentucky. By the time young Jefferson was immersed in his studies at Transylvania Joseph had become a highly successful and influential member of the Mississippi bar. He was prominent in the drafting of the Constitution under which the state joined the Union in 1817, and in the mid-twenties he was wealthy enough to purchase several thousand acres of land south of Vicksburg and undertake a new career as slaveowner and cotton planter in the upper echelons of Mississippi's self-made aristocracy.

The power and influence that Joseph Davis had so abundantly

acquired could now be brought to bear in his younger brother's behalf. It was undoubtedly the brother and not the father whose connections secured the cadetship at West Point, in a day when competition for each appointment was keen. It was certainly Joseph who persuaded his brother to accept this appointment; Jefferson, it appears, had his eye on the study of law at the new University of Virginia. Neither West Point itself nor the prospect of a military career had much appeal for him, and his reluctant acceptance of the cadetship came only after Joseph promised that a transfer to Virginia would be forthcoming if Jefferson were dissatisfied with the Military Academy at the end of his first year. The youth gave in. The only consolation he could find, as he prepared to enter the institution that would shape so many of his future activities, was that his friend and hero of Transylvania days, handsome Albert Sidney Johnston of Kentucky, had gone to West Point two years earlier and would be there to greet him.

No such academic choices confronted young Abraham Lincoln, whose formal schooling—acquired in bits and pieces under an assortment of back-country teachers in Kentucky and Indiana, the total instruction adding up to less than a year—was well ended when Jefferson Davis reluctantly assented to a trial at West Point. Perhaps this particular contrast, for all its sharpness, is less important than it appears. Davis was, to be sure, a well-educated man by contemporary standards. His intellectual curiosity, which seems to have been no more than average in pre-college years, was clearly stimulated by exposure to higher learning, and the omnivorous reading that he began at Transylvania would remain a lifelong habit. College acquainted him with a breadth of literary, historical, and philosophical classics which Lincoln, reading strictly on his own, could discover only piecemeal and by accident. Davis's intellectual awareness was further heightened by formal instruction in a variety of subjects that ranged from trigonometry and surveying through history and philosophy to Latin and Greek (his knowledge of the latter so impressing the officials at West Point that a large portion of his entrance examination was apparently waived).

The curriculum at Transylvania brings into bold relief the well-worn image of young Lincoln in the backwoods snatching every idle moment from axe or plow to pore over *Robinson Crusoe* or Scott's *Lessons in Elocution* or Weems' *Life of Washington*. The Indiana of Lincoln's boyhood contained few books, and his reading was confined to the stray volumes that occasionally turned up in nearby frontier homes: the measure both of this scarcity and of Lincoln's appetite is most terrifyingly illustrated by his painstaking absorption, while still in his teens, of a five-hundred-page edition of the *Revised Laws of Indiana*. In a way this is part of the point. The boy Lincoln was a bright youngster with a fund of intellectual curiosity that was almost consuming; he learned the rudiments of reading before he was seven years old, and acquired on his own a voracious hunger for the printed word that antedated and equalled, if it did not surpass, Transylvania's legacy to Jefferson Davis.

All Lincoln lacked was access. In the eighteen-thirties both young men continued to devour reading matter—Davis in the new plantation carved from his brother's vast holdings along the Mississippi, Lincoln amid his political activities in the Illinois legislature—and Lincoln on balance appears to have narrowed the gap somewhat: Shakespeare, Gibbon, Burns, Paine, Volney, and other writers were added to the sparse boyhood stock. Lincoln also read every newspaper he could lay a hand on, and scanned with special interest the great political speeches that thundered periodically out of Washington; this was the Augustan age of American political oratory, and a man could add no little to his education from a careful study of the utterances of Clay, Webster, Calhoun, Benton, and Hayne. Along with these ventures, in the thirties, Lincoln was studying law. He had long since made the Bible an essential, living item in his literary experience. All that he read became a part of him, and taken together it provided an intellectual awareness and enrichment fully tantamount to a good education by the rather easy standards of the day.

Nor is it wise to assume that educational differences were primarily responsible for the gradually diverging political and social philosophies of the two men. From his earliest manhood a nationalist of the Clay-Whig school, Lincoln slowly evolved a theory about the ultimate meanings of the democratic experiment, a theory that emerged more sharply as the sectional conflict cast its deepening shadow in the eighteen-fifties. The reading he had done on his own—steeped as it was in a study of the Declaration, the Constitution, and American political origins generally—was blended with the direct experience of men and politics garnered in Illinois to produce a well-reasoned, democratic creed that no academic training could possibly have made more profound.

Davis drew in like manner upon nonacademic roots for his philosophy. Extensive travels in the army and afterward contributed strongly to his intense nationalism—the devout belief that the continued expansion of America and its form of government would redound to the lasting benefit of mankind, a belief that Davis retained with slowly gathering disillusionment until it was virtually torn from him by the advent of disunion in 1860. His faith in the beneficent future of America had two important modifiers—both essentially acquired, like the nationalism, from outside the classroom. Private reading, to the accompaniment of long, serious conversations with brother Joseph during the gentle plantation days in Mississippi, produced the conviction that the nation's future greatness depended on strict adherence to the Constitutional principles of the founding fathers; if these principles were abandoned, even the Union might not be worth preserving. And finally, his plantation experiences convinced him that the unparalleled blessing of democracy was strictly the white man's heritage; that slavery, as the only constructive answer to the problem of the Negro in America, must flourish and expand without hindrance as the nation grew.

Clearly, the external forces that brought significant contrast to these two lives lay not in education but in the pervasive influences of home and environment. Whatever traces of the raw frontier that might otherwise have clung to Jefferson Davis had been expunged by college, West Point, his brother's wealth, and the dignified reserve that Samuel Davis and his wife had bequeathed to their children. His manners polished and courtly, his dress and carriage immaculate, Davis was socially at home and at ease in the best of drawing rooms. An aggrieved critic on the floor of Congress might refer to him as a member of an "illegitimate, swaggering, bastard scrub aristocracy," in sneering reference to his parvenu origins, but Jefferson Davis from early manhood was able without effort to act the gentleman.

For Abraham Lincoln the circumstances of youth had been different, and from beginning to end he was never able—probably he never tried—to shed the unmistakable signs of manner and speech that gave away his back-country origins. While Sam Davis was striking southward from Kentucky on the long wagon trail to the deep South in 1810, Lincoln's father was still shifting uncertainly from one to another of the three small farms he had purchased at various times in Hardin County. None of his titles to this scattered acreage was secure, and after several vain attempts to litigate through the conflicting claims which Kentucky's free-wheeling system of survey and settlement had attached to a vast portion of its real estate, Thomas Lincoln gave up in disgust and decided to move elsewhere. Remarking morosely that Kentucky was no place for a poor man to live, he took his family northward across the Ohio into Indiana. It was an understandable choice. In Indiana, under the careful terms of the Ordinance of 1785, the land survey had been systematic and titles to homesteads were correspondingly clear. With this inducement alone the territory had become a popular target for thousands of disgruntled Kentuckians who shared Thomas Lincoln's sentiment.

The family moved in the early winter of 1816-1817. Young Abraham, who had spent enough weeks in a Kentucky log school to master the elements of reading and writing, was not quite eight; his sister Sarah, the only other child, was two years older. The four Lincolns crossed the Ohio by ferry at the Indiana town of Troy, roughly midway between Louisville and Evansville, and settled about sixteen miles north of the river in what is now Spencer County.

Hard years followed. Southern Indiana was a grim frontier wilderness, heavily forested and sparsely settled. The Lincolns spent most of their first winter in a makeshift shelter enclosed on three sides by logs and boughs, the open side protected by a fire that blazed constantly to provide some warmth. Before the winter was over the father had erected a rough log cabin; with the coming of spring began the endless task of felling trees to make room for a crop; by the end of their first year in Indiana Tom Lincoln had been to the government land office at Vincennes to enter his claim and make a down payment of twenty-five per cent on 160 acres.

From this alert beginning the Lincolns settled into a normal frontier routine of toil and monotony, punctuated by heartbreak. Abraham's mother died in 1818, felled by one of the lingering back-country ailments which few pioneer families were able to escape. When Nancy Hanks Lincoln died her husband's cabin was still floorless, her two children wandering ill-clad and barefoot among the few stump-filled acres of corn and wheat and oats that he had managed to clear. This was sheer rock bottom, but the unhappy father stuck it out. In early 1819 he made a brief trip to Kentucky and returned to the Indiana farm with a second wife: the former Sarah Bush Johnston, an industrious, level-headed widow with three young children of her own, who quickly restored order and brought some neatness to the unkempt Lincoln household. At his new wife's insistence Thomas cut puncheons and floored the cabin, while young Abe and his sister were tidied up and enrolled in a nearby school.

On such foundations Lincoln's Indiana boyhood took shape. Thomas hacked and grubbed away at his hard-won quarter section for thirteen years before yielding to a relative's glowing description of the better life in nearby Illinois, and in these years the son grew into manhood and acquired character, uniquely his own yet stamped indelibly with the jagged ill-shaped brand of the American frontier. Lincoln's Indiana had all the trappings, distinctly unglamorous save in retrospect, that later generations have learned to associate with life on the farther reaches of civilization. It was a land of dense somber forest, teeming with wild game, broken only by the log cabins in isolated clearings or the meandering wagon trails that linked the cabins to straggling village communities growing up about a country mill or church or general store. Cash was scarce; men raised small lots of grain or hogs or livestock which they bartered, if they could not sell, for the necessary store goods. Clothing was homemade; the food coarse and the diet monotonous; life in the small cabins at best unrefined and at worst overcrowded and unsanitary.

The people that Lincoln grew up with exhibited a unique blend of qualities: at once rough-mannered and generous, patriotic and narrowly provincial, superstitious and ignorant yet often eager for education, hard drinking and boisterously violent yet God-fearing, democratic, gregarious. They were individualists. Their humor tended to be bawdy, their liquor hard, their religion deeply emotional. As a national type they gave ante-bellum America its underlying flavor and many of its greatest leaders, and perhaps they were, as their admirers have claimed, the backbone of American democracy. These were Lincoln's people, and in all the years ahead he was able to make them respond.

(By and large, the people and the way of life in frontier Mississippi were strikingly similar. But slavery had a way of altering the pattern, and cotton was a money crop which enabled a man with a small stake to rise comfortably above the bottom-rung crudities of one-room cabins and earthen floors. Nothing in Indiana within Tom Lincoln's reach paid cash dividends so promptly, and Abraham remained a backwoodsman while Jefferson went to college.)

Bright and curious and full of offbeat energy, young Lincoln quickly rose to local prominence in the humdrum backwater of Spencer County. On three separate occasions, for a few weeks or months at a stretch, Mrs. Lincoln saw to it that her stepson attended some nearby school. He learned to read, write, and cipher with such skill that he became a sort of intellectual window for the ill-educated community, in demand wherever a letter or newspaper or column of figures was beyond the capacity of its owner. Always tall for his age, with a wiry, muscular strength that formed another ingredient in the popularity accorded him in his rough-and-tumble environment, Lincoln shot toward full height during early adolescence, his figure rapidly assuming its unforgettable proportions of lanky angularity.

His love of reading, quickly developed, was accompanied by a bright sociability and fondness for human companionship. When opportunity offered, he could seldom resist putting aside the axe or the plow to join the idlers and visitors at a nearby store for a round of yarn-swapping and general talk. A born entertainer, he soon became the animated center of such groups, producing alternate rounds of chuckles and guffaws with his quick sallies, droll manner, burlesque mimicry, and humorous stories. When not so engaged he was apt to be found poring over a book or inscribing his thoughts on a slate or plank, and these habits—particularly the reading—brought increasing annoyance to his father, who saw only that Abe's affinity for books and words was impairing his efficiency as a worker. On these frontier farms the round of chores was endless, and Thomas Lincoln kept his son as busy as the son's nature would permit, hiring him out to work on neighboring farms whenever he was not needed at home.

Abraham Lincoln had little liking for physical labor. He had the strength and dexterity to perform the rough tasks with competence, but to him it was so much time away from books and storytelling, and only one of his varied assignments did he perform with any enthusiasm. At the age of seventeen he took a job as assistant to a ferryboat operator in the town of Troy on the Ohio River, where the family had crossed into Indiana ten years before. This was his first glimpse of the outside world, and it fascinated him. He watched the unending parade of traffic on the big river, the produce-laden flatboats, scows, keelboats, rafts, and above all the lordly steamboats, puffing majestically by in midchannel or putting in to Troy to tie up for the night and take on wood.

The youth felt the tug of the river. In the spring of 1828, just turned nineteen, he and another young man contracted with a nearby storekeeper to take a cargo of produce down the Ohio and Mississippi to New Orleans. They traveled by flatboat, and Lincoln gazed with keen interest—as the boy Davis had done on a trip of similar proportions a few years before—at the broad panorama unfolding endlessly along the great waterway. After a few days of gaping wonderment at the bustling cosmopolitan splendor of New Orleans, he returned to Indiana by steamboat (one is repeatedly tempted to wish that Lincoln had lived long enough to read the works of Mark Twain) at about the time young Jefferson Davis was being graduated from West Point with the commission of second lieutenant.

For Davis, West Point was a proving ground of uncertain quality. In his four years as a cadet he achieved little in the way of academic distinction, ranking twenty-third in a graduating class of thirty-three. His best grades, significantly, were in the subjects of rhetoric and political philosophy, but he did poorly in mathematics, which formed a vital and extensive part of the curriculum. On the drill field, however, and in the other soldierly aspects of his training, the fledgling officer performed with snap and grace. Well-formed and handsome, he was an impressive figure in his trim uniform, acquiring a degree of straight-backed military bearing that he never lost, and adding to his already visible quality of dignified reserve. The dignified reserve, it should be noted, did not extend to the realm of deportment, where Jefferson displayed a fun-loving nature that rolled up sizable blocks of demerits each year and got him into a variety of scrapes in nearby taverns and barrack-room escapades.

Cadet Davis also made important additions to his circle of friends and acquaintances; the West Point of this generation contained an impressive number of future Civil War generals. He soon became an intimate member of the "set" surrounding Albert Sidney Johnston. In the Johnston group Davis befriended Leonidas Polk, who was destined to achieve the command of Confederate armies by way of a career as Episcopalian bishop. Davis also liked Cadet Robert Anderson, the commander of Fort Sumter in 1861, and before graduating he met Lucius Northrop, his future commissary-general, and John B. Magruder, whose theatrical maneuvers with a handful of troops on the Peninsula in 1862 would delay McClellan's advance on Richmond. In the class immediately below Davis were the two young men who would figure most prominently in his own Civil War career: Joseph Eggleston Johnston and Robert E. Lee.

Upon graduation from the Academy in 1828 Lieutenant Davis vacationed briefly with his family in Mississippi, spending most of the time on his brother's estate near the broad curving bend of the river a few miles below Vicksburg. He reported to St. Louis in the fall to receive his first military assignment. It was the beginning of a seven-year hitch in the regular army, spent largely on isolated posts in the upper Mississippi Valley. This was still unsettled wilderness in the eighteen-twenties, richly green and starkly handsome, inhabited largely by a scattering of fur traders and Indian tribes and an abundance of wild game, little changed since the days of the French voyageurs. But the advancing tide of American settlement was rolling toward the region, with the usual result. Periodic clashes between disgruntled Indians and overeager white settlers provided employment and constant headaches for the small detachments of United States regulars scattered about the upper valley, and most of Lieutenant Davis's military activities were related to such episodes: the climax came with the campaign against Black Hawk in 1832.

Davis took readily to army life. The hardships and recurrent danger were a challenge and a stimulant. There was ample time for reading, which he continued with his customary avidity, and he thoroughly enjoyed the solid male companionship of fellow West Pointers on the various frontier posts. He proved a good officer, repeatedly demonstrating the prime qualities of firmness, tact, disciplined courage, quick decision, and resourcefulness, which his profession demanded. In 1834, after a promotion to first lieutenant, he was appointed adjutant in a newly formed regiment of dragoons; the final year of his military service was spent with a detachment of this regiment in western Arkansas, helping to ride herd on the tribes that the nation had decided to transplant in its Indian Territory on the southwestern border.

In his years in the upper valley he served under Colonel Zachary Taylor, at Fort Crawford on the Mississippi above Prairie du Chien, and in these years, also, he nearly died from a prolonged bout with pneumonia in the remote winter fastness of central Wisconsin. Both Colonel Taylor and the pneumonia left their mark. His early friendship with the gruff commander was se-

verely interrupted when Davis married Taylor's daughter, much
against the old man's wishes: the stern parental opposition was
partly responsible for Davis's decision to quit the army in 1835.
The friendship was renewed when Davis again came under Taylor's command in the Mexican War, and it ended on an unhappy
note just before the old general's death in 1850 when Senator
Davis and President Taylor found themselves on opposite sides
in the bitter controversy over slavery in the territories acquired
from Mexico. The pneumonia provided a recurrent handicap; he
was thereafter susceptible to frequent colds and an acute neuralgia
that nearly blinded him on occasion and punctuated his future
labors in Washington and Richmond with sharp physical pain.

Into central Illinois in 1830, well behind the vanguard of settlement that was keeping Lieutenant Davis busy a few hundred
miles to the northwest, came the Lincolns, in search once more
of the opportunity that had stayed out of reach in Kentucky and
Indiana. Guiding one of the family's three laden wagons was
lanky Abe, just turned twenty-one, increasingly restless since his
trip down the Mississippi two years ago, soon to shake loose from
the confining atmosphere of life with old Thomas and strike out
for opportunities of his own. The family settled near Decatur and
shifted to Coles County at the end of their first year in Illinois,
but Abraham did not accompany this latter move. In the spring
of 1831 he agreed to take another cargo of goods to New Orleans,
making the trip with a stepbrother and a cousin on a homemade
raft. On his return from the deep South in July he took up
residence by himself in the straggling infant hamlet of New Salem
on the Sangamon River, a few miles from the county seat in
Springfield and close to the spot where Lincoln and his mates
had launched their raft.

At this point in his life Lincoln felt anchorless and uncertain,
"a piece of floating driftwood," as he put it, but it did not take
him long to become well established and popular in his new home.
He unquestionably found New Salem more congenial and inspiring than southern Indiana. The new community was similarly raw
and primitive, exhibiting many of the same frontier characteristics

and inhabited by the same breed of transplanted Kentuckians, but the atmosphere was vitally different. Where Spencer County had been a stagnant backwash in the westward movement, central Illinois was bustling and alive and confident, crossed by the main traveled roads. New Salem, moreover, was a town—small enough, to be sure, its bright aspirations soon unfulfilled, but a town for all that, with stores and a post office and artisans and a small sprinkling of folk with some education and professional training. It offered, in short, a modicum of the activity, sociability, and intellectual stimulation that Lincoln craved.

In New Salem he worked for a few months as clerk in a store recently opened by the country merchant who had contracted with him for the trip to New Orleans. The community quickly learned that this was no ordinary young man. Not long after his arrival Lincoln won the friendship and undying support of the village roughs by beating their leader in a frontier-style wrestling match, and within a few months he captivated the local intelligentsia by joining and taking active part in the village debating society. The droll young spinner of humorous yarns was also, it turned out, an effective public speaker who argued with clarity and forceful logic; "all he lacked," as the admiring president of the society remarked after one of Lincoln's debates, "was culture." It was a lack that most of his fellow-townsmen were readily prepared to overlook.

His confidence and ambition stirred by the popularity that New Salem quickly accorded him, Lincoln decided without much soul-searching that his future lay in politics. The choice was easy and eminently practical. Politics was interesting, absorbingly so to a man of Lincoln's nature, and in the West of his day it offered one of the quickest avenues to success. He aimed high enough, certainly: his decision to seek office came in the spring of 1832, and the office he chose was a seat in the Illinois legislature. This was a fairly lofty aspiration for a youth of twenty-three who had lived less than a year in his community, less than two in his adopted state, who lacked experience, education, wealth, family connections, and political backing.

But this was the American West in the age of Jackson. The

region was abuzz with ambition and political strife, and many
of the brightest careers had risen from positions no loftier than
Lincoln's. Party politics the country over was in a state of flux.
The old Federalist organization had died out and the Republicans
who had run the country since Jefferson's time were splitting into
factions and realigning behind regional leaders. One such leader,
Andrew Jackson, had reached the White House in 1829, and under
the broad mantle of his popularity his political managers were
busily putting together the loose national coalition that was about
to emerge as the Democratic Party. His enemies had found, as
yet, neither the leader nor the national coalition with which to
oppose him. They had several prominent aspirants, notably Henry
Clay of Kentucky and Daniel Webster of Massachusetts, and
before the end of Jackson's second term they would assemble
the framework of a national organization and call themselves
Whigs. But when Lincoln entered political life all of this was
still in process. On the local level, party labels were apt to be
confused, inconsistent, or totally lacking. Where organizational
backing did not exist, many contestants for local office either ran
as supporters of some state or regional leader or campaigned on
specific issues or their own popularity. Under such conditions it
was easily possible for a man of Lincoln's meager background
to get a start in politics and go as far as native skill and ingenuity
would take him. Lincoln decided to give it a try.

He failed on his first attempt, being completely unknown in
his district outside the immediate vicinity of New Salem, but he
ran well enough to keep his ambition alive and aim for a second
effort in 1834. He campaigned as an adherent of Henry Clay,
always his favorite political hero, and he soon became identified
with the emerging Whig organization in Sangamon County. In
his stump speeches he stressed the need for governmental spending in behalf of internal improvements, one of Clay's pet projects
and an object of vital concern throughout the West, a central
issue in Illinois politics for years to come.

His future political guidelines thus sketchily laid out, Lincoln
whiled away the interval before the canvass of 1834 in a variety
of pursuits. A few weeks' militia service in the Black Hawk War

had preceded his unsuccessful campaign in 1832. He mustered out in July, took his defeat in October (placing eighth in a slate of thirteen candidates, of whom the top four won seats in the Assembly), and looked about for something to do. He first tried storekeeping, buying a local store on credit in partnership with another young man, but neither had much talent for business, and all Lincoln had to show for a few brief months of mercantile endeavor was a debt that took him years to pay off. Desperate for employment, he worked at splitting rails, husking corn, assisting a local merchant, and whatever odd jobs came to hand.

In 1833 his local friends, recognizing his need for a steady income, secured his position as postmaster at New Salem, which he held during the remaining three years of his residence there. Shortly afterward he also got the post of deputy surveyor for Sangamon County, and with the aid of a nearby schoolmaster and some independent reading he managed to learn the essentials of this task and perform his duties with competence. His two government jobs enabled him to travel about the district, meet people, do a bit of quiet politicking, and indulge with renewed fervor in his favorite pastime of reading. During this period he made the acquaintance of Shakespeare and Gibbon and other authors, and as postmaster he had access to an abundance of newspapers, which he read regularly with painstaking care. When the new campaign opened in the spring of 1834 he was in a much stronger position politically, enjoying the favor of both the local party organizations.

Above all, Lincoln had won the favor and friendship of John T. Stuart, the Whig leader in Sangamon County. Two years Lincoln's senior, a handsome, well-educated Kentuckian of quiet manner and considerable ability, Stuart ran a law office in Springfield and labored cannily in behalf of the Whig Party. The two had met during the Black Hawk campaign. Lincoln was a captain in Major Stuart's battalion, and when both returned to county politics Stuart took the measure of the gangling, ambitious youth and liked what he saw. In 1834, on Stuart's advice, Lincoln accepted the overtures of local Democrats and ran as a nonpartisan candidate; Stuart's Whig organization was also working for him, and with this dual support he won handily—carefully avoiding, this time, any Whiggish speeches or statement of principles which might damage his popularity with Sangamon Democrats. But it was as a confirmed advocate of Henry Clay Whiggery that the new delegate, flushed with his first political triumph, looked forward to the opening session of the legislature in December. During and after the campaign, as his friendship with Stuart deepened, he listened to more advice from the young Springfield attorney, procured copies of Blackstone's *Commentaries* and Chitty's *Proceedings*, and began the study of law.

Abraham Lincoln and Jefferson Davis had reached the major turn in the road at almost identical moments. When Lincoln took the stage from Springfield to the capital at Vandalia in the closing weeks of 1834, on the threshold of his career in law and politics, Lieutenant Davis had begun giving serious thought to the idea of quitting the army. His romance with Sarah Knox Taylor, now a secret engagement, continued to meet stern opposition from old Zachary. His military duties among the itinerant Indians in western Arkansas were far from inspiring; and Joseph Davis, ever mindful of his brother's welfare, was losing his former enthusiasm about the future possibilities of a career in the regular army. Military achievement and renown depend solely on war, and in the eighteen-thirties there were no wars in sight: the large-scale Indian campaigns were apparently over, and America had no disputes with foreign neighbors that seemed likely to result in military action. The country was concentrating on domestic affairs, and the big opportunities were all in civilian life, in land or trade or politics or the professions.

In early 1835, while Lincoln began mastering the intricacies of debate and maneuver at Vandalia, Jefferson Davis was on furlough in Mississippi to discuss his future with Joseph. They soon arrived at a decision. Jefferson and Sarah Knox Taylor were now determined to marry, with or without her father's consent, and Joseph offered to allot his brother some 1800 acres out of his vast Warren County holdings, lend him money for the purchase of slaves, and help him become established as a cotton planter. The

young couple were married on June 17, 1835, the old Colonel
having given a grudging consent that lacked the slightest trace of
approval, and the lieutenant's resignation from the army became
effective on June 30. Plans were immediately laid for a new Davis
plantation adjoining Joseph's along the great river.

The decade that followed was extremely important for both
men, each pursuing his separate way toward a rendezvous with
national politics and the slavery controversy. They were busy
years. Lincoln served four successive terms in the Illinois legislature, acquiring influence and power in the state Whig organization
and steadily adding to what eventually became an enormous fund
of knowledge about the American political process. In the legislature he voted the party program, and worked hard in behalf
of three hotly contested measures which dominated the Illinois
politics of his day: a huge internal-improvements program that
called for state aid to a staggering array of railroad, canal, turn-
pike, and navigation projects; a group of bills and resolutions that
collectively upheld the principle of a national bank and the rights
and charters of two state banks; and a bill to transfer the state
capital from Vandalia to Springfield. The bank and internal-im-
provement measures were standard Whig fare, the move to Springfield a project that Lincoln and other Sangamon delegates pushed
through against the determined opposition of Vandalia, Alton,
and other hopeful candidates. Soon a leading member of the party
delegation, Lincoln thrice served as Whig floorleader and helped
win the passage of his favored measures by mastering and apply-
ing the stock assortment of political devices: pressure, cajolery,
debate, logrolling, and a labyrinth of parliamentary tactics.

The Illinois legislature in the eighteen-thirties was a rugged
training ground in practical politics. Its membership contained
many men whose skill and shrewdness were on a par with Lincoln's own, including several who would attain national prominence and cross his path again in years to come. There was John
Stuart, of course, whose long friendship with Lincoln would none
the less find him in Congressional opposition to Lincoln's emancipation policy in 1863 and 1864. Another staunch Whig was Orville

Hickman Browning, a young lawyer of Kentucky origins, stately and elegant, destined to figure in Lincoln's nomination for the presidency and to support his administration in the Senate during the early months of the war. Another was John Hardin, quiet and deceptively artless, who would contest with Lincoln for the nomination in Congress in 1846 and die a hero's death in Mexico a few months later.

Among the Democrats was another Kentuckian, John A. McClernand, expansively eloquent, an ambitious, clever, tactless climber whose political influence would ultimately bring him a major general's commission in the Union army and provide a multitude of headaches for his Commander in Chief. In the session that began in 1840 Lincoln met another astute young Democrat of future prominence, one who would be a powerful Republican ally in years to come: the quiet, courteous descendant of a famous Connecticut family, Lyman Trumbull. Finally, there was an absurdly short, broad-shouldered, hard-fighting political strategist of unquenchable spirit and boundless ambition, Stephen A. Douglas.

The young Whig politician was also a lawyer now, expanding his horizons in this new direction when the legislature was not in session. Admitted to the Illinois bar in 1836, Lincoln promptly quit New Salem for Springfield to enter a partnership with John T. Stuart. Thereafter, amid legislative duties and political fence building, in rather slipshod fashion but with growing competence, Lincoln practiced law until his departure for Congress a decade later. He left Stuart in 1841 to enter an office with the meticulous, hard-working Stephen T. Logan, an eminent Springfield attorney with political aspirations who, unlike Stuart, also had an interest in the legal profession for its own sake rather than as a mere pathway to political advancement. Logan's rigid insistence upon exactitude and careful preparation was excellent discipline for the rather easygoing Lincoln, but conflicting temperaments and ambitions led to an amicable dissolution of this partnership in 1844. Lincoln's third and final partner was energetic young William H. Herndon, nine years Lincoln's junior, son of a fellow delegate in the legislature, a bright, high-strung, fun-loving youth who had idolized Lincoln since the beginning of their acquaintance a few years before.

In successive collaboration with this oddly assorted trio Lincoln tried cases in Springfield and on the judicial circuit, enjoying the companionship and excitement of court week in the distant towns and hamlets, arguing before juries in a hundred dusty courtrooms, adding steadily to his experience and legal ability. He soon became a most effective advocate, his courtroom manner friendly and casual, giving away point after point without argument until what he regarded as the nub of the case was reached. Then he went after it relentlessly, guiding the argument back to his main point again and again, restating and clarifying with a superb use of homely analogies which the rustic jurymen readily grasped. Homely analogy was by no means his only weapon. Before the end of his first decade of practice he was known throughout the Eighth Circuit as a master of logic, lucidity, and forceful argument.

In moving to Springfield Lincoln had reached the center of the state's social and political activity. New Salem, never more than a village, had reached the limits of its growth and was already starting to decline when Lincoln left; Springfield, a few miles to the east, was a growing town of some two thousand inhabitants, with hotels and two newspapers and a variety of stores and business houses, its future assured by the recent legislative triumph that had made it the state capital. Though still in most respects an unpolished frontier community, Springfield had an urban flavor and a budding class structure new to Lincoln's experience, led by an upper circle of prominent, reasonably affluent, well-educated families that constituted a distinct social elite.

Springfield high society was recruited almost entirely from Kentucky. John Stuart was a member of this set, as were the Edwardses, Todds, Logans, and other families from the Bluegrass. As Stuart's partner and a rising power in Whig Party councils, Lincoln gained ready access to Springfield's new aristocracy. He moved about in it with awkward familiarity, discarding little of his country manner and almost none of his irrepressible wit and

homely stories. While making the social rounds he met a cousin
of Stuart's named Mary Todd, youngest daughter of a prominent
Kentucky family. Mary had recently come to live in Springfield
with her sister, Mrs. Ninian W. Edwards, whose husband was
another member of the upper circle. For Abraham and Mary
there ensued a spasmodic and highly uncertain courtship, and in
1842, after much backing and filling on Lincoln's part, and somewhat to Springfield's amazement, the lanky politician and the
plump Kentucky belle were married. A few months later the
young couple bought a house in town; a son, Robert Todd Lincoln, was born in 1843; another, Edward Baker Lincoln, in 1846.

The momentous addition of Mary Todd to the forces at work
upon his character was made at the outset of Lincoln's involved
quest for a seat in Congress. At the end of his fourth term in the
legislature he concluded that he had earned the right to higher
office, and sought to build support for the Whig Congressional
nomination in 1843. Since Lincoln's district was a Whig stronghold which made nomination tantamount to election, his quest
brought him into conflict with the ambitions of two erstwhile
legislative colleagues, John Hardin and Edward D. Baker. In the
three-cornered test of strength that followed it was Hardin who
finally corralled a majority of the delegates and won the nomination.

To preserve party unity, Lincoln supported Hardin's candidacy
and promoted what he thought was an understanding with his
two rivals concerning the future. Lincoln's idea was rotation in
office, whereby Hardin would be followed by Baker, then Lincoln,
as the party nominee for successive terms. In practice it worked
out that way, although neither Baker nor Hardin seems to have
understood that there was any prearranged agreement. In any
case, Hardin was duly elected in 1843 to the Twenty-Eighth Congress, which assembled in December, Baker in 1844 to the
Twenty-Ninth, and Lincoln in 1846 to the Thirtieth, after a brief
vigorous attempt by Hardin to ignore the rotation idea and seek
another term. Lincoln had worked and waited his turn, and was
now successful. In the fall of 1847, as the opening of the new
session neared, he and Mary leased their home in Springfield,

gathered up their two sons and packed their belongings, and set out for the capital on the Potomac.

Jefferson Davis reached Congress two years earlier, without so much as a day's apprenticeship in any other political office. In the deep South the plantation often conferred political eligibility, and the office sometimes went in search of the man. So it was with Davis. The decade that saw Lincoln immersed in Illinois politics, working upward through the ranks, was spent by Davis in the privacy of his new estate on the Mississippi, laying effective but far different foundations for a national career.

During much of this period it was an unplanned career, except in the mind of brother Joseph. Jefferson's own ambition went into sudden and prolonged eclipse in September, 1835, when his bride of a few short months contracted malaria and died at the home of Davis's sister in Louisiana. Heartbroken, the young widower spent all but a fraction of the next eight years in voluntary retirement from public affairs, grimly immersed in the task of building a home and founding a plantation on the uncleared land that Joseph had put at his disposal. With his brother's advice and assistance Davis bought slaves, drew up plans for a house, stable, slave quarters, and other outbuildings, and supervised the laying out and clearing of acreage for the planting of cotton.

Davis became a model Southern planter, the type that apologists in his own time and for generations afterwards insisted upon regarding as typical, as both example and proof of the beneficence of the civilization built on cotton and human slavery. His new home, which he called Brierfield, was not the gigantic resplendent mansion of Scarlett O'Hara tradition, but a spacious, comfortable, one-story house with wide doorways and porticoed verandas. There were thoroughbred horses in the stable, well-thumbed books in the library, and twin rows of neat slave cabins flanking the house at a respectful distance. Davis ran his own plantation at all times, supervising every activity, scrupulously attentive to each varied detail.

Like his brother Joseph, who had even installed a species of limited self-government for his slaves, Jefferson treated his

Negroes with extreme kindness and care. Force was sparingly used. The more responsible slaves were entrusted with the management of the plantation storerooms and outbuildings. Each slave was allotted a patch of ground of his own and could sell the yield on the plantation or on the open market, as he chose. Davis's overseer and executive officer, who shared the managerial responsibility and ran the estate himself when Davis was absent, was the able Negro James Pemberton, faithful body servant and companion since army days. As lord of the manor, in feudal tradition, Davis unfailingly provided gifts and services with each birth, wedding and burial. Among the "fringe benefits" available to a Davis slave were medical and dental care, a plantation nursery, and religious services. Under this kind of management, a faithful echo of his brother's well-run establishment, close adjoining, the labor force thrived and the plantation prospered.

When the Davis brothers were not riding about their fields or balancing their books they were apt to spend hours at a time in Joseph's big plantation library. Both men were constant readers, and they regularly sharpened their explorations in history, philosophy, literature, or current newspapers by a thorough discussion of everything they read. These long, stimulating conversations with Joseph were the anvil on which Jefferson Davis's fundamental beliefs about his country and its institutions were hammered out: the reverence for the strict constitutional principles of the founding fathers, a belief in state sovereignty and national expansion and a balanced republican form of government. These were essentially Jeffersonian principles; Thomas Jefferson was for the sons, as he had been for the father, the fount of political wisdom. Thus, untempered by argument or practical application, did the Davis philosophy emerge. No loosely held, pliant, or transitory affair, this philosophy; emerging with it, clearly visible then and thereafter, was a deep conviction that it was *right,* that no honorable man could possibly see things any other way.

In 1843, after eight years of almost unbroken seclusion amid his fields and his books, the outside world recaptured the young planter-scholar. Politics reached him first. The Davises were Democrats—out of reverence for Jefferson, not Jackson, for whose principles they shared a growing Southern distrust—while most of their fellow planters in the prosperous Vicksburg-Natchez region were Whigs. The Mississippi Democrats, hopeful of cutting into this Whig stronghold (when their overconfident opponents ran two candidates for a single seat in the state legislature), persuaded Davis to come out of retirement and contest the election. Perhaps the Democrats hoped that a new face was what they needed; Davis remembered later that a week before the election the party became dissatisfied with their regular candidate and withdrew him. Davis attended a county nominating convention on October 31, 1843, and in reporting the affair the Vicksburg *Sentinel,* a Democratic organ, revealed the line that the party would take in promoting their new man:

"It will be seen that JEFFERSON DAVIS, Esq. received the unanimous nomination of the party, a gentleman, who, should he be elected, will do honour to himself and his constituents. Mr. Davis is a sterling Democrat, a man of unsullied private character, talents of a superior order, extensive political information, and judging from the structure of his remarks before the convention, a fine public speaker. There may be some in the county to whom Mr. Davis, from the secluded privacy in which he has lived, is unknown, to these we repeat, Mr. Davis is what we have stated, *a man, every inch a man,* of whom the Democracy of Old Warren should be proud."

The Whigs of Old Warren were sufficiently alarmed to close ranks behind a single candidate and rush one of their best orators into the county to strengthen their cause. Davis was duly defeated, although he proved a good campaigner who debated with a restrained, persuasive eloquence and ran a good race, polling more votes than Warren County Democrats normally received. Impressed, the party employed his talents in a larger framework. In the campaign of 1844 he was a Democratic presidential elector, speaking on Polk's behalf throughout the state, and in the following year he agreed to run for Congress.

On the two leading questions of the day in Mississippi Davis took firm, forthright stands that broadened the basis of his appeal.

On the national side, he stood strongly on Polk's platform and called for the annexation of Texas, which delighted the expansion-minded Democrats; locally, he opposed his party and spoke against the repudiation of the bonds that Mississippi had issued in great profusion a few years back to support a pair of now insolvent banks, thus delighting the business-minded Whigs. Dignified and handsome, obviously intelligent, his integrity beyond cavil, speaking with earnest eloquence, Davis made a good impression everywhere and won his Congressional seat after a vigorous campaign.

Even as politics beckoned, romance also reached out to pull the young planter from seclusion. In 1843, at a Christmas party on his brother's estate, Davis met young Varina Howell of Natchez, seventeen years old, daughter of a long-time friend of Joseph's. Varina was dark haired and full lipped and charmingly intelligent, and when it became obvious that Jefferson found her interesting, Joseph quietly saw to it that the couple had ample opportunity to get acquainted. The Howells were aristocrats and Whigs, and at seventeen Varina's first estimate of her future husband remains as keenly incisive a judgment as anyone ever made of him:

"I do not know," she wrote her mother, directly after their first meeting, "whether this Mr. Jefferson Davis is young or old. He looks both at times; . . . He impresses me as a remarkable kind of man, but of uncertain temper, and has a way of taking for granted that everybody agrees with him when he expresses an opinion, which offends me; yet he is most agreeable and has a peculiarly sweet voice and a winning manner of asserting himself. The fact is, he is the kind of person I should expect to rescue me from a mad dog at any risk, but to insist upon a stoical indifference to the fright afterward. . . . Would you believe it, he is refined and cultivated, and yet he is a Democrat!"

What the refined and cultivated Democrat first thought of Varina is unrecorded, but a courtship was soon under way, and in February, 1845, the couple were married in the Howell mansion near Natchez. After a honeymoon in New Orleans the Davises returned to Mississippi to prepare for the coming campaign. Victory followed, and in late November, two years ahead of Lincoln, the Representative-elect from Mississippi and his excited young wife boarded an upbound steamboat and set out for Washington.

Congress and the Mexican War provided an important watershed for both men. Davis's career received a sharp boost, hastening the day when the Southern states would turn to him for leadership; while Lincoln returned to a soul-searching obscurity in Illinois that later proved the making of him. Davis stayed in Congress six months. He made his customary favorable impression, even winning a sober tribute from a shrewd, venerable opponent on the other side of the aisle, John Quincy Adams, who had been in the United States Senate before Davis was born. Davis vigorously supported the Polk administration in its policy toward Mexico, cautioned moderation in the negotiations with Great Britain over the Oregon question, and managed as a good Jeffersonian Democrat to go on record against internal improvement and protective tariff legislation.

An ardent expansionist, convinced of the justice of American claims against Mexico and thrilled by the preliminary exploits of Zachary Taylor along the Rio Grande, Davis resigned his House seat in June, 1846, to accept the command of a regiment of Mississippi volunteers. The young colonel drilled his troops, joined Taylor's army in southwest Texas, and served with gallantry at Monterey and Buena Vista. Displaying tactical brilliance as well as valor, Davis emerged from the war a national hero, the toast of his section and his state, with a glittering military reputation and the prospects of a bright future ahead.

Congressman Lincoln pursued a different course, and for him the Mexican War appeared to mark an end rather than a beginning. He entered Congress in December, 1847, with hostilities virtually over and a rancorous debate over the justice and ultimate meaning of the conflict in full blast. A loyal party man, with few firm convictions of his own about Texas or the quarrel with Mexico before he entered Congress, Lincoln quickly adopted the Whig line and joined in denunciations of the Polk administration for having initiated and waged an unjust war of conquest.

Among certain elements, notably in the East, this Whig attack on the war enjoyed wide support, but in this instance it was Davis and not Lincoln who had correctly gauged the sentiment in the expansion-minded American West—which included not only Davis's Mississippi but Lincoln's Illinois. Beyond the Appalachians, from the Great Lakes to the Gulf, the majority had responded fervidly to the appeal of Manifest Destiny and exulted in the triumphs of Zachary Taylor and Winfield Scott. The angry debate over slavery had not yet obscured this western expansionism. Volunteers from Mississippi and Illinois and every western state had fought side by side in Mr. Polk's war, and they resented those who maligned it.

As a result, Lincoln's persistent attacks on the war in Washington were severely criticized in his home district. Under a cloud, his record in the Thirtieth Congress marked by diligence rather than distinction, Lincoln campaigned strenuously for the Whig ticket in 1848 but held to a previous political agreement—rotation in office again, this time in favor of his old law partner Stephen T. Logan—and did not seek re-election. His chances would not have been promising. As it was, a majority of his Illinois constituents were so disenchanted by his antiwar record in Congress that they voted against Logan in 1848. Lincoln did not accept the territorial appointment offered him by the incoming Taylor administration, and returned home rather disconsolately in the spring of 1849, bearing few laurels and fewer prospects. His national career had sputtered out within eighteen months. Meanwhile, the glamorous Colonel of Mississippi Volunteers, his dignity only enhanced by the crutches he wore from the effects of a bullet wound at Buena Vista, had reappeared in Washington in 1847 to take his seat in the United States Senate.

By any objective measurement, Davis had more than earned his eminence, Lincoln his obscurity. The new Senator from Mississippi was a truly national figure. Extensive travels, the wide variety of his military experiences, and long hours of study had given him a broad national viewpoint. He had grasped the scope and dimensions of the young republic, and if he was acutely conscious of the peculiar needs of his own section, he still thought in national terms. His patriotic speeches in behalf of national expansion and America's united destiny carried the eloquence of conviction. He had surpassingly demonstrated the qualities of leadership—on the frontier posts, against Black Hawk, in Mexico, on the plantation, in politics. Disciplined and able, a tireless worker and effective speaker, his youth enhanced by a dignity that compelled respect and a charm that seldom failed to captivate, the gifted Jefferson Davis bore all the earmarks of a great national statesman.

Davis, in short, had reached the height of his powers; Lincoln very definitely had not. The real contrast was not between the polished, cosmopolitan dignity of the self-assured plantation aristocrat and the awkward small-town lawyer with the rustic manners and droll frontier stories. What mattered, at this point, was the difference in outlook. Lincoln's breadth of view, unenforced by education or travel, was still bounded essentially by the shabby confines of backroom politics in Illinois. As yet Lincoln had not risen above the level of party hack. For all his ready wit, honesty, and alert intelligence the man still lacked maturity and depth, and some of the character traits he had exhibited thus far were ill-becoming. In his maneuvers against political opponents he was not merely devious, which perhaps went with the job, but conniving, thoughtless, and sometimes petty. Only when challenged to a duel by the peppery James Shields in 1842, for instance, did Lincoln learn to stifle a malignant habit of impugning the character of his opponents by means of anonymous letters in the daily press.

For Lincoln, the full maturity and self-mastery that Davis had already achieved would soon emerge, but there was one other column of figures on the ledger. Davis's broad range of experience stopped just short of the one arena where Lincoln was most fully at home. Provincial shallowness notwithstanding, by the time of the Mexican War Abraham Lincoln knew the art of practical politics, and when the great test finally came there would be no substitute for this knowledge. The American democratic process was ungoverned and contradictory and full of dangerous cross-currents, and Lincoln was well on his way to mastering it. Americans see only enough of this strange process to conclude that it is basically sordid and not very nice, and they are partly right, but somehow all of the elements that respectable citizens disapprove of most highly—compromise, logrolling, pressure, "steamroller tactics," and the rest—can on occasion be put to work in behalf of the noblest ideals. If, as a consequence, the ideals come out a bit tarnished, one is yet forced to the conclusion that they can become part of the law of the land in no other way.

Lincoln reveled in the rough give-and-take of politics, and Davis, whose political experience when he reached the Senate consisted mainly of studying bills and making speeches, detested it. On the higher levels of statecraft Davis was talented and sometimes brilliant, but his pride and dignity would never let him don the back-slapping, buttonholing geniality whereby votes are lined up and deals made. His first impression of political Washington was gained on a visit in 1838 and apparently lasted his lifetime. "Washington," he wrote, "that hotbed of heartlessness and home of the world's worldly." Davis had uttered a fact of life. His tragedy was that he never learned to live with it.

At bottom, there was more involved than politics. Most of Lincoln's contacts, from his Indiana boyhood to the back roads and villages and county courtrooms of Illinois in later years, had been with a big cross-section of rural, frontier America: the type of folk orators had in mind when they talked, in reverent capital letters, about The People. In nineteenth-century America there were a great many of them, and when these people moved—to the West, for instance, or to the city, or to war—the nation moved with them; if they stopped, it would stop. Lincoln understood them all his life, and his sixth sense, or instinct, or whatever it was, seldom failed to tell him how a majority would be likely to respond.

Jefferson Davis, too, was sprung from this great American bedrock, but he quickly lost his sense of belonging to it. Despite his wide travels and varied experiences, most of the people he knew were of another sort. The social circles in which he moved—at college, in the Army, or among the plantation gentry and their range of Northern friends—were more or less consciously insulated from the grass roots. Nor, obviously, could this deficiency be supplied by the lower strata that Davis did know at first hand: neither regular army privates nor Negro slaves were in the American mainstream. Davis's image of the country was projected on a wide screen, but parts of it—especially outside the South—were never quite in focus.

Davis's strength, in fact, was also his weakness. From earliest manhood he had been *in command,* and his qualities of leadership were undisputed. He could lay the best of plans, and give orders with firmness and clarity. He could command respect and obedience; he could exhort; he could often inspire. But always as the commander, the man on horseback out beyond the ranks. Someday this grass-roots democracy would don uniforms and take sides and go to war against itself. And perhaps, in the final accounting, each side's best effort would depend less upon numbers or technology or fighting quality than upon the breadth and depth of understanding that existed between democracy in uniform and its Commander in Chief. Call it the common touch, if you will: the elusive, intangible, unfailing contact that Lincoln never lost and Davis never quite had, the one quality, for good or ill, that no successful American leader can ever afford to be without.

What this might mean for the future of the republic began to take dim form as soon as the status of slavery in the territories became the prime legacy of our war with Mexico. The legacy was bequeathed before the war itself had fairly begun.

[T H R E E]

S U N L I G H T   &   S H A D O W

The issue was bound to come up, and if David Wilmot had not raised it someone else would have done so.

At the time of the Mexican War, American leaders had managed to keep the slavery controversy more or less out of national politics for twenty-five years. The most pressing issue had seemingly been settled by the Missouri Compromise of 1820. Missouri had been admitted to the Union as a slave state, and the balance was kept even by letting Maine detach itself from Massachusetts and enter as a free state. The original union of thirteen commonwealths had grown to twenty-four, twelve free and twelve slave, equally represented in the national Senate and as yet showing no great disparity in population.

Central feature of the Compromise, however, was the provision that determined the status of the vast, virtually unpopulated trans-Missouri portion of the Louisiana Purchase territory, so that no arguments over slavery need intrude upon the making of future states. Missouri's southern boundary ran along the line of 36°30′ North Latitude. This line was simply extended due westward beyond Missouri to the national border, which then zigzagged north and west from the mouth of the Sabine to the Rocky Mountain divide, intersecting 36°30′ about three hundred miles west of Missouri. By the terms of the Compromise, slavery was permitted to enter American territory south of 36°30′ but was permanently excluded from the much larger region north of the line.

It was all very neat and tidy, and Americans hailed the Missouri Compromise as a just and businesslike solution to what had threatened to become a nasty problem. Slavery was secure in one domain, freedom in another. The sectional balance, which practically guaranteed that neither side could muster a hostile majority against the other, seemed in no danger. True, 36°30′ had awarded freedom the lion's share of the trans-Missouri country, but most of this region was labeled the Great American Desert on contemporary maps, and men were content to let it go at that; from such an area few states, certainly none in the foreseeable future, would emerge to upset the comforting free–slave balance in the Senate. For most Americans the issue was settled, although a few important voices were raised in warning. Thomas Jefferson, a sage in retirement on his Virginia hilltop, might confide that the sudden argument over slavery in Missouri had awakened and terrorized him like a firebell in the night; and John Quincy Adams might define the controversy as a preamble, "a title-page to a great, tragic volume"; but on the whole the nation was thoroughly satisfied with its adjustment of the controversy.

As a permanent solution, the Missouri Compromise was going to be effective only so long as both the American conscience and the American frontier stood still. Both refused. In the thirties and forties the American conscience found expression in the agitation of a small but vocal group of abolitionists, whose printed fulminations against slavery were tabled in Congress and destroyed by Southern postmasters until a tiny Congressional minority, led by the grimly high-principled John Quincy Adams, defended the rights if not the cause of abolitionism by invoking the Constitutional guarantee of freedom of speech. In 1845 Adams forced the repeal of the so-called Gag Resolutions, by which all antislavery literature had been kept off the floor of Congress, and the issue was once again free to air itself in national councils.

The American frontier was also on the march. In the twenties it sent a vanguard across the border into Mexico, the larger por-

tion to settle in Texas and the smaller to exploit the opportunities
of the Santa Fe trade. In the late thirties it began curling another
tentacle far into the pine-topped Pacific Northwest—the Oregon
territory, joint possession of Great Britain and America, hitherto
occupied solely by fur traders and largely a preserve of the powerful Hudson's Bay Company. By this time, too, Yankee mariners
and mountain men were describing an idyllic, fertile Arcadia of
vineyards and white-walled mission houses in the Mexican province of California. The Americans in Texas threw off Mexican
rule in 1836 and set up an independent slaveholding republic,
their avowed desire to join the United States thwarted only by the
reluctance of national leaders to reopen the slavery controversy.

Expansion was a double-barreled and quite potent mixture. It
was democracy with its eye on the main chance, eager to spread
the blessings of the world's most beneficent government into the
farthest reaches of the continent and show a profit on the transaction. The idea found its golden voice in the publicist and editor
John L. O'Sullivan, who described continental expansion as America's Manifest Destiny, and it found its national leader in James
K. Polk of Tennessee, who swept into the White House in 1845 on
a platform that called explicitly for the annexation of Texas and
the acquisition of Oregon, the respective claims of Mexico and
Great Britain to be bought off or crushed, as the case might be.

Great Britain was willing to negotiate the Oregon question, and
after a round of bellicose tub-thumping, Manifest Destiny was
willing to settle for the southern half of the territory, below the
forty-ninth parallel. Mexico decided to fight for Texas—thereby,
in the end, losing her New Mexico and California provinces as
well. And thus in the early summer of 1846, with the Oregon
transaction still pending and the hostilities with Mexico barely
underway, the stage was set for young David Wilmot, a portly,
earnest, reform-minded Congressman from Pennsylvania, to intro-
duce his fateful proviso in the Lower House and block out the line
that the conflict over slavery would follow thereafter.

Wilmot's measure demanded, quite simply, that slavery be excluded from any and all territories that might be acquired from
Mexico as a result of the present war. It was a deliberate echo

of the Northwest Ordinance of 1787, which had banned slavery from the area north of the Ohio and east of the Mississippi, and it voiced the sentiment of growing numbers in the North who had come to feel that slavery must not be allowed to expand beyond its present area. Only the barest fraction of these Northerners were abolitionists. Most of them had no intention of interfering with slavery in the Southern states, but they were determined to block its further spread. Almost every Northern legislature gave ringing endorsement to the Wilmot Proviso in the months that followed, and the measure was introduced again and again in Congress from 1846 to 1849—Lincoln voted for it five times by actual count and later recalled, humorously, having done so thirty or forty times, so frequently was the issue before the House. On this question both national parties tended to divide along sectional lines, an ominous portent that did not go unnoticed. The North, now far ahead of the South in population, could occasionally muster a majority in favor of the Proviso in the lower chamber, but a Senate still evenly divided between slave and free states was always able to block final passage of any such measure.

The Proviso was defeated, but the issue would not down. Debate over the status of slavery in the territories would crop up again and again during the eighteen-fifties, each time with increasing bitterness, each time with greater numbers of men from the South arrayed against greater numbers of men from the North. Southerners, forming ranks quickly behind the powerful intellect of their greatest spokesman, John C. Calhoun, met Wilmot's proposal with the Constitutional doctrine that slaveowners were entitled to the equal protection of the laws in every square inch of national territory. Deprive us of this, warned Calhoun, and the Southern states would be justified in withdrawing from the compact of Union drawn up in 1789.

Northerners listened to a babel of voices: to moderates like Clay and Webster, who would compromise on slavery in order to keep the Union intact; to democratic realists like Stephen A. Douglas, who suggested that the people in any territory be allowed to settle the slavery question for themselves; to radicals like Seward of New York and Chase of Ohio, who followed Wilmot and demanded

that slavery be contained within its present limits; to out-and-out
abolitionists like William Lloyd Garrison, who would end slavery
throughout the country, immediately and at one stroke.

Beneath the Northern confusion, however, was a clear principle
that sliced through the babel like a peal of trumpets. The man
who sounded this note, again and again, until a majority of
citizens in the North came to realize by slow steps that it summed
up what they really felt, was Abraham Lincoln. "Slavery is
founded in the selfishness of man's nature," he said in 1854, "opposition to it is in his love of justice. . . . Repeal all past history,
you still cannot repeal human nature. It will still be the abundance
of man's heart, that slavery extension is wrong."

Arrayed against this was another principle, equally clear. Jefferson Davis was displaying the hard core of Southern opinion
as early as 1848. Slavery, said Davis, "is a common law right to
property in the service of man; its origin was Divine decree—the
curse upon the graceless sons of Noah." God had blessed the
institution. So had the Federal Constitution—a scarcely less than
scriptural authority in the South—and "simple justice" (this
was Calhoun's phrase) demanded that slavery be protected in
federal territory, wherever it chose to go. These two principles
were truly, as Lincoln pointed out, "an eternal antagonism." They
might coexist for a time, but ultimately one or the other must
prevail.

America continues to present a confusing spectacle in that last
frenzied decade before the Civil War. Because it ended in a
bloody conflict that shook the very roots of our national existence
and embedded itself deeply in the national conscience, touching
our heritage with a fire at once tragic and sublime, the quarrel
over slavery is apt to distort the picture of the eighteen-fifties.
The record seems to indicate that the nation was all-engrossed by
the slavery question—that it talked slavery, thought slavery, lived
slavery, and barely existed on any other plane. Surely nothing
else mattered. This was the decade that riveted the national attention on crisis after crisis, always over slavery, a grim roll call
of episodes that whipped up emotions and ultimately summoned

forth armies on the march: Fugitive Slave Law, *Uncle Tom's Cabin,* Bleeding Kansas, Bully Brooks, Dred Scott, Lecompton, John Brown.

A black shadow had cast itself across the bright landscape, darkening everything it touched. In Calhoun's graphic metaphor, the great cords that bound the Union were snapping, one by one. The Northern press rang with denunciations of the aggressive Southern slave power; Southern editorials responded with blasts at the fanatic abolitionist Yankees who sought to destroy a social system and a way of life. The two largest Protestant denominations, Baptist and Methodist, split over slavery into Churches North and Churches South. The national parties broke up and regrouped along sectional lines. First the Whigs disintegrated, rudderless with the passing of Clay and Webster in 1852, their cohesion shattered by the slavery issue. Then the ephemeral Know-Nothing Party came and went, its transient conglomeration of nativists, opportunists, displaced Whigs, and conservative nationalists unable to withstand the North-South controversy. And finally the Democracy, the great party of Andrew Jackson, broke completely in 1860 and yanked the kingpin from the ramshackle structure of national politics. While the old parties died or split, a new party—the Republican—took shape in the Northern states. Fear of slavery and its implications brought this party into being and widened its circle of adherents until it commanded a majority throughout the North. Fear of this party and what it might do in national office drove the Gulf states into disunion.

All of this was high tragedy and absorbing emotional drama, sometimes ludicrous but more often grim, carried out in fear-laden atmosphere to the tune of angry debates on the floor of Congress and the defiant mutterings of a restless people convening spasmodically in mass meetings or local conventions from one end of the country to the other. The American experiment had apparently produced two distinct societies, the one free and the other slave, each with its own set of values and goals, standing now face to face in open antagonism bred of fear and suspicion, North and South at daggers drawn, war drums throbbing offstage, a house dividing, a nation rent in half. This, surely, was the essence of American history in the fifties.

It was only part of the essence. The long crescendo of sectional conflict was bound up with a greater drama, less spectacular and less sharply focused but even larger with meaning for the nation's future. What would happen to slavery, in fact, was ultimately dependent on this mightier fabric, into which all the varicolored strands of change were woven. During these years an incredible amount of energy and effort was spent outside the realm of sectional discord. If these were the worst of times, they were also the best of times. Men kept an anxious eye on the close-fought elections and the heated debates; they responded emotionally to fraud and bloodshed in Kansas and physical violence in the national Senate and other milestones along the path to war; but they were also hard at work in one of the busiest and most prosperous decades the country has ever known. In all save the one tragic sector it was a period brimful of energy, achievement, optimism, and material progress.

Modern America was in the making. An awesome process was at work, visibly and powerfully, a tangled and barely co-ordinated process of gears and pistons and clanking hammers that ground the old familiar patterns into powder and harnessed every phase of human existence to its strident mechanic tempo. Change was pounding across the land. The machine drove it forward; its breath was the hiss of steam, its cry the deep-throated bass, mellow treble, or high-pitched shriek of the steam whistle, its grimy signature a plume of coal smoke. A highly centralized industrial nation was emerging from the loose-knit, pastoral self-sufficiency of former years. Nothing would ever again be quite the same, and if the people involved were unable to grasp the full implications of what was happening they sensed that it was big and that they were a part of it.

Moreover, they were able to profit by it—for the most part handsomely, now and then enormously. A continental treasure house was unlocking its varied doors in the eighteen-fifties, and Americans scrambled toward them with a whoop and an exultant burst of energy. Gold almost poured from the streams and mountains on the far Pacific slope, drawing hungry-eyed men from all parts of the world to grub for wealth amid jerry-built tarpaper cities that sprang into being overnight. From the California boom towns the rivers of gold flowed far and wide, enriching every channel of commerce and finance, boosting prices, restoring the balance of America's trade with industrial Europe. Near the end of the decade rich mineral strikes in Nevada and Colorado gave further evidence of the treasure lodes that veined the Western mountains. Longhorns fattened on the rich prairie grass in Texas and the great central plain. Every summer the fields in the lower South lay beneath a white cotton blanket that stretched from the Cape Fear to the Brazos. From Ohio westward to Iowa stood the amber waves of grain—and among them, equally important if less inspiring, ran the squealing droves of hogs. Vast stands of virgin forest awaited the locust hosts of lumbermen in Maine and Michigan, Wisconsin and Minnesota, Georgia and the Pacific Northwest. Copper was discovered in Michigan's upper peninsula, oil along the streams in western Pennsylvania.

And above all, rich seams of coal darkened the rock-slabbed Appalachian hillsides in Pennsylvania and Maryland and western Virginia, and huge rust-flecked beds of iron ore lay along the southern coast of Lake Superior. Here was the combination that became the mainspring of America's industrial transformation and made mockery of Southern boasts that cotton and slavery would remain at the center of the universe. The idea that cotton was king, that the trade and welfare of the western world were dependent upon it, took firm root in the Southern mind at an early day and remained there until the blue-clad infantry columns were filing into the streets of Charleston and Richmond. Actually, cotton wore an uneasy crown from the moment in 1855 when the Sault Ste. Marie Canal was open for traffic in the remote northern woods, permitting the laden ore boats to descend from Superior to the Lower Lakes. A new axis had formed, its poles in the northern ore beds and the Appalachian coal fields, its center in the glowing furnace-lined valleys of Lehigh and Mahoning and Monongahela. Even before the Soo Canal, the iron deposits in Pennsylvania were pointing the way ahead; King Cotton was deposed neither by Federal soldiers nor by King Wheat (as Midwestern editors liked to call it), but by the efficient, mundane triumvirate of coal and iron and steam.

If continental abundance underwrote the Big Change, technology performed it. Each year during the fifties the Patent Office clerks toiled longer to keep pace with the growing list of mechanical devices and improvements which Yankee inventors were busily adding to their piecemeal assembly of an industrial system. American mechanical ingenuity gained worldwide respect on a wide range of fronts, from locks and watches to printing presses and steam locomotives. In almost every field of human endeavor the machine was steadily taking over more of the work.

And the change came. The Northeast was becoming a region of industrial cities and growing mill towns and a few sprawling centers of commerce and finance, its farms strictly tributary to the tasks of the mill hand at spindle or forge, the stevedore along the waterfront, the clerk behind his desk. The great urban magnet was at work. It pulled upcountry farmboys into New York and Boston and Philadelphia and a hundred smaller cities, and blended them—none too smoothly—with the restless, searching tide of newcomers from County Cork and Rhine Valley and the Scandinavian fjords.

The urban flow was matched—perhaps still surpassed in these years—by a steady flood of settlers rolling westward, dissatisfied farmers from the older states joining immigrants in search of fertile acres, in the gigantic American breadbasket that stretched from Ohio to the prairies of Kansas and Nebraska. This region, still known as the Northwest, was also in the grip of change. It grew mightily, and while farming remained its major activity, it was farming with a difference. Technology had caught up with agriculture and yanked it abruptly from the Middle Ages to the present: a revolution of untold proportions that broke the old, confining ratio of land to labor and checked, if it did not destroy, the grim predictions of Thomas Malthus. The timeless man with the hoe was giving way to the reapers of Cyrus McCormick and the steel moldboard plows of Charles Deere and a growing assortment of mowers, threshers, drills, horserakes, and other implements. While agricultural output expanded at a dizzy pace, industrial towns and trade centers sprouted and flourished amid the newly mechanized farmlands of the Northwest, diversifying and enriching the economy of the nation's fastest growing section.

The machine had also conquered distance. In the last prewar decade Americans were busily enlarging and improving a loose-jointed but increasingly efficient transportation network that tied all of the nation's varied activities together and made a single economic unit out of its diverse far-flung regions. The moving parts of America's dawning industrial system were the most dramatic evidence of the technological impact, unforgettable symbols of the transformation then in process.

The old and the new were picturesquely blended in the fifties. Canal boats still floated in leisurely fashion across upper New York state, beside the Potomac, and elsewhere on a once proud system of waterways now becoming obsolete. The covered wagon and the cart still creaked along country roads, and high-wheeled stages yet survived in frontier communities and remote towns. There were still an abundance of flatboats and rafts on every river, hundreds of schooners and sloops at work along the coast, dozens of tall square-riggers in the transatlantic trade. The farthest sealanes of the world were yet briefly thronged with America's graceful winged clipper ships, surpassingly beautiful, final match-less product of the age of sail.

But this was the age of steam; the combustion engine was the noisy herald of things to come. Every waterway had become main street for the busy steam craft. Walking beams and smoking fun-nels were more and more in evidence on every Great Lakes water-front, in every major bay and river along the eastern coast. The steamers of Samuel Cunard and E. K. Collins had usurped pri-macy from the lordly sailing packets in the transatlantic trade, and the riverboat was supreme on the Mississippi.

And by 1850, the railroad was in the bright midmorning of its ascendancy. Its impact and potential had captured the imagina-tion of dreamers and realists the country over: no one, from Henry David Thoreau in his Walden solitude to the hardest-headed financier on State Street or Wall Street, entertained the slightest doubt that modern America was riding in behind the locomotive. Frontier opportunities once narrowly bound by the forbidding cost of wagon transport or the water level in a nearby stream had been linked by the iron trail to the markets of the world; Iowa corn and Illinois pork now fed the Lancashire mill hand and the soldiers of the Light Brigade. Provincial ways of thought were shattered with each daily arrival of the steam cars bearing mail and newspapers and travelers from distant places.

The railroad was vitally necessary, and ambitious promoters built new lines as fast as capital or the promise of capital could be obtained. Before the Civil War the New England and Middle Atlantic states were spiderwebbed with iron rails. A similar network had taken rapid shape in the Northwest, and the two regions were bound together shortly after midcentury with the completion of four trunk lines across the Appalachian mountains, connecting the rich meat-and-grain country of the Great Lakes and upper Mississippi Valley with the smoking factory cities on the eastern seaboard. (The four lines helped determine the Civil War alignment: in 1860 the Northwest still used the Mississippi but no longer depended upon it, and relied chiefly for its markets and supplies on a direct rail traffic with the East. Southerners who dreamed that the Northwest might be neutral or even an ally in the event of civil conflict should have looked more closely at the endless parade of freight trains clattering across the mountains between the ocean and the Lakes. The Northwest would never disrupt this traffic for the sake of King Cotton.)

The revolution in transport and communication was nationwide. Although the slave-land-cotton economy in the lower South soaked up surplus capital, enterprising promoters had succeeded, by 1860, in putting together the outline of a rail network in the slave states. In the West, the first tangents shot across the Mississippi into Iowa and Missouri, and throughout the decade men planned and sought Federal assistance for a transcontinental road that would bind the Pacific coast more effectively to the rest of the nation—a project thwarted by the crippling effect of the slavery controversy. The railroad's close working partner, the telegraph, had also put in its appearance, and a web of poles and wires spun out along the nation's roadbeds and beyond, spanning the continent by 1861, centralizing and modernizing the jumbled apparatus of marketing and finance. Both Europe and America celebrated the temporary success of the new transatlantic cable in 1858, which spanned the ocean with a finger's touch.

The economic trend was unmistakable. Every technological advance—the railroad, the steamship, the telegraph, the new machines for farm and factory—pointed in a single direction, toward national unity and a complex industrial society and close integration with world economy. Rural self-sufficiency and isolation, except in detached, receding pockets, had given way to commercial production for distant markets both national and international. A war in the Crimea or a panic on the Paris Bourse or a drop in interest rates by the Bank of England now touched off seismic shocks that rippled into Merrimac textile mills and Pittsburgh iron foundries, into distant Iowa cornfields and the wild grasslands of western Texas. In the field of transportation the corporate organization had superseded partnerships and individual owners and was opening up a shadowy, boundless new world for management and finance.

Cotton grown in Mississippi was spun and woven in Fall River and worn by farmers in Wisconsin and railroad section hands in Ohio and Illinois. Timber cut near St. Paul was transshipped at New Orleans and gave employment to carpenters in New York and coopers in Baltimore. Ice from Walden Pond cooled drinks for Southern planters; shoe factories in Lynn turned out footwear for Georgia fieldhands and Illinois stock drovers. Scranton rails and Pittsburgh spikes and Michigan crossties were spliced together on the newly graded roadbeds in Indiana and Missouri. Country stores on the farthest frontier now sold Philadelphia carpets and Waltham watches, rifles from Connecticut and plate glass from Pittsburgh, oysters canned in Baltimore and blankets made in Worcester from wool clipped in Vermont. In these and a thousand similar combinations the new order stamped its complex imprint on the land, stitching it together with iron and wire, making the diverse parts a whole. Here, in all its harsh splendor, altering even the dark drama of sectional conflict, was the essence of the prewar decade and the shape of things to come.

What was coming would take many shapes, some exciting and others ugly, but all of them totally unlike the past. And far from incidentally, the two items for which there was absolutely no place in the emergent scheme of things were disunion and slavery. Technology and commercial enterprise had woven the tight fabric of a national economy into every corner of the land. The various regions were interdependent and tightly interlocked, free-flowing currents of trade and travel already well established. It was too late for artificial political barriers; disunion was a false vision which economic reality would resist from the outset and ultimately negate.

The United States was going to remain one and indivisible and it would some day put an end to slavery: only the time and the circumstance remained in doubt in the fifties. A powerful, deep-rooted, moral indignation against slavery hastened its demise, but even had the moral indifference of a Stephen Douglas prevailed over Northern antislavery sentiment, the institution was headed for extinction. If it did not die of violence, technology demanded that it evolve into something better, and there are no permanent way stations (as the republic is still in the process of learning) between slavery and full citizenship. By 1860, if not before, it was possible to predict with certainty that the typical American of the future would be a mechanized farmer, a factory hand, a clerk, a businessman, an engineer, a skilled worker or plant manager, a man with professional education and training. These demanded a range of skills that slavery in the main neither possessed nor sought to acquire—a recognition, this last, of the grim truth that the safest slave was an ignorant slave, that lessons in carpentry or mechanics are lessons in intellectual advancement which in turn bring freedom closer and make it an object of educated desire. Many Southerners saw the logic in all of this quite clearly, and in the end, tried to escape by pulling loose from a system that was greater than their own, and at fundamental odds with it.

What industrial development might have done to slavery, if allowed to operate unchecked, was beside the point. Slavery was

far more than a labor system, and the economic differences between the South and the rest of the nation were more apparent
than real. The Southern states formed an integral part of the
national economy. Like Northern businessmen, the planters of
cotton, tobacco, sugar, and rice were capitalist entrepreneurs in
the classic nineteenth-century tradition. They invested money in
capital goods—in this instance primarily land and slaves—sold
their products competitively on the open market, balanced their
books, and showed a profit or loss at the end of each year. The
South was in the mainstream of national development; it traded
heavily with other parts of the country and provided the most
important single items in America's foreign commerce—the sale
of the cotton crop, as Southerners were delighted to point out,
pulled the nation out of its financial slough following the Panic
of 1857.

The South was in the mainstream, but it came to fear the speed
of the current. Up to a point, slavery had permitted the South
to develop within the national framework at a rapid pace. In
1850, or thereabouts, the point was reached, and from then on the
land of cotton could only choose between readjusting its system
or falling behind. Economically, readjustment would not have
been difficult; despite their preoccupation with land and slaves,
Southerners were able to block out a rail network in the fifties
and experiment here and there with the beginnings of an industrial
system. That slavery was at least partly adaptable to a diversified
and advancing economy was evidenced by the number of slaves
systematically hired out for nonagricultural work, much of it
skilled or semiskilled, in the towns and on the steamboats and
the railroad lines.

The dawning transition was destroyed by a pervasive mixture
of complacency and fear. To many individuals, if not to the section as a whole, plantation slavery was attractively profitable.
Much argument was expended at the time, and much has been
expended since, to disprove this contention. Critics have depicted
slavery as a wasteful, backward system that kept the South in
a status of primitive colonial dependence on the North, that
exhausted the soil and used up both capital and manpower and

impoverished or held back the majority of Southern whites in the tight and narrow interests of a feudal plantation oligarchy. Apologists, pointing to the chronic indebtedness of most planters and the numberless headaches of running a plantation, have suggested almost tearfully that the institution was harder on the master than on the slave. There were elements of truth in these arguments, but they did little to dispel the overriding faith held by a majority of slaveowners in the basic soundness of their system. This faith went far beyond the familiar counterargument that waste, exploitation, and poverty were equal if not greater byproducts of the Northern industrial process; it did not content itself with the plea that many of the South's ills were attributable to soil, climate, Northern greed, and other factors having nothing to do with slavery.

Quite simply, a man could show handsome profits from owning a plantation, and as wealth was counted in those days there were as many substantial fortunes in the South as in the North. The measurement may have been based on faulty bookkeeping (a science still in its infancy, poorly understood and shoddily practiced by factory owners and railroad managers as well as by planters), and plantation wealth consisted largely of assets which were tragically unconvertible, when need arose, into locomotives and shoes and cannon; but it was wealth all the same, genuine enough, with luck and careful management, to permit as splendidly attractive a manner of living as anything America had yet known.

In short, the plantation ideal had laid its firm grasp upon the Southern imagination, and a good portion of the South's unwillingness to recast itself in the Northern mold was due to a frank admiration of things as they were. The North denounced this attitude as stagnant and unprogressive, when in truth it was simply a Southern version of the American success story: a chance to move into the ranks of the great planters, the possibility of a porticoed mansion with vast rolling acres and a hundred slaves. If the barest handful of aspirants reached this goal, the thing could be done—Joseph Davis provided a striking example—and after all, the number of Astors and Lowells in the North was equally small.

(Americans, as the colonial lotteries and the modern policy racket suggest, have seldom insisted that there be many winners, but have always responded to any system that permits a tiny few to win big.)

For the most part, Southerners saw little point in diverting their assets from land and slaves into transportation or industry. A country estate was where a man ought to live, and for his major investment a dozen prime fieldhands were more rewarding than a textile mill, a thousand acres of land infinitely preferable to a thousand shares of stock. Southerners were far too content with the real evidences of slavery's wealth and opulence to think seriously about the alternatives. They would add that value went beyond dollars and cents, anyway. Their system, in contrast to the turbulent, frenzied, money-grubbing North, was comfortingly stable; it allowed for gracious living and underwrote cultural progress, and it was all made possible by slavery. (It was pointless to argue that the stability relied ultimately on the methods of a police state, that the gracious living was confined to a tiny minority, and that what was genuinely praiseworthy in the Southern way of life was not due to slavery and could have been preserved apart from slavery. The people clung to their faith the more fiercely as its basic inconsistencies and flaws became demonstrable.)

Fear as well as complacency went into the Southern decision to keep plantation slavery at the center of their society. Whether profitable or not, slavery was recognizably more than a labor system. It was a social system, the only supportable answer to a race problem, and here the white South was almost a unit in closing ranks against change—from the planters, great and small, through the townsmen and the huge middle grouping of farmers with one or two slaves and farmers with no slaves at all, down to the ragged poor whites who existed on the squalid fringes of Southern life. In 1850 the slave population in the states of the deep South almost equalled the white population, and in the richest Southern counties the slave majorities ranged as high as eighty and ninety per cent.

A nightmare of violence and terror and degradation, it was universally believed, would follow any adjustment in the complex system that controlled the lives of those whom Jefferson Davis had called the graceless sons of Noah; the nation blundered into civil conflict in 1861 not because the Negro was a slave, but because the slave was a Negro. To tinker with slavery was to loosen it; to industrialize was to train fieldhands in the ways of freedom, to expose the South to the winds of change. Southerners had what they wanted; they preferred to stand still. They would enlarge their system, if they could, to keep pace with the growing free-state population—Manifest Destiny might well add the rich Caribbean lands to slavery's domain—but they would never change it.

There was one more dimension to the institution of slavery, of course, which guaranteed that any attempt to handle the problem was going to run into difficulty. Slavery was also a moral question. It had to be, and practical realists of a later generation who have deplored the fact that the moral argument prevented a gradual, bloodless solution to the slavery problem are apparently suggesting that one of the mightiest ideological currents in the history of the western world should somehow have flowed around this one issue. The nineteenth century was not all materialism and coal smoke; faith in progress and human betterment and a movement for humanitarian reform were powerful impulses on both sides of the Atlantic. An age that concerned itself increasingly with the rights of women, convicts, seamen, laborers, and the mentally ill was not going to overlook the bondsman; and all the varied promptings of western civilization had made it the abundance of man's heart, as Lincoln put it, that slavery was wrong. It was an

> ". . . unjust thing,
> That some tamed into mercy, being wise,
> But could not starve the tiger from its eyes
> Or make it feed where beasts of mercy feed."

The tragedy was not that morality had injected itself into the question and thereby rendered it more difficult to solve; the moral aspect was inherent and unavoidable. The race problem was equally basic, and tragedy came because the South was too hypnotized by the racial factor to accept any moral condemnation whatever, while the North was so blinded by moral indignation that it overlooked the race problem. There was an awesome complexity to this issue which is yet taxing all the resources of a later and more sophisticated generation, and North and South on slavery a century ago were like the proverbial blind men touching different parts of the elephant: neither description was inaccurate, yet each was fatally incomplete. And so the question was quickly raised on both sides to the level of high moral principle, slavery a positive blessing to be defended at all costs or an unmitigated evil to be attacked and destroyed. The voice of compromise, always present, complaining that people had lost sight of reality for the sake of an abstraction, was succinctly answered by a Southern newspaper in 1861: "There is a habit of speaking derisively of going to war for an *idea*—an abstraction—something which you cannot see. This is precisely the point on which we would go to war. An idea is exactly the thing that we would fight for. . . ."

This did not happen all at once. It took nearly a decade and a half for the opposing principles raised during the Wilmot Proviso controversy to crystallize and become the focus for majority sentiment on either side of the line, and between Wilmot and Fort Sumter the path to civil conflict was neither clear nor direct. Only a few leaders, North and South, took the extreme positions right from the start. For several years after 1846, the great majority of Americans were inclined to take a moderate stand. But they exhibited a fatal tendency to mistake postponement for solution, and it finally developed that even the Northern moderate and the Southern moderate had drifted into positions too far apart to be bridged.

Characteristically, Davis and Lincoln moved at different speeds toward the opposing vantage points on which the battle lines would someday form. Davis moved faster—partly due to circumstance, to be sure, but more fundamentally because his deepest thinking on the subject of slavery had already been done. Nor would anything that happened between Mexico and Sumter (and on to Appomattox and beyond, for that matter) materially alter his views. He first entered the United States Senate at the end of 1847, still wearing the laurels and scars of Buena Vista, and he quickly joined the territorial debate touched off by David Wilmot. First and last a man of principle, always acting out of sincere conviction, Davis saw no reason to hesitate. He spoke on behalf of Southern rights as a man defending the cause of justice, which was precisely how he pictured it.

Echoing Calhoun, whose disciple he had become, the handsome Mississippian announced that Congress would violate the Constitution whenever it legislated against the rights of slaveowners to take their property into federal territory. To Davis, this was the outer bastion, the first line of Southern defense; abandon it, and the inner citadel of slavery would soon be open to assault. The North-South conflict, he announced in 1848, had arrived: "It is a struggle for political power, and we must meet it at the threshold." The same view, enlarged now to demand that Congress legislate positively to *protect* slavery in the territories, he sounded with equal firmness in 1860, with a military overtone that carried grim meaning: "The power of resistance consists, in no small degree, in meeting the enemy at the outer gate." In the years that separated these statements Davis would veer somewhat in response to changing circumstance, but he never doubted that the South must take its stand on this line whenever the issue arose.

Behind this defense of slavery in the territories was a philosophy of slavery itself, and here Davis revealed that his meditations on the subject had transcended the normal Southern viewpoint. To be sure, slavery was a positive good—these were, after all, the graceless sons of Noah, inherently the white man's inferior—but he frankly defined the institution as transitory rather than permanent, and the evolution he foresaw, however dimly in the distant future, sounded strangely on the Southern tongue.

"Sirs," he told the Senate in 1848, "this problem is one which must bring its own solution; leave natural causes to their full effect, and when the time shall arrive at which emancipation is proper, those most interested will be the most anxious to effect it." The Negroes must first be "elevated by association and instruction: or, instead of a blessing, liberty would be their greatest curse." There were elements of wisdom and foresight in this view. From most slaveowners such a statement could be dismissed as pious cant and rank hypocrisy, but Jefferson Davis never uttered a syllable save from honest conviction, and his exemplary treatment of his own slaves bore him out. In a far-off, mystic sense this man was an emancipationist, although his predictions were couched in terms that would never disturb the South, satisfy the North, or solve the problem.

Lincoln moved more deliberately. He had to examine every facet of this tangled question; like the mills of God his mind ground slowly, but ground exceeding small. Lincoln, too, was in Congress during part of the Wilmot debate. He had always disliked slavery. In the Illinois legislature he had introduced resolutions emphasizing its basic injustice; in Congress he framed a bill calling for the gradual emancipation of slaves in the District of Columbia; he voted for the Wilmot Proviso on five occasions. But his opposition had always been restrained and temperate, and he took little part in the angry Congressional debates, nor gave support to the more radical antislavery measures. Abolitionism, he felt, was both wrong and dangerous; slavery was too complex a problem to be eliminated at one stroke.

As yet the issue had not assumed urgent dimensions in his mind, and for five years after his retirement from politics in 1849 there was no occasion for him to speak or act on the subject. He had not stopped thinking about it, however, and with the sudden appearance of a new national crisis over slavery in 1854 he concluded that the thing had to be faced, and could be faced in only one way. Slavery extension was wrong, morally wrong—and more important, people who thought so had to stand up and be counted, because everything of value in the nation's heritage was somehow tied to this question. He had now discovered the abundance of man's heart, and would follow it unswervingly to ultimate fulfillment. In a sense much less mystic and far-off, Abraham Lincoln was an emancipationist, too.

Increasingly, the citizens of the Northern states found what they were groping for in Lincoln's approach to slavery. It was moderate and cautious, but it was forthright, and it might just possibly be content with the gradual erosion of slavery by industrial forces or with the millennial transformation predicted by Jefferson Davis. But there was a quiet urgency about the Lincoln position, together with a growing awareness that the South would resist any attempts to modify its social structure, be they ever so gradual or long-range. With the underlying Southern view —that slavery was a positive good which had every right to expand—the Lincoln position must sooner or later collide. An eternal antagonism, he had called it. The ideas were what counted, and the economic forces that might have recast slavery into something better by slow degrees would instead be used to smash it to fragments, and much that should have been preserved would be smashed along with it.

At bottom, the conflicting ideologies and the emergent economic system were symptomatic of a social order singularly ill-equipped to cope with a problem as complex as slavery. The leaders of the prewar decade—whether as cool-headed as Davis and Lincoln and Stephen Douglas, as doctrinaire as Charles Sumner and James H. Hammond, as expedient as William Seward and David Atchison, or as inflammatory as William L. Yancey and Wendell Phillips—were no longer debating the question, but simply shouting back and forth without listening. The quarrel had picked up a momentum of its own, and the politicians were doing little more than running before a wind they had blown up themselves— usually with the best of intentions, seldom with a view of the nation that encompassed enough of its sprawling diversity or internal disorder. Running before the wind was all this fragmented society itself could do, for that matter. It had no other leaders to follow. It was incapable of producing any other kind, and the ones it got—as able, by and large, as Americans of any epoch—did not mislead their generation so much as mirror it.

Yet the fault went deeper than this. The philosophy of John Locke, filtered imperfectly and incompletely through the minds of America's revolutionary leaders, had been applied to the new nation with all the rational confidence of the eighteenth century. By the mid-nineteenth this application had produced a degree of individual freedom that was the wonder of the western world and a degree of social irresponsibility that was the despair of it. Vast empty acres, abundant resources, advancing technology, the immigrant, the combustion engine, and the corporation multiplied opportunities for the free individual while they systematically shattered the relative cohesion and order of colonial society.

Individualism unfettered could accomplish much, alone or in combination, as the railroad, the pony express, the lyceum, Fall River, the cotton kingdom, the Yankee clipper, and the over-worked patent office bore witness, but the problem of Negro slavery was harder to subdue than a continent. In tackling slavery the nation first lost its patience, then its temper, and finally its unity because all three were of unstable and deteriorating quality before the controversy began, rendered so by a guiding philosophy that eroded older attitudes of social obligation and tossed the stable colonial heirarchy of more or less interdependent classes into chaos, then back into irresponsible and competing interest groups. Extreme social mobility and broadening opportunity combined to wipe out old class lines; new ones were measured only in monetary or material terms; and the anxieties and habits of mind engendered by the profit motive replaced *noblesse oblige* with narrow self-interest.

At the same time, manhood suffrage and party politics did away with a recognized, quasi-patrician class of leaders and substituted a species of professional politician whose interest in lining up an immediate majority tended to obscure a national viewpoint and put constructive statesmanship at a discount. At the lowest level this meant demagoguery and appeals to prejudice, and even at the highest it encouraged saying what one's audience wanted to hear or risking defeat at the hands of a rival who never said anything else. Under the circumstances it is remarkable that the nation bred leaders as relatively high-minded as Lincoln and Davis and a handful of others, not remarkable at all that none of these could gain a national hearing or rise too far above the babel of sectional and private interest groups who recognized no responsibility save to themselves.

The gods did not first have to make Americans mad in order

to destroy them; it was only necessary to turn them loose. Once at large, they would energetically remove the props from a stable social order—after which, given a problem utterly unanswerable in terms of competing self-interest, they would unfailingly proceed to destroy one another.

[FOUR]

MODERATION
CHALLENGED,
1 8 4 6 – 1 8 5 4

To Southerners, the attempt to bar slavery from the territories
was a naked act of aggression on the part of the North. They
accepted the challenge of the Wilmot Proviso with the hair-trig-
gered dignity of self-conscious aristocrats whose honor (and more,
much more) was at stake—determined, in Davis's phrase, to meet
the enemy at the outer gate.

The issue was immediately compounded by a variety of related
topics. The South wanted a much stronger Federal slave law,
one that would make the recapture of runaway bondsmen in the
North less liable to obstruction by a hostile citizenry. Many
Northern spokesmen wanted to abolish the wholesale slave trade
in the District of Columbia, disgusted that the very seat of democratic government should have to witness lines of manacled
human chattels being paraded to the auction block. Some Northern leaders hoped that slavery itself might be abolished in the
nation's capital. Texas, already admitted to the Union as a slave
state, claimed large slices of the new territory acquired from
Mexico, and the Texas boundary could not be settled until the
status of slavery in the disputed region was determined. Agreement on the territorial question was rendered urgent in 1849 by
the rapid influx of population to California goldfields. Almost

[80]

overnight, California was host to a growing, acquisitive multitude whose need for laws and the machinery of government produced an immediate demand for territorial organization, first step on what was bound to be a rapid road to statehood.

In no time the debate became a quarrel, savage and angry. As each side presented its demands with increasing vigor and showed scant signs of retreating from positions which the other side refused to accept, people began to realize that the problems posed by the Mexican War and David Wilmot had paralyzed the national government and might well destroy it. Insults and blows were exchanged on the floor of Congress. Party discipline was rent by hostile Northern and Southern factions, and legislative machinery ground almost to a halt. Southerners would not vote to organize California, or any of the former Mexican provinces, unless slavery was permitted to go there; Northerners would support only bills that kept it out. The Lame Duck session of the Thirtieth Congress adjourned in early 1849 without acting on the territories or much of anything else, and the opening session of the Thirty-first in December was so hamstrung by sectional discord that it took three weeks and sixty-odd ballots merely to elect a Speaker and get organized.

The fullness of the disaster that threatened the nation was given dramatic utterance from a familiar quarter. In January, 1849, John C. Calhoun spoke his mind at an important meeting of the entire Southern delegation—Whigs and Democrats, Senators and Representatives. Calling for a new all-Southern party that would present a united front against its foes, the aging, defiant South Carolinian issued a grim manifesto that prophesied a break-up of the Union unless Northern aggression against slavery were stopped. This aggression, Calhoun warned, did not begin with Wilmot. It went way back to the Missouri Compromise and the Northwest Ordinance of 1787, each forming pieces in a carefully matured Northern design to halt the spread of slavery. The recent organization of the Oregon territory with a ban on slavery was a late example; Lincoln's abortive bill to emancipate the District of Columbia was another. The expanding, hostile North sought to monopolize federal territory and add to the number of free states until it could muster the votes to destroy slavery by Constitutional amendment. In short, ruin and ultimate degradation lay ahead unless the Southern states banded together as a unit to thwart the Northern plan.

Calhoun's Southern Address had said it all, though few in either section realized it at the time. As prophecy it was matchless. Calhoun was genuinely afraid. He feared the North, and he feared for the future of slavery, and his fear would spread like a contagion through the South until it produced, in the years to come, something approaching the unity he demanded in 1849. For its own security, said Calhoun, slavery must be allowed to expand: here was the core of Southern policy in the decade ahead. Sudden emancipation would bring poverty, upheaval, anarchy, and racial strife to the South. To avoid this dread contingency, he repeated, the slave states as a last resort would break up the Union, even at the cost of civil war. If David Wilmot had opened Pandora's box, John Calhoun had described with pitiless accuracy what lay inside.

Among the signers of this remarkable document, which was printed and circulated in both sections as a warning and a call to arms, was Senator Davis of Mississippi. But Calhoun and Davis had momentarily overreached themselves. Many Southerners were not ready for so extreme a position, and the call for unity met so limited a response that Northerners tended to laugh it off as one more bit of fiery but meaningless Southern bravado. Members from the border slave states, including such influential figures as Thomas Hart Benton of Missouri, Sam Houston of Texas, and John M. Clayton of Delaware, refused to sign the Address; so did the rising Georgia triumvirate of Alexander Stephens, Robert Toombs, and Howell Cobb; so did a host of others. Southern Whigs generally backed away from the idea, seeing in it a move to swallow up their party in a new organization dominated by Democrats. A Southern-rights convention, assembled in Nashville by adherents of Calhoun in early 1850 with a view to rallying disunion sentiment, was a distinct fizzle, captured by moderates and poorly attended.

Public sentiment on both sides had been aroused by the territorial controversy, but it was not yet ready for a showdown. There was time for one more of the great compromises that Americans had come to rely on in moments of crisis, and there were still great national leaders on the scene who could rally moderate opinion behind such an effort. The leaders came forward. In 1850, after weeks of earnest debate and careful political maneuver, a compromise was hammered out and jammed through both Houses of Congress against bitter opposition. Though many able hands went into the effort, the chief architects of compromise were Clay, Webster, and the ambitious, capable young Senator from Illinois, Stephen A. Douglas.

Vivid scenes, unforgettably dramatic, attended the creation of the Compromise of 1850. Midcentury was a watershed in American politics. An older generation was passing and a new one was coming of age, and for a few brief months the spokesmen of both were mingled together in the national forum to decide the country's fate.

Recent arrivals, mostly younger men, were adding their voices, already reaching out for the leadership soon to be theirs. In the Lower House the votes in favor of compromise were laboriously marshaled by the competent young Georgians: pale, sickly Aleck Stephens, lion-hearted Robert Toombs, and the genial, curly-headed Howell Cobb. Among their backers was an ardent, sensitive Unionist from Tennessee named Andrew Johnson; their opponents, the extremists and radicals from both sections, included David Wilmot and a sharp-tongued, sardonic fellow Pennsylvanian named Thaddeus Stevens.

In the Senate the men of tomorrow were also present. Now it was beak-nosed William H. Seward of New York, addressing the upper chamber with negligent ease, hands in his pockets, announcing in husky voice that there was a higher law than the Constitution which had ordained the doom of slavery. Now it was Seward's second in the fight against compromise, the handsome, humorless Salmon P. Chase of Ohio, zealous antislavery leader, shaking hands proudly with the fire-eating proslavery extremist from Louisiana, Pierre Soulé, when the compromise was momentarily beaten down by a coalition of Northern and Southern radicals. Now it was Davis of Mississippi, archfoe of compromise in the name of Southern rights, rising with dignity to read the defiant resolutions of the Mississippi legislature. "We will not permit aggressions," he rasped. "We will defend our rights." Now it was stocky little Douglas of Illinois, shaking his loose mane in quick nervous gesture as he bustled energetically in search of the compromise formula that could steer its way through the hostile factions.

But the center spotlight still played on the older men. This was the last great drama for the Senatorial giants who had overshadowed the political scene for a generation and more, and few who saw them rise to do battle in the bright sunset of their careers would ever forget it. They saw the majestic, combative old Roman from Missouri, Thomas Hart Benton, a Senate fixture for thirty years, outspokenly eloquent, a slaveowner who fought the extension of slavery—Benton rising to denounce the Southern leaders and advancing in a rage upon peppery, bald-headed Foote of Mississippi after a bitter exchange, Foote nervously brandishing a pistol, and Benton, seeing it, roaring: "I am not armed. I have no pistols. I disdain to carry arms. Let him fire! Stand out of the way and let the assassin fire!"

They saw Calhoun sit in grim silence, his throat bandaged and his stern face haggard with approaching death, following every word while his final speech to the Senate in defense of Southern rights was read by a colleague—John Calhoun, a tired, proud, gray hawk still glaring defiance while he perched high on the outer ramparts of the South for the last time.

They saw Henry Clay on his feet again and again to defend his compromise proposals and plead for national unity, still alert at seventy-three, his famous charm undimmed by age, his voice still able to captivate and compel, urging now that the nation was more important than the transient discontent of individual men. "What is an individual man?" he asked. "An atom . . . a drop of water in the great deep . . . a grain of sand . . . Shall a being so small, so petty, so fleeting, so evanescent, oppose itself to the onward march of a great nation, to subsist for ages and ages to come . . . ? Forbid it God!"

And they heard the mightiest voice of all, old Daniel Webster pouring out his last eloquence in behalf of compromise and union, deep-set eyes still glowing beneath the black brows. "I wish to speak today," he said, while the tense galleries rustled into silence, "not as a Massachusetts man, nor as a Northern man, but as an American . . . I speak today for the preservation of the Union. 'Hear me for my cause.' " The giants were passing, but they would not pass unheard.

The eloquence of Clay and Webster, ably reinforced by the political adroitness of Douglas and a host of others, ultimately carried the day. When a weary Congress finally adjourned in the early fall of 1850, it had tacked a patchwork compromise over every visible rent in the national fabric. California, true to its expressed sentiment, was admitted to the Union as a free state. Texas, its ambition mollified by a handsome financial recompense, gave up its vast territorial claims and accepted its present boundaries. In the rest of the domain acquired from Mexico the new territories of Utah and New Mexico were organized, and the vexatious slavery problem was swept beneath the rug by adopting the principle—men called it popular sovereignty—whereby the decision to permit or exclude slavery would be made by the inhabitants of the two territories, rather than by Congressional legislation. Slavery was retained, the slave trade abolished, in the District of Columbia. The South was rewarded with a stronger Fugitive Slave Law.

In general, the nation expressed itself as satisfied. The Compromise of 1850 was admittedly patchy, but it might hold together. No one liked all of it, and there was abiding bitterness against it in both North and South, extremists on either side maintaining that the agreement was a complete sellout to the enemy. The Fugitive Slave Law stuck painfully in the Northern throat, and many took a silent oath along with Ralph Waldo Emerson that they would not obey it. The South regretted the admission of free California with no guarantee that a new slave state could be found to match it, "the balance of power between the sections of the Union," as Davis crisply observed, having thus been destroyed in freedom's favor. No one quite knew what "popular sovereignty" with respect to slavery in Utah and New Mexico was going to mean (time and broader application would show that it meant disaster), and for the moment radicals could simply grumble, according to their persuasion, that slavery should have been banned or legalized in both territories by positive enactment. Despite all the carping, however, popular sentiment went increasingly on record in favor of the settlement. To most people, giving way here and there on slavery was not yet too big a price to pay for national unity.

Three and a half years of relative calm—the last the nation was to know for over a decade—followed the Compromise of 1850. To Jefferson Davis, who had opposed the measure at every step, popular acceptance of the Compromise dealt a sharp political setback and forced him temporarily into retirement, a lesson in the majesty of public opinion that Lincoln had learned in similar fashion a few years before. Every Southern state gave a more or less qualified endorsement to the compromise in the months following its passage. Southern extremists who advocated disunion at this time were defeated, narrowly in some states, overwhelmingly in others, both by a resurgence of union sentiment and by a sharp break in their own ranks. In the areas where Southern-rights feeling was strongest—the cotton belt generally, and South Carolina and Mississippi above all—opponents of compromise were fatally divided between "immediate secessionists," who sought to break up the Union right away by individual state action, and "cooperative secessionists" who preferred to wait until some or all of the Southern states could act as a unit. Of the two groups, the latter were more moderate, by far, and when the halfhearted efforts at cooperative action got nowhere, these men joined the unionist element in their respective commonwealths in voting against secession. The South might show its concern by applauding the Georgia resolutions of 1851, which endorsed the Compromise while warning that any Northern violations of it would force something akin to an agonizing re-appraisal, but Calhoun's stark fear was still far from dominant in the Southern mind.

Davis found this out in 1851, when the supporters and foes of compromise vied for supremacy in his home state. The South-ern-rights candidate for governor was rugged, bewhiskered John A. Quitman, Davis's brigade commander in the Mexican War, a devout believer in slavery extension and Southern resistance to Northern aggression. His opponent on the Unionist ticket was Henry S. Foote, of pistol-brandishing fame in the recent alterca-tion with Senator Benton. Volatile, coarsely eloquent, and fiercely combative, Foote was a born maverick who had first championed slavery extension, then shifted radically to become a strong defender of the Compromise in the Senate.

Foote was now out to demonstrate that Mississippi approved his new stand. He campaigned so well against Quitman that the Southern-rights element took alarm and importuned Davis, their most eminent spokesman, to resign his Senate seat and replace Quitman in the gubernatorial race. Davis consented. He and Foote, once good friends, had broken on the compromise issue in the Senate and formed an abiding personal enmity that would return to plague the Confederate president a decade later. By the time Davis took the stump against Foote, the tide in Mississippi was already running strongly against the extremists. A Unionist majority was elected to the convention that had been called to decide the state's relations to the Union—in other words, to con-sider secession—and Foote was visibly gaining support wherever he went. Forced on the defensive, Davis virtually came out on the side of compromise when he admitted that immediate secession was inadvisable. This retreat, added to the personal popularity he had enjoyed in Mississippi since Mexican War days, enabled him to make a good race of it, but Foote and the cause of Unionism won a clear victory in the autumn of 1851. Davis found himself back in private life, and returned to Brierfield to meditate ruefully on the ways of public sentiment.

Actually, Davis was not at this time, nor until the very last, an out-and-out secessionist. He had signed Calhoun's Southern

Address in 1849 and defended its principles for the next two years, both in Mississippi and in Washington, not because he wanted the slave states actually to withdraw from the Union, but because he agreed with Calhoun that only a united South could bring an end to Northern attacks on slavery. This was meeting the enemy at the outer gate, standing resolute and united to force a return to the Constitutional principles of the Founding Fathers. Davis still loved his country. The vision of an expanding America under a beneficent republican government burned as brightly as ever in his mind's eye. But the country he loved could not, must not, interfere with the peculiar institution, and when it threatened to do so the South was justified in talking secession as a counter-measure. Firmest of Davis's firm convictions was the belief that every state had the constitutional right to secede—this was standard Southern doctrine, derived directly from Calhoun and by rather tortuous logic from Thomas Jefferson, another much-disputed point over which Davis and Lincoln would someday marshal the opposing hosts—but a state should only exercise that right as a last resort; the *threat* of secession would be enough to beat off the Northern assault.

As a nationalist, Davis never saw the twin dangers in this approach. If Southern leaders continued to use secession as a bargaining point to win concessions from the other side—in short, as a bluff—the South was very apt to start believing that secession was a good idea, as a small but determined minority in each of the cotton states already did by 1850, and the North was some day apt to call the bluff. Moderate Southern leadership in the decade ahead never quite faced up to the dilemma that would confront them if this happened.

Davis's involuntary retirement from politics was cut short in early 1853 when the incoming Democratic administration, headed by the genial, pliable Franklin Pierce, tendered him a cabinet post. Unionists and backers of compromise in both sections were horrified at the selection of this archdisciple of Calhoun, but from Pierce's standpoint it was an understandable choice. Pierce and

Davis had known and liked each other since 1838, when the young planter visited Washington for the first time and ate at a Congressional "mess" with the young Representative from New Hampshire. They had been fellow officers under Taylor in Mexico. The Secretaryship of War was a natural post for a man with Davis's military background, and it seemed advisable, since cabinet making was primarily a matter of rewarding as many areas and factions as possible, to choose a Southern Democrat of high standing who represented not the extreme fire-eaters but the solid core of state-rights sentiment in his section. Davis, who had campaigned actively for Pierce in more than one Southern state during the canvass of 1852, first declined the offer, then agreed to visit Washington during the early winter of 1853 for a chat with the President-elect, and finally allowed himself to be persuaded.

In the cabinet, Davis was soon able to demonstrate in fairly convincing fashion that he thought in national rather than sectional terms. He was one of the ablest Secretaries of War the nation has ever had, and most of his far-ranging activities were sincerely aimed at strengthening and unifying the country. Never would he display greater breadth of vision or boldness of intellect; seldom were his real executive talents and statesmanlike qualities more strikingly in evidence.

Approaching his duties with characteristic earnestness and remarkable energy, he undertook nothing less than a complete overhaul of the country's military establishment—an intensive muscular build-up which no dreamer of secessionist dreams could possibly have desired. Under Davis the regular army was enlarged, reorganized, and strengthened. He prescribed new infantry tactics and a new model rifle, modernized forts, secured pay increases for all grades, founded the army medical corps, and battled (vainly) for promotion by merit rather than by seniority. In conjunction with his old classmate Robert E. Lee, now commandant of West Point, he embarked on an ambitious program of enlarging the facilities and improving the quality of training at the Military Academy. He saw to it that the army adopted a newly invented, cone-shaped, expansive rifle bullet known as the Minie ball, with which a great many thousands of American youths would soon become acquainted.

The well-known experiment with Arabian camels in the desert region of the American Southwest was his idea; so, essentially, was the mission of James Gadsden to Mexico for the purchase of an extra strip of territory in that same area, with an eye to the best route for a Pacific railroad. His interest in this rail project, which he saw as a great bond of national union, culminated in an exhaustive, competent, War Department survey of the American West in ten massive volumes. Davis closely supervised this mammoth compilation and took a keen interest in it, with the result that it was crammed with useful scientific data as well as likely railroad routes. He planned and executed the addition of the Capitol's present wings, and directed the construction of the fine new aqueduct at Cabin John, a few miles above Washington. His devotion to the principle of state-rights did not prevent him from interpreting the military clauses of the Federal Constitution broadly enough to justify government spending in behalf of railroads and river improvements: like his namesake and political patron saint, Jefferson Davis did not hesitate to adopt the Hamiltonian outlook when it suited his purpose. Under Davis's leadership the War Department became a vigorously active, highly competent agency for cementing national unity and building national strength.

It was partly true, as Northern critics darkly noted then and later, that many of his projects seemed unduly helpful to the South. His expansionist views, which the Pierce administration pushed with great vigor and greater clumsiness, were aimed at Mexico and the Caribbean and above all Cuba, areas of benefit to slavery; his diligent labors in behalf of a Pacific railway pointed strongly to the cotton states. But this was by no means inconsistent with the Davis brand of nationalism. The South must grow and prosper with the rest of the nation, in order to preserve a healthy sectional balance. Slavery was a distinct blessing—a gradual, all-wise process of civilizing and elevating the Negro race—

and as such its expansion into new areas would merely extend its benefits.

Moreover, unlike the majority of Southern leaders, Davis both recognized and approved the economic transformation at work in the United States, and his advocacy of a Southern Pacific railroad and navigational improvements in the lower Mississippi valley were frankly designed to give the South a greater stake in the new order. Take a leaf from the Northern book, he warned his section in 1849, diversify and grow strong: "let us get together and build manufactories, enter upon industrial pursuits and prepare for our own self-sustenance." Such policies, to be sure, would strengthen the South for conflict, if and when it came; but in Davis's view they were primarily aimed at bringing the South into line with economic progress and thereby rendering conflict more easily avoidable.

It was also true that Secretary Davis exerted a great deal of influence in the Pierce administration, and there was no denying that this influence was strongly Southern in tone. Something of the sort was almost bound to happen. Davis was a strong-willed character who would always tend to dominate the men around him, especially the lesser men. Franklin Pierce was the very incarnation of the lesser man, the type who simply had to be dominated by someone, and he and Davis adopted such a relationship with the ease and mutual satisfaction of a trained mount and an experienced rider.

Pierce was heavily predisposed in favor of the South anyway. Detesting abolitionism and endorsing the Southern view that slavery deserved security from such attacks, Pierce was thoroughly typical of the appeasement element in the North—men unmoved by the moral assault on slavery, who would preserve the Union by giving the South everything it wanted. (This element was quite strong in the North during the early fifties; Southerners, who drew their Northern friends entirely from this quarter, would fatally overestimate its strength in 1860, even as Republicans fatally overvalued the power of the Southern Unionists.) There were also two Northern strong men in the Pierce cabinet, but Attorney

General Caleb Cushing of Massachusetts was as staunch a defender of Southern rights as Davis himself, while bushy-browed William L. Marcy of New York, the Secretary of State—he had coined the well-worn maxim about the victor and the spoils—found himself unable to exert much counterinfluence against the strength of the Davis-Cushing bloc, reinforced as it was by all of Pierce's natural inclinations.

As a result, the Pierce administration was Southern-oriented. Avowedly expansionist, it sought to turn Manifest Destiny in a southerly direction, toward regions hospitable to slavery. It bought the Gadsden territory from Mexico and talked of acquiring more, displayed a suspicious want of energy in blocking the attempts of its own citizens to carry out schemes of private conquest in Central America, and maneuvered for the purchase or seizure of Cuba from Spain with an inept zeal that bordered on the fantastic. Although these matters were theoretically within the purview of Secretary Marcy, the impetus and guidance were more often provided by Davis and Cushing. It was only by asserting himself at the last minute that Marcy was able to avert a war with Spain and use neutrality against a private organization—led by Davis's long-time comrade John A. Quitman of Mississippi—which sought to liberate Cuba by means of an expeditionary force recruited and equipped in the United States and launched from American soil.

None of this really mattered, however, when placed beside the administration's pro-Southern stand on the Kansas-Nebraska Bill.

The man primarily responsible for what may have been the most fateful single piece of legislation in all American history was Senator Douglas of Illinois. When Douglas reported the Kansas-Nebraska Bill from the Senate Committee on Territories in January, 1854, he was setting in motion a chain of events that led unswervingly into civil conflict. The new measure repealed the old Missouri Compromise, destroyed the three-year truce that had followed the Compromise of 1850, reawakened and instilled new vigor into the controversy over slavery in the territories, summoned Abraham Lincoln from retirement, created a new political party and split an old one down the middle, induced fraud and bloodletting on the remote Kansas prairies, touched off some sort of process in the disordered mind of a tall, bearded mystic named John Brown, and added immeasurably to the mutual fear and distrust that were making a cold war out of the North-South relationship. Before Kansas-Nebraska the country's chances of avoiding a civil war were problematical, but fair; after Kansas-Nebraska they were virtually nonexistent.

That Stephen Douglas should be the man to release the brake and start the country down the last long slope was ironic, to say the least. A patriot and believer in national unity, he made disunion infinitely harder to avoid; a loyal party man, he invoked the controversy that was almost bound to split his party in two. Few men were more indifferent to the moral and emotional aspects of the quarrel over slavery, yet few men did as much, in a single legislative enactment, to insure that the moral and emotional features would dominate every remaining phase of the controversy. He is an arresting figure, this Stephen A. Douglas. His country will always find him easy to misjudge but impossible to ignore, and it must end however reluctantly by pronouncing him a great man. They called him the Little Giant, and it fitted superbly; a short man with broad shoulders and massive brow and commanding presence, highly able, harshly eloquent; a battler who fought with the same courage and tenacity for the loftiest and shoddiest of causes; an ambitious politician of coarse habit and unscrupulous tactic who ultimately learned to wear the mantle of statesmanship without stumbling; a materialist who took his final stand on the ground of high principle.

In framing the Kansas-Nebraska bill Douglas undoubtedly had the best of intentions, although his logic was hampered by one enormous blind spot. The measure called for the creation of two new territories out of the vast, unorganized region that stretched from the western boundaries of Missouri and Iowa to the Rocky Mountain divide and from the Canadian border to 36°30′, the prairie version of the Mason and Dixon line. This much was routine; what gave the Douglas bill its toxic quality was the clause that specifically repealed the Missouri Compromise of 1820 and permitted slaveowners, with their chattels, to settle at will

in the region north of 36°30′, which the law of 1820 had pronounced "forever free." Douglas had originally planned to side-
step this explosive issue—even he recognized that it would "raise
a hell of a storm" in the North—until a few Southern senators
warned him that the South would oppose the measure if it did
not unequivocally reopen the Kansas-Nebraska region to slavery.
The bill was so amended, and Congress had to decide whether
it wanted to legislate the Missouri Compromise out of existence.

There seemed no need to reopen the slavery question. The
country was highly prosperous, still enjoying the relative political
calm ushered in by the Compromise of 1850. The status of slavery
had been settled by legislative enactment in every square inch
of the national domain. Abolitionists and Southern fire-eaters continued to exchange denunciations with undiminished virulence, but
extremism was clearly in the minority, still smarting from the
triumph of moderate sentiment in 1850-1851.

There were trouble spots, of course. The South made new enemies each time a runaway, real or alleged, was brought before
the harsh terms of the Fugitive Slave Law in some northern city.
In 1852 young Harriet Beecher Stowe began to sear the Yankee
conscience with the hot, effective lash of *Uncle Tom's Cabin*—a
vivid, highly imaginative, best-selling, and altogether damning
indictment of slavery that roused a counterindignation among
Southerners both because they thought Mrs. Stowe's portrait un-
true and because the North was so willing to believe it. (In men's
minds, reality was giving way to images, and the images were
irredeemably hostile: from now on the Southern stereotype in
Northern eyes was something akin to Simon Legree, even as the
South would shortly come to identify the typical Yankee with
John Brown.) But in 1854, with the thorny question of territorial
slavery out of national politics, there was yet reason to hope that
the barometer of ill feeling would not drop to the danger point.

It began to drop, steadily, from the moment the terms of the
Kansas-Nebraska Bill leaked out to the Northern press. Though
he had foreseen this—with pathetic dimness, as it turned out—
Douglas felt that the benefits of his measure would far outweigh
its drawbacks. Several considerations were prompting him. He was

an Illinois Democrat, a self-appointed and highly popular spokesman for the land-hungry, expansion-minded Northwest, and a
staunch advocate of material progress. Organization of the Kansas-
Nebraska region, he knew, would appeal strongly to the Western
homesteader and could not be long delayed in any case, since
the advance guard of settlement was already spilling across the
Missouri at Independence and Council Bluffs. His bill would also
further the cause of a Pacific railroad, a project dear to Douglas's
heart, by permitting exact location of the route and making land
grants available.

In reopening the new territories to slavery, Douglas thought
he had found a formula at once democratic and practical. He
would apply the principle of popular sovereignty: open Kansas-
Nebraska to all, keep Congressional hands off, and allow the
settlers themselves—the sovereign people—to decide whether they
would erect free states or slave states. Long a champion of the
popular sovereignty idea, Douglas had been instrumental in apply-
ing it to the Utah and New Mexico territories under the Compromise of 1850. He could thus point to precedent, and he could argue,
with some logic, that letting the people decide was the very essence
of democracy and the American way. The principle, once accepted,
would permanently remove the troublesome slave-territory issue
from the arena of Congressional debate.

Popular sovereignty was supposed to perform one other important service. A loyal Democrat with his eye on the White
House, Douglas was acutely distressed at the squabbling, drifting, divided condition to which a year of Franklin Pierce had
reduced the Democratic Party. Douglas actually seems to have
felt—a practical politician whose instinct in this case was guiding
him approximately 180 degrees off course—that Kansas-Nebraska
and popular sovereignty would provide the great winning issue
around which (and behind whose author) his faction-ridden party
could unite. Popular sovereignty would appeal to the strong democratic sentiment in the Northwest and in the country generally,
while the opportunity to take slavery into an area formerly closed
to it would appeal to the South.

He saw no cause for Northern antislavery opinion to get excited.

Senator Douglas was a practical man, and he had figured it out this way: Kansas and Nebraska were geographically unsuited to slavery, which was a specialized labor system able to thrive only in subtropical regions. Material considerations always determined the issue. "Whenever a territory has a climate, soil and productions making it the interest of the inhabitants to encourage slave property," Douglas said, "they will pass a slave code and give it encouragement. Whenever the climate, soil and productions preclude the possibility of slavery being profitable, they will not permit it. You come right back to the principle of dollars and cents." It followed, then, that the legal right to take the slaves to Kansas was form without substance. Nature had already decreed that the new territories would be free soil, and the Missouri Compromise ban on slavery above 36°30′ had never been necessary. Removing this ban would calm Southern feelings without the danger of adding a single square mile of territory to slavery's domain.

Armed with this brand of logic, backed by an administration that readily accepted his measure and did not hesitate to enforce party discipline upon recalcitrant Democrats, the Little Giant tugged and clawed and barked his controversial bill through both Houses of Congress. It took nearly four months of stormy debate and intricate political maneuver, but in the end neither the bitter opposition of a large Congressional minority nor the roar of protest from every Northern state was able to forestall the combined skill and pressure tactics of Senator Douglas and the Democratic machine.

The victory was dearly bought. Although Southern Democrats were nearly a unit in their support of the bill, the opposing free-soil block in either House was joined by Northern Whigs and border state moderates and, more ominously, by nearly half of the Northern Democrats, all of whom were torn between party loyalty and the angry protests from their home districts. When Southern enthusiasts celebrated the passage of Kansas-Nebraska by firing cannon in the small hours of a Washington morning, Senator Chase of Ohio paused on the Capitol steps to answer the reverberations with a prophetic charge, thoroughly in character: "They celebrate a present victory, but the echoes they awake shall never rest until slavery itself shall die."

Senator Douglas was a practical man, but he was now addressing himself to an issue which the country had long since lost its ability to consider in practical terms. Slavery had far outgrown the American genius for pragmatic solution, and it is not enough to blame this on a handful of demagogues and extremists, whose reckless, willful appeals to blind emotionalism (so the argument goes) were alone responsible for the failure of a realistic approach. At best this was a half truth, certainly less than half an answer. The demagogues and extremists were an effect, not a cause; the reality of slavery went well beyond geography and climate and dollars and cents, Stephen A. Douglas to the contrary notwithstanding.

His one mistake, of course, was a fatal underestimate of Northern feeling on the subject. Abolitionism was little more than a fringe of this feeling. Most Northern citizens were quite willing to leave slavery alone in the states where it already existed, but they were strongly opposed to letting it expand. Douglas's practical geographic arguments about the inability of slave labor to thrive on the Kansas prairies were beside the point. For over thirty years the Missouri Compromise had been part of the law of the land, and throughout the free states the ban on slavery north of 36°30′ was regarded as a time-honored principle at once sacred and inviolable, a permanent bulwark against the encroachments of an institution that could not be tolerated unless it stayed put. Although with some exceptions the Northern homesteaders were both antiabolitionist and anti-Negro—here they stood arm-in-arm with Senator Douglas—their version of the good society was based on free soil and free labor. In practical terms they were convinced that sharing Kansas with slaveowners would rob free labor of both its dignity and its profit, and in principle they believed that slavery extension was morally wrong.

Acute myopia, amounting almost to blindness, clouded Senator Douglas's vision at precisely this point. Himself hugely indifferent to the moral aspects of slavery, he never understood the dimension that this side of the question could assume in the minds of others.

He knew, of course, that his Kansas-Nebraska bill would evoke the customary shrieks from abolitionist quarters, but he believed that after a momentary shock the great majority of Northerners would see the truth in his geographic argument and respond happily to the democratic appeal of popular sovereignty. The "hell of a storm" would soon blow itself out, and a vigorous, reunited Democracy would elect its vigorous young leader to the White House in 1856.

Few political calculations have been wider of the mark. News of the Kansas-Nebraska bill was greeted with mounting cries of protest from Maine to Minnesota, and the sustained response of newspaper editors, ministers, state legislatures, and indignant mass meetings soon dispelled any notions of a brief or moderate storm. Reaction to Kansas-Nebraska was lethal and cyclonic, a wind that would blow with undiminished force until it disrupted both the party and the country that Stephen Douglas aspired to lead. And from the distant prairies of his own state of Illinois, not long after Congress began debating the Kansas-Nebraska measure in the early months of 1854, rose the voice that would point out to him, repeatedly and with unmistakable clarity, just how grievously he had erred.

Abraham Lincoln was completing his fifth year of political retirement when a startled North learned the details of the Douglas bill. Though immersed in the details of law practice and family life, he had kept a watchful eye on national affairs since returning home from Congress in 1849, and his decision to re-enter politics in opposition to the Kansas-Nebraska Act was based upon a careful, prolonged analysis of the real issues at stake in the sectional controversy. In these years of retirement a new depth and maturity had been added to the quick wit and partisan cleverness of his earlier career; if the distinction has meaning, the politician, now and henceforth, was also a statesman. The process was by no means complete, and the "new Lincoln" was a logical extension rather than a sharp transformation of the old. The statesman would remain a politician. Personal ambition was enhanced, not eclipsed, by his new dedication to principle. He had found his cause, but he had not found all the answers. Neither the growth nor the groping, least of all the uncertainty that marked his long quest for ultimate truth, would cease until the last, slow train ride home in the far-off spring of 1865. But it was unquestionably this five-year abstention from political activity—a period marked by sober reflection—that recast the frontier lawyer's intellect and laid the foundation for his rise to national leadership.

Certain character traits, always present but less strikingly in evidence before midcentury, had now become more pronounced. Chief among these, undoubtedly, was a passion for understanding, a desire to probe to the heart of a question and emerge with an answer that most nearly satisfied the evidence. Some restless inner craving had deepened and broadened the bright intellectual curiosity of his younger days, and friends in Springfield and on the judicial circuit constantly bore witness to the intensity of Lincoln's mental absorption in the problem of the moment. When not actually ferreting after the truth in some legal matter, he was apt to be reading or lost in thought, methodically enveloping an idea and turning it about until he had the essence of it. In his desire to learn he read Euclid, studied astronomy, deepened his acquaintance with Shakespeare, and read the newspapers in order to understand the course of politics and national affairs.

Lincoln strove not merely to understand but to be understood. From his earliest speeches he had tended toward a forthright, uncluttered prose and an easy directness of manner, in contrast to the rolling periods and ornate grandiloquence that often embellished the oratory of his day. Maturity of thought and purpose was accompanied by a growing maturity of style, aided by his study of the mathematical symmetry of Euclid and the lyric power of Shakespeare, reinforced by a sustained, working familiarity with the King James Bible, seasoned with the restraint and clarity of the best newspaper writing. When Lincoln rose in 1854 to dissect and demolish the Kansas-Nebraska Act, the clarity and eloquence of the war years were unmistakably present, and the consummate stylistic mastery that would finally endow the coming struggle with the highest of its many tangled meanings was fairly on exhibit.

This much was impressive, as those who watched him try a case or listened to his sharp indictment of the Douglas bill were quick to testify. Yet the underlying power in Abraham Lincoln went beyond intellectual precision and literary grace; the new-found moral purpose did not draw on these roots alone. If the less tangible elements housed within this restless spirit seem contradictory, each item added its peculiar force to his nature. It was in the combined hardness and flexibility of Lincoln's total strength that all the disparities were fused.

People now noted, for example, that the affable, story-swapping, gregarious Lincoln of old was basically something of a loner, a man whose long-time craving for human companionship was surpassed by a deeper craving for the contemplative solitude of his own thoughts. For all his drollery and love of talk, which never left him, there was a visible quality of remoteness about the man, a quiet dignity that kept easy familiarity at arm's length. When sociability claimed him it was on his terms and at a time of his choosing. Even to his friends he was Lincoln rather than Abe, and behind the easy geniality was a reticence and a brooding loneliness—brilliantly tailored, as it turned out, for the august office that some have called the loneliest job on earth.

No one ever mistook this aloofness for coldness. He was both respected and liked, and what constantly attracted people and led them to confide in him was not the wit nor the fund of anecdotes but the personal warmth that came from genuine sympathy and human understanding. The one quality perhaps closer to the core of Lincoln than any other was compassion: the enduring legend that took shape after his death did not have to magnify this quality, and the legend endured in part because compassion was its vital ingredient. "Malice toward none" was neither hyperbole nor cant; in a generation rapidly learning to hate well, the man was fundamentally incapable of hatred, and his strong sense of justice and love of fair play owed less to academic morality than to an abiding tenderness of heart that exempted no one, not even his enemies.

And yet no single quality provided the answer. Even his closest friends found him more or less a mystery. If his aloofness was anything but cold, those who mistook the tender-hearted warmth for softness did so at their peril. Somewhere along the way—perhaps in his marriage to Mary Todd, whose own psychological problems and increasingly unstable temperament punctuated the genuine affection that underlay their relationship with fierce emotional outbursts and a current of domestic tension—Lincoln had mastered the quality of infinite patience, and he had learned self-discipline. But when his goal was set and his delicate sense of timing told him that the moment had come, the brooding thinker could act fast and act hard; the patience resolved itself into decision; the man of compassion could show a streak of something very like ruthlessness and drive toward his object with all the compassion of a steamroller.

The man of intellect who strove for rational exactitude and read Euclid and acted, in a sense, on the belief that by taking thought one could add a cubit to one's stature—this man was also a mystic and a visionary, a believer in dreams, a fatalist who saw human destiny under the control of some higher power. His sense of humor and love of laughter were very real, but the merriment he frequently sought was primarily a form of relief from the profound inner melancholy that, in William Herndon's apt phrase, fairly "dripped from him as he walked." This melancholy was chronic, deep-rooted, often pervasive. In his youth and early manhood it had welled up now and then in the form of severe attacks, acute derangements that sapped his vitality, clouded his brain, and overcame him with despair. In the course of learning to live with himself and his wife he succeeded in bringing this affliction under more or less effective control, although it clung to his spirit until the very end; the Lincoln of mystic melancholy and vague portentous dreams would find nothing incongruous in the thought that destiny had already arranged his bizarre appointment in Ford's Theater a few years hence.

It was with the profoundest conviction of principles at stake and a cause to be joined that Abraham Lincoln decided to re-enter public life in opposition to the Kansas-Nebraska Act. Thousands of his Northern countrymen felt a similar urgency, and the protests

that greeted the very introduction of Senator Douglas's new measure were soon translated into political action of revolutionary
proportions.

Four political parties of varying size and composition existed
at the outset of the Kansas-Nebraska debate in early 1854. The
Democrats, by far the strongest in terms of organization, prestige,
and numerical support, could alone lay claim to a truly national
following. The Whigs were still powerful in several areas, but
they had split on the slavery issue in 1852 and now possessed
neither a program, national leadership, confidence, nor appreciable
Southern support outside the border slave states. A new organization, the American or Know-Nothing Party, seemed on the verge
of achieving major-party status in the middle fifties, on the basis
of a general appeal to patriotic sentiment and an all too specific
appeal to the anti-immigrant, anti-Catholic prejudices of older
stock Americans. Finally, there were the Free-Soilers, a tiny, vocal
band of Northern antislavery enthusiasts whose zeal could not
offset the fact that they had polled less than five per cent of the
popular vote in the presidential election of 1852.

Even before Kansas-Nebraska the political situation was fluid;
with his fateful bill Senator Douglas transformed fluidity into
a turbulence that bordered on chaos. None of the four existing
parties was in a position to derive more than local or short-range
profit from the upheaval. The Democrats, of course, faced a ruin-
ous split, the kind that had already destroyed the cohesion of the
Whigs and would confront any national party as long as the
slavery question remained alive. Kansas-Nebraska was first and
last a Democratic measure, introduced and guided through Congress by one of the foremost Democratic leaders, supported by
all of the influence and pressure the Democratic administration
could bring to bear. Northern Democrats who disliked the Douglas
bill—and they were many—could either voice their opposition
within the party, which meant battling against the formidable
powers of the entrenched state and national organizations, or they
could leave. The true depth of Northern feeling on the subject was
most dramatically underscored by the fact that thousands of

Democrats chose the latter course, even though there was no convenient place for them to go.

They could hardly join the Whigs, traditional archenemies since the days of Jackson and Clay a generation ago, drifting and rudderless now, their power and prestige conspicuously ebbing. Even less attractive were the Know-Nothings, whose arrant nativism deeply offended the egalitarian instincts of old Jacksonians and the sensitivities of the Irish and German immigrant groups, confirmed bulwark of party support in the urban areas of the East and Middle West. Although Democratic wrangling over Kansas-Nebraska enabled Whigs and Know-Nothings to profit locally, neither could enlarge its membership at Democratic expense; whatever the anti-Nebraska Democrats did, they were not going to make permanent cause with such inveterate and distasteful foes. This left the Free-Soilers, whose own hostility to the Douglas bill seemed to offer a convenient rallying point. As a party, however, the Free-Soilers were far too insignificant, and they suffered from an abolitionist taint. Anti-Nebraska sentiment was much too big for such a splinter group; the Free-Soilers could join this movement, but they were totally unequipped to absorb it.

A new organization was needed, and it was not long in coming. In state after Northern state during the spring and summer of 1854 the dissidents met and denounced the handiwork of Stephen Douglas—anti-Nebraska Democrats, Free-Soilers, antislavery-minded Whigs and Know-Nothings coming together in spontaneous and unco-ordinated fashion, old party differences blurring rapidly before a common grievance. The focus, quite simply, was anti-Nebraska—that is, unalloyed hostility to the repeal of the Missouri Compromise and unbending determination to halt the further spread of slavery. "Anti-Nebraska" was a potent battlecry, but the movement needed a better title than this, and in more than one state the fusionists quickly adopted the name Republican, which had a suitably Jeffersonian flavor. The name took hold. The new party, still a disconnected assortment of local organizations whose one common bond was a desire to contain the institution of slavery, steadily gained cohesion and continually drew added strength from the older parties until, a bare six years after the first rudimentary gatherings in 1854, the Republicans commanded a majority throughout the North and forced the slavery controversy to its climax.

The most indignant anti-Nebraska men joined one of the new Republican organizations right away, but others tended to be more cautious, preferring to study the political situation before casting off old party ties. The Republicans could easily collapse, after all. They lacked the machinery and tradition that enables a going party to maintain itself, and in 1854 it was hard to predict with certainty that so unco-ordinated and motley an assortment of political malcontents represented the shape of the future. It was hard, too, for old-line Democrats and old-line Whigs to bury the animosities of long standing and unite in a new organization, however much they might agree on the iniquities of Kansas-Nebraska. Voting together for the restoration of the Missouri Compromise was one thing; shedding the loyalties and rivalries of a lifetime for the sake of some ephemeral new party was quite another.

Abraham Lincoln reasoned this way at the outset, and for several months after his return to political life in 1854 he saw no need to change his mind. To him the issue was what counted; he would co-operate willingly with anti-Nebraska men of all political stripes in fighting the spread of slavery, but he saw no necessity for a new party. He was an old-line Whig, and proud of it, and after twenty years of service working upward through the ranks he had the professional politician's distrust of abandoning power and perquisites by casting loose from a going machine. The Whig organization in Illinois, unlike too many of its counterparts elsewhere, was still fairly strong; Lincoln had not given up hope that the party might yet regain its national following and restore its sagging fortunes. The Nebraska issue itself could do this, if the Whigs held together while the Democrats fell out. With such goals in mind Lincoln and his former law partner Stephen T. Logan tried to rally Whig sentiment by running for the state legislature in the fall of 1854 and campaigning vigorously for the re-election of an anti-Nebraska Whig Congressman from the Seventh District.

When Congress finally adjourned in August, 1854, exhausted and rancorous after its Kansas-Nebraska struggle, Stephen Douglas hastened back to Illinois to mend his fences. The opposition was in full cry. Burning Douglas in effigy had come into sudden vogue in many parts of the North, and the Democrats were in trouble from Maine to Iowa; every political weathervane pointed to a party debacle in the fall elections. Irascible, sharp-tongued old Thomas Hart Benton of Missouri had capsuled the prevailing sentiment in an explosive outburst against Douglas's presidential ambitions. "He won't do, sir!" Benton snapped. "His legs are too short, sir. That part of his body, sir, which men wish to kick, is too near the ground!"

Douglas was sobered, but undismayed. A born fighter, he counterattacked his foes in Illinois with characteristic vehemence and energy. He had committed himself to the principles embodied in the Kansas-Nebraska bill from the moment it reached the floor of Congress, and he now repeated to his own constituents the whole range of arguments—a mottled blend of logic and sophistry—that he had employed so vigorously in Washington. Jeers from the opposition only spurred him on.

He began to make progress, too. The Little Giant was an effective debater, skilled in the art of emphasizing the strong points in his argument and submerging the weak ones beneath a flood of oratory. His enemies, he continually reminded wavering Democrats, were an odious compound of nativism, abolitionism, and expedient Whiggery. The major theme in his defense of the Kansas-Nebraska Act was popular sovereignty, and this doctrine, as he had calculated all along, was potent in its appeal to the spread-eagle democracy of the Old Northwest. What was fairer, what more American, than letting the settlers in a new territory decide their own institutions? Dividing the country along a line such as 36°30′ was arbitrary and sectional, he said, while popular sovereignty was democratic and national. The new law was not only just, but necessary: the country would profit in several ways from a rapid development of its unsettled territories, and homesteaders deserved immediate access to the empty acres beyond the Missouri. Besides, Douglas would invariably add, geography had rendered the Kansas-Nebraska region inhospitable to slavery; it could never take root there.

All in all, this formula was fairly effective. As Douglas stumped from Chicago to downstate Illinois in the early fall of 1854 his crowds grew larger and more friendly. There was a good chance that he might yet retain the bulk of his popularity and restore his party's ranks.

When Douglas reached Springfield, still denouncing his political opponents and defending Kansas-Nebraska with undiminished vigor, Lincoln seized this opportunity to deliver his first major speech on the subject. With a state fair in progress and the political campaign moving into high gear, the capital was jammed with visitors. Douglas addressed a huge crowd on October 3, repeating what was now a stock discourse in praise of popular sovereignty, and Lincoln spoke to much the same audience on the following day. He had worked hard on this speech, buttressing his opposition to the new law with long hours of research in the newspapers and statute books, carefully studying the legal history of the slavery controversy from the Revolutionary era to the present.

Standing tieless and shirt-sleeved before a packed hall on a warm October evening, perspiration matting his hair and soaking through his shirt, voice shrill at first but taking on a modulated resonance as conviction drowned his nervousness, Lincoln subjected the Kansas-Nebraska Act to an eloquent, impassioned scrutiny, while Stephen Douglas scowled intently from his seat in the first row. Point by point, line by line, frequently interrupted by bursts of applause, he dissected every argument Senator Douglas had advanced, exposing all the half-truths and distortions in these arguments and all the weaknesses and dangers in the measure itself. His prose was clear and compelling; few could miss the substance of this indictment or fail to be impressed by its logic. Lincoln was not destroying Stephen A. Douglas at one stroke— the Little Giant was an old campaigner, full of resource and frontier courage, and he did not destroy easily, ever—but the tall lawyer with the awkward gestures was providing the inchoate anti-Nebraska sentiment with a creed and a focus that would enable it to survive and cohere, and ultimately to triumph.

Part of Lincoln's speech was devoted to practical objections. The need to organize the new territories, he pointed out, did not call for a repeal of the Missouri Compromise. A Nebraska bill with no repeal clause attached had been introduced late in the Congressional session of 1852-1853—had actually passed the House, in fact, and was meeting no real opposition in the Senate when Congress adjourned; the same bill was reintroduced early in the next session, and could probably have passed without causing undue mischief had Senator Douglas not chosen to inject the slavery issue.

As for Douglas's geographic arguments, which averred that slavery could never establish itself on the Kansas prairies, Lincoln pointed to a whole tier of border slave states lying as far north as Kansas—a tier that stretched from Delaware to Missouri—and suggested that physiographic conditions offered free soil no guarantees whatever. In particular, and with telling effect, Lincoln talked of northwestern Missouri. Slavery in Missouri was most deeply entrenched in those very counties that adjoined the new Kansas territory. Missouri was widely expected to provide Kansas with the nucleus of its prospective settlement, and slaveholding Missourians were already boasting that they would transplant the institution promptly and without difficulty. Certainly, Lincoln added, what was now flourishing on the Missouri side of the river could hardly be expected to wither and die on the Kansas side.

Lincoln then took a long, cold look at popular sovereignty, Kansas-Nebraska's most heralded attraction. He questioned the idea that the institutions in a new territory should be decided solely by the inhabitants. This was the national domain, and the use made of it was the concern of every citizen, not merely of those who settled there. He emphatically denied Douglas's claim that the popular sovereignty clause in the Compromise of 1850 in any way "superseded" the Missouri Compromise or erased the chalk-line of 36°30′ from the territorial blackboard. Northerners had conceded popular sovereignty in Utah and New Mexico in 1850 in exchange for Southern concessions elsewhere—in California, for example—but this was all part of a definite bargain over the lands acquired from Mexico. By no stretch of the imagination was the principle thus transferred to the Kansas-Nebraska region.

Moreover, Lincoln pointed up a fundamental ambiguity in the popular sovereignty idea. According to the new law, the actual settlers would "decide" for themselves whether they wanted to form free states or slave states. But how decide, asked Lincoln, and when? The law was silent. Did the people vote to admit or exclude slavery as soon as the first band of settlers arrived, or when the population reached one hundred, or one thousand, or several thousand? Was the first decision binding thereafter, or would each new influx necessitate a recount? It made quite a difference, and in the meantime the law's silence only guaranteed confusion and misunderstanding.

Popular feelings about slavery being what they were, Lincoln went on, the confusion and misunderstanding could have but one outcome. In the absence of procedural legislation, there was no guarantee that popular sovereignty in action would take the form of orderly processions to the ballot box. Quite the contrary, said Lincoln: "Some Yankees, in the east, are sending emigrants to Nebraska, to exclude slavery from it. . . . But the Missourians are awake too. . . . They hold meetings, and pass resolutions, in which not the slightest allusion to voting is made. They resolve that slavery already exists in the territory; that more shall go there; that they, remaining in Missouri, shall protect it; and that abolitionists shall be hung, or driven away. Through all this, bowie-knives and six-shooters are seen plainly enough; but never a glimpse of the ballot-box. And, really, what is to be the result of this? Each party *within,* having numerous and determined backers *without,* is it not probable that the contest will come to blows, and bloodshed? Could there be a more apt invention to bring about collision and violence, on the slavery question, than this Nebraska project is?"

In this passage Lincoln was predicting with hairline accuracy what would be afoot on the plains of Kansas for the next three years. He then put his forecast into broader perspective. "If this fight should begin," he warned, "is it likely to take a very peaceful, Union-saving turn? Will not the first drop of blood so shed, be the real knell of the Union?"

Some few, at least, among that packed Springfield audience might have shivered a little. The distant drum was beating louder now. It had tapped a warning when David Wilmot rose in Congress eight years before, and it had rumbled at a faster tempo behind Calhoun's prophetic Southern Address in 1849. As Lincoln spoke it seemed to roll again, and the endless ranks of future armies quivered in the shadows beyond the flicker of the lamps.

Grievous though the law's practical shortcomings undoubtedly were, Lincoln reserved his heaviest fire for the theoretical implications of the Kansas-Nebraska Act. On this aspect of the question he had done his deepest thinking. "Let no one be deceived," he said flatly. "The spirit of seventy-six and the spirit of Nebraska, are utter antagonisms; and the former is being rapidly displaced by the latter."

Lincoln took some pains to spell this out. In facing the problem of slavery, he asserted, the fathers of the republic had recognized it as a necessary evil—too well entrenched and complex a problem to be eradicated at one stroke, but too fundamentally at odds with the principles of the Declaration of Independence to be encouraged or allowed to flourish unchecked. So they had carefully hedged the institution "to the narrowest limits of necessity," hoping that they were setting it on the road to ultimate extinction. In framing the Constitution they had scrupulously avoided the words "slave" and "slavery," revealing their distaste by such euphemisms as "person held to service or labor."

What Lincoln meant by the "spirit of seventy-six" was, quite simply, government by consent of the governed—the very "sheet anchor of American republicanism." Slavery was a "total violation" of this principle, as the revolutionary generation knew full well. But now, Lincoln said, the authors of Kansas-Nebraska are claiming, as a matter of high principle, the right of slaveowners to take their property to Nebraska—and, by obvious intent, "to every other part of the wide world, where man can be found inclined to take it." The spirit of Nebraska, in other words, was proclaiming slavery not an evil to be tolerated but a sacred right to be extended. This was the very antithesis of the Declaration, for it assumed "that there can be MORAL RIGHT in the enslaving of one man by another ... a sad evidence that, feeling prosperity, we forget right—that liberty, as a principle, we have ceased to revere."

Lincoln was here squarely confronting what the nation as a whole had been trying for decades to avoid: the frank admission that the Negro was a man. If he were something less, then there could be no wrong in slavery. And yet, Lincoln went on, turning to the South itself for answer, the Southern attitude toward slave traders and the very nature and complexity of slavery's legal code were proof that a Negro was not property in the sense that a hog was property. The difference, like it or not, lay in the Negro's essential humanity. This did not mean, Lincoln hastened to add, that he was advocating social and political equality for the colored man. (White Americans, including most of those who disliked slavery, were still far from accepting that idea.) Nor was he advocating that slavery in the South be abolished. Like the Founding Fathers, he knew a necessary evil when he saw one, and confessed that with "all earthly power" he would not know what to do with the existing institution. Characteristically, too, he pointed no accusing finger at the South—"They are just what we would be in their situation"—and he frankly admitted that slavery was a national, not a Southern, responsibility.

All the same, as far as Abraham Lincoln was concerned the Negro was a human being, and because the nation had tacitly agreed with him it would have to make a choice. Either the Declaration of Independence or the "spirit of Nebraska" was wrong. By accepting the handiwork of Stephen Douglas the people were denying their birthright. One of the major guidelines in Lincoln's political philosophy depicted America as a great experiment in democracy, a tentative banner of hope for lovers of freedom all over the world. Right now the banner was faltering; "in our greedy chase to make profit of the Negro, let us beware, lest we 'cancel and tear to pieces' even the white man's charter of freedom."

In his peroration Lincoln pleaded for a repudiation of the Kansas-Nebraska Act and a restoration of the Missouri Compromise. "Let us turn slavery from its claims of 'moral right' back upon its existing legal rights.... Let us re-adopt the Declaration of Independence.... If we do this, we shall not only have saved the Union; but we shall have so saved it, as to make, and to keep it, forever worthy of the saving."

Lincoln had found his position, and would take his stand there from this point forward. Slavery extension must be fought and fought hard. When this position led the nation to its larger choice in 1861, there would be multitudes enough who thought the Union worthy of the saving, and without quite grasping all the implications they would fundamentally accept Lincoln's premise that the self-evident truths of Thomas Jefferson were the reason why.

M O D E R A T I O N
I N   R E T R E A T ,
1 8 5 4 – 1 8 5 8

Although Lincoln's Springfield speech of 1854 made quite an impression, its impact was entirely local; in the great debate raging elsewhere over Kansas and Nebraska that fall his name was yet unknown. In Illinois, however, he proved a most effective campaigner along the lines laid down at Springfield, repeating much the same address at Peoria a few days later and stumping energetically for the Whig ticket both downstate and in Chicago. His political fortunes slowly began to improve. In keeping with the trend that moved with varying intensity over every Northern state in the elections of 1854, the anti-Nebraska forces in Illinois elected fifty-nine out of one hundred state legislators, including Lincoln and Stephen T. Logan, and won five of the nine Congressional races. As predicted, the first referendum on the Kansas-Nebraska Act had dealt a sharp setback to Douglas and the Pierce administration.

Of major importance in Illinois was the expiring Senate term of James Shields, a Douglas Democrat, whose seat the incoming legislature was slated to fill in early 1855. Lincoln, his reputation much enhanced by the campaign, cast an acquisitive eye in this direction almost at once. If anti-Nebraska sentiment were ever to summon the strength that could repeal the hated enactment of

Stephen A. Douglas, it would have to do so in the national Senate, where a powerful coalition of Southern leaders and cooperative Northern Democrats was in firm control. As the Illinois campaign reached its climax, many politicians were sufficiently impressed by Lincoln to talk of sending him to the Senate, although the idea, as his partner William Herndon suggests, was far from moving on a one-way street. "That man who thinks Lincoln calmly sat down and gathered his robes about him, waiting for the people to call him, has a very erroneous knowledge of Lincoln," Herndon wrote. "He was always calculating, and always planning ahead. His ambition was a little engine that knew no rest. . . . His canvass . . . was marked by characteristic activity and vigilance. During the anxious moments that intervened between the general election and the assembling of the legislature he slept, like Napoleon, with one eye open."

Lincoln was not the only thoughtful observer who knew where the big decisions were customarily made. From his post in the War Department Jefferson Davis, too, had been making plans and nursing political ambitions, and from personal experience he could share Lincoln's respect for the power and prestige of the United States Senate. Still regretting his defeat by the Unionist Henry S. Foote in the Mississippi gubernatorial contest of 1851, which he had quit the Senate in order to enter, Davis wanted to refurbish his standing as a Southern-rights champion at home. The only endorsement that would demonstrate this in convincing fashion was a return to the Senate; neither his great influence in the Pierce administration nor the challenge of his duties in the War Department was as important to him.

Davis tried, consequently, to muster support in the Mississippi legislature for the Senate vacancy to be filled in January, 1854, even though a victory would have meant resigning from the Cabinet less than a year after he had entered it. But this Senate campaign, conducted of necessity by long distance from his desk in Washington, got absolutely nowhere. His supporters in Mississippi mismanaged things so monumentally that his name was never even presented as a candidate, and the legislators ignored him in favor of a former governor and long-time Jacksonian, the astute, voluble Albert Gallatin Brown. As of 1854, Davis's desire to re-enter the Upper Chamber with a ringing mandate from his home state was conspicuously unfulfilled. Soon afterward he began to lay his plans for another try in 1856.

Lincoln's Senate campaign in 1855 likewise ended in failure, although he lost by the narrowest of margins and had the satisfaction, even in defeat, of striking another blow at the Douglas Democrats. The anti-Nebraska majority in the Illinois legislature was an unwieldy coalition of rebellious Democrats, old-line Whigs, and a few spokesmen for the infant Republican Party. They could agree on opposing the Kansas-Nebraska Act but not on a candidate, and their failure to unite very nearly enabled the Douglas forces to win the election. Only a last-ditch move on Lincoln's part—at his own expense—upset the Douglas strategy.

The contest was marked by intensive maneuvering, crisscrossed with plots and counterplots that bore eloquent testimony to the divided, unstable condition of Illinois politics. In the weeks before the legislature met, Lincoln wrote dozens of letters and kept in close touch with a variety of political leaders in an attempt to build support for his candidacy. The prospects seemed good, at first. The Whigs favored him, with varying degrees of enthusiasm, as did several anti-Nebraska Democrats, but Lincoln's real strength was less impressive than it looked. On the first ballot he received forty-five votes, only six short of a majority. Then his support began to fade, and it became increasingly obvious that he would be unable to hold his following in line. Many anti-Douglas Democrats were adamant in their refusal to consider any Whig candidate, mutual hatred of Kansas-Nebraska notwithstanding, and others who began by voting for Lincoln were soon attracted to another contender: Lyman Trumbull, a widely respected Democrat of known ability and impressive record in state politics, whose opposition to the Kansas-Nebraska Act was no less determined than Lincoln's. As the balloting proceeded Trumbull's support crept up while Lincoln's gradually dwindled.

The regular Democrats, meanwhile, were following a strategy of their own. For several ballots they voted as a bloc to re-elect the incumbent, James Shields, then abruptly shifted to the wealthy, influential Joel Matteson, a popular ex-governor who had maintained a discreet silence on the explosive Nebraska question. With the forty-one regulars a unit behind him, Matteson needed to pick up only ten votes from among the wavering ranks of the anti-Nebraska Democrats. It was an expedient move; the Douglas men had no great love for Matteson, but he was infinitely preferable to the only other candidates with any chance of success— Lincoln, of the hated Whigs, and Trumbull, whom they regarded as a traitor to the party and hated even more.

The surprise switch from Shields to Matteson came within a whisker of success. Matteson's strength quickly jumped from forty-four to forty-six votes, then forty-seven, while Trumbull shot up to thirty-five and Lincoln dropped to fifteen, only the staunch old-line Whigs remaining in his column. With Matteson clearly about to go over the top, Lincoln at the last minute instructed his fifteen supporters to vote for Trumbull on the next ballot. This final switch elected Lyman Trumbull to the Senate without a vote to spare, and Lincoln, who had resigned his newly won seat in the legislature in order to seek the higher office, was left once again with his law practice and thwarted hopes.

The loss was a personal disappointment, but Lincoln drew much satisfaction from the knowledge that his own defeat represented a strategic victory for the anti-Nebraska cause; he and Senator-elect Trumbull saw eye to eye on the slavery question and would soon be close political allies. "I regret my defeat moderately," Lincoln wrote, but "on the whole, it is perhaps as well for the general cause that Trumbull is elected. The Neb [raska] men confess that they hate it worse than anything that could have happened. It is a great consolation to see them worse whipped than I am."

For the next twelve months Lincoln moved dutifully ahead with his private practice and kept an eye on the political situation, clearly waiting for an opportune moment to re-enter the struggle. Despite his absorbing interest in politics, which grew steadily as the slavery controversy waxed hotter in national affairs, the legal profession was by no means a stopgap or petty sideline for Lincoln in the eighteen-fifties. He was now a man of stature and repute in the Illinois bar. The nature of his practice displayed a growing complexity—token not only of legal competence but of the economic ferment that was altering the shape and texture of rural America. Increasingly, Lincoln served as counsel in suits involving the corporation. He variously fought or defended the interests of banks, insurance companies, business firms, and railroads, groping thoughtfully amid the intricacies of patent fights, corporate tax litigation, and navigational disputes.

But the abiding interest was still politics, and amid the press of other duties both the lawyer from Springfield and the United States Secretary of War were intently gazing at the political scene. Each was aware that the slavery problem, transposed to a new and harsher key in 1854, was moving ominously toward some sort of climax.

No two men in all the nation held views about the crisis with firmer conviction than did Abraham Lincoln and Jefferson Davis, and inescapable tragedy lay in the fact that neither man was an extremist. Save on one crucial item they stood in fundamental agreement. Both loved the Union and hoped in all sincerity that it might be preserved. Both deprecated the irresponsible radicalism of the Northern abolitionist and the Southern fire-eater; neither bore the opposing section the slightest ill will. Lincoln asked only that slavery be contained within its present limits, Davis that it be rendered secure from attack. They agreed, actually, on the real nub of the case: that slavery, once firmly contained and barred from expanding into new areas, would someday perish.

From this emerged the one disagreement—which was, unfortunately, basic; moderation and extremism here became indistinguishable. To Lincoln, all that gave meaning or value to the American experiment demanded, however distantly, an end to slavery—which meant blocking its growth right now. With equal earnestness Davis insisted that slavery must be defended—which meant allowing it to expand. Here, certainly, was the "eternal antagonism" Lincoln had so recently described in his Springfield speech, and any hope of compromise was lost because each man felt with what amounted to religious certitude that he had assumed a position from which no retreat was possible. The trumpet in Julia Ward Howe's famous Battle Hymn never sounded with more clarity than these.

In those darkening months of 1855 and 1856 both men had much to contemplate. The alarm bells were clanging everywhere. In Kansas, popular sovereignty was working precisely as Lincoln had said it would. Emigration to Kansas touched off a savage contest between proslavery and free-soil groups which magnified the normal lawlessness of a frontier area and found expression in ballot-box stuffing, intimidation, demagoguery, and incitements to mob action. Proslavery Missourians crossed the border in organized bands to vote illegally on a mass scale, and before long there were two rival "governments" in the territory, one proslavery, the other free-soil, the former based entirely on fraud, the latter having no legal basis whatever. Brawls and scattered violence were frequent, always threatening to erupt into open civil war. In late 1855 an armed clash was averted at the last minute by the territorial governor, but the administration's attempts to keep order were largely ineffectual, marred by lack of vigorous leadership from the White House and the absence of specific procedures for the implementation of popular sovereignty.

In 1856 the pot boiled over. A ragged proslavery "army," replete with cavalry and cannon, marched on the free-soil town of Lawrence and proceeded to sack the place—burning shops, bombarding the hotel, destroying newspaper presses, and generally laying waste. A life or two was accidentally lost in the process, and while the indignant Northern press ran scare headlines about "bleeding Kansas" and evoked lurid visions of mass slaughter on the western prairies, a brooding Kansas free-soiler named John Brown decided to retaliate. Misinformed about the exact death toll in Lawrence, vaguely prompted by the Old Testament maxim of an eye for an eye, Brown armed a small band of sons and followers with heavy cavalry sabers and conducted a ghastly midnight raid among the scattered cabins of proslavery settlers, butchering five men in cold blood.

It was now the turn of the Southern press to cry havoc. Events in the troubled territory provided a field day for the press and brought out the very worst in most editors. Kansas bled far more copiously in newsprint than on the ground, but there were enough real episodes to keep the story alive; the Brown raid touched off a species of guerrilla warfare, punctuated now and again by small pitched battles, and Kansas towns took on the look of armed camps. Toward the end of his term Franklin Pierce finally found a territorial governor who made real progress in stabilizing the troubled area, but it was obvious that no final solution had been reached. In its struggle to determine whether it would enter the Union with or without slavery, Kansas yet contained enough disruptive force to shatter Democratic Party unity.

Elsewhere, too, the storm signals flashed. Since Mexican War days adventurous citizens had dreamed, planned, and occasionally tried to execute schemes of conquest in Latin America and the Caribbean. Between 1849 and 1854 Cuba was the target of several abortive thrusts. Other filibusters, as these military adventurers were called, made attempts here and there in Central America and in the Mexican province of lower California. Since the usual object of these forays, along with personal enrichment, was the establishment of a regime that would sooner or later join the United States, the more bellicose Southerners tended to applaud such expeditions with enthusiasm, hailing them as the glorious march of Manifest Destiny—and slavery—into the rich lands south of the border. Northerners, correspondingly, tended to regard the filibusters as paid agents of an aggressive, expanding "slave power."

In the late spring of 1855 occurred the most spectacular and successful of these irruptions (many of which, despite or perhaps because of the deadly seriousness of the participants, are imbued in retrospect with a slightly comic-opera touch), this time under the dynamic leadership of William Walker of Tennessee, ablest filibuster of them all. There was little of the comic opera about Walker. Recruiting and equipping his force in the United States, he sailed from San Francisco with sixty-odd followers in a dilapidated brig, landed on the Pacific coast of Nicaragua, fought his way inland, and brought the entire country under his control within five months. His force was steadily augmented by new arrivals of American volunteers. Jubilant Southerners talked of a great slaveholding republic in Central America, with Walker's Nicaragua the nucleus. When President Pierce received Walker's emissary in May, 1856, thus in effect recognizing the regime, and when Walker decreed the establishment of slavery in his new domain two months later, Northerners saw it all as evidence that the "slave power" was about its evil work. Sectional animosity fed on such episodes, which threatened to multiply in the wake of Walker's success.

Anxious observers did not have to look as far afield as Kansas or Central America to find cause for alarm. In May, 1856, just as Walker's Nicaraguan emissary arrived in Washington, as news of Lawrence and the John Brown raid flashed across the headlines, violence strode into the august chamber of the United States Senate. Focus of this outburst, which perhaps did more than any other single episode to raise sectional ill feeling on both sides to an enduring fever pitch, was the tirelessly controversial Charles Sumner of Massachusetts.

Adjectives can never measure a man; they merely serve as identification tags, and Charles Sumner is none the easier to encompass for being supremely, unmistakably, almost awesomely identifiable. He entered the Senate in 1851, just turned forty, a tall, heavily handsome, altogether imposing figure of a man, elegantly costumed, his wide, slightly downturned mouth, firm jaw, and normally uncompromising stare framed by rich brown hair, his self-assurance unshakable. Boston-born and Harvard-educated, comfortably at home in the best New England society, widely known and respected in Europe as scholarly traveler and man of letters, Charles Sumner brought to the Senate an eloquence at once polished, classical, and offensively vituperative, an ego that managed to stand out even among the most egotistical assemblage in the United States, an unswerving set of high moral principles, and a sincere, abiding hatred of the institution of slavery. Sumner was by conscious choice a member of that unsettling and (perhaps fortunately) rare breed: the moralist in politics. He had come to rally public opinion by inveighing boldly and immoderately against the evils of slavery, under the firm conviction that, in his own words, the proclaiming of a "moral blockade" would ultimately lead an aroused public to repeal the laws protecting the hated institution and set the bondsman free.

Clearly, here was a man with both the intent and the capacity to make trouble, and what finally happened to him in the Senate chamber, if not exactly predictable, was a logical by-product of his own campaign. When Sumner rose to condemn—he did little else, as befitted the self-appointed spearhead of a moral blockade—he could not refrain from dealing in personalities. He did so insultingly, and with apparent relish. This habit, accompanied by a lofty, sanctimonious manner that was almost as infuriating as the actual content of his speeches, could not fail to inflame the rather easily ignited Southern temper. The New England Senator quickly became the embodiment of everything the South most despised and feared, the very prototype of the aggressive, fanatical, self-righteous Yankee abolitionist.

In May, 1856, Senator Sumner delivered a ponderous, carefully prepared denunciation of what he called "The Crime Against Kansas." Most of the speech was a routine criticism, in Sumner's cadenced, stinging, pompous oratory, of the various proslavery enactments and policies that were subverting the cause of freedom and justice in Kansas. But Sumner could not let it go at that. He added a few remarks "of a general character," admittedly "not belonging to the argument." The gist of these was a vivid analogy depicting slavery as a foul harlot, "polluted in the sight of the world," yet lovely and chaste—they were Sumner's adjectives—in the eyes of the slaveowner.

As an exercise in brilliant bad taste this in itself would have been sufficient, but Sumner had gone a step further. Never content to criticize evil in the abstract, Sumner not only personified the institution but identified the slaveowner. For this purpose he chose a colleague, white-haired Andrew Pickens Butler of South Carolina, a courtly, dignified plantation aristocrat. Although Senator Butler's personal relations with Sumner had always been cordial, the South Carolinian had been a leading defender of administration policy and the rights of slaveowners in Kansas. Butler was therefore singled out to make his vows and profess his devotion to the harlot slavery in Sumner's speech; there were related slurs of a lesser nature directed at Senator Douglas, still a popular target for Northern shafts. Sumner also lashed out at Butler's native state of South Carolina.

Sumner's intemperate language startled the Senate and infuriated the South. Stephen Douglas, who had been at the game long enough to take personal insults in stride, knew how the less equable Southern temperament was apt to respond. "That damned fool," he muttered, during the harlot-slavery portion of Sumner's speech, "will get himself killed by some other damned fool." Butler was absent on this particular day, but many of his friends were not, and Congressman Preston Brooks of South Carolina, a young kinsman of Butler's who heard the speech from the Senate gallery, concluded wrathfully that Sumner's calculated, gratuitous attack was the sort of wrong that demanded redress. A few days later, at the close of Senate business on May 22, Brooks strode across the nearly empty chamber and stood beside Sumner's desk, where the unsuspecting New Englander was busily franking copies of his speech. He had refused to take seriously the notion that some aggrieved foe might seek him out. (It was a blind spot of Sumner's that in his crusade against evil it always came as a surprise when people took personal attacks as a personal affront.)

Brooks was armed with a stout gutta-percha walking stick, carefully selected for the business at hand. (For treating insults from an inferior, the Southern code prescribed a horse-whip or a cane.) Confronting Sumner at his desk, Brooks solemnly announced that the recent speech had libeled his kinsman, Senator Butler, and his state, South Carolina. Before Sumner could rise, Brooks proceeded to beat him about the face and shoulders with increasing force until the cane broke. Though Sumner finally wrenched clear of his desk, which was bolted to the floor, he could not ward off the rain of blows. Even after the cane snapped, Brooks continued the assault with the splintered stump, and Sumner, bleeding heavily, staggered about the Senate aisle in a blind daze and finally slumped unconscious to the floor, his fall partly broken by a colleague. The whole affair had taken less than a minute.

Of itself, the episode was deplorable enough. The reaction was tragically ominous. Charles Sumner and Preston Brooks had blundered into the vintage where the grapes of wrath were stored, and the more vocal element in the South frankly exulted at the news that a United States Senator had been clubbed into insensibility. Even the less extreme Southerners could not restrain a twinge of inner satisfaction; if there was regret here, it stemmed primarily from an awareness of the political profit the South's enemies could derive from the affair.

The South's enemies were indeed in full cry, but the protest that mattered came in angry spontaneity from everyday folk across the scattered byways of the North. In the hundreds of letters that poured in to the stricken Sumner was evidence that iron and something very akin to hatred were entering men's souls —and, perhaps more significantly, women's souls as well. (Wars are fiercer when the women hate, and under the tutelage of such as Harriet Beecher Stowe, John Brown, and Preston Brooks the women of America were fast learning how.) "The instant Papa told me," a Massachusetts girl wrote Sumner, "it seemed exactly as if a great, black cloud was spread over the sky. . . . I keep always thinking about it, and no matter what I am doing I have a sort of consciousness of something black and wicked." And from a schoolgirl in Connecticut: "I don't think it is of very much use to stay any longer in the High School, as the boys would better be learning to hold muskets, and the girls to make bullets."

Here was the spirit that sent armies off to battle, and little that happened in the next four years would allow it to diminish. Northerners had long since rejected the punctilious code of honor by which Preston Brooks had brought Sumner to account. They saw, with a "consciousness of something black and wicked," not honor but savage brutality, a relic of the less civilized past, and in their minds it was of a piece with the whip and the branding bar, the auction block and the bloodhounds and every other patent flaw in the dark mosaic of slavery. There was no room, in the image of the South that had already formed and was now hardening in the Northern mind, for the gentler and happier features of Southern society. Instead, the image was of a people who sent Missouri border ruffians into Kansas to uphold the rights of slavery with lynch law and fraud, who plotted conquest for slavery's sake in Latin America, who encouraged and applauded the use of a bludgeon in response to the exercise of free speech. Such a people, obviously, must be resisted, such tactics fought. With near unanimity the Massachusetts legislature re-elected Sumner to the Senate in 1857, fully aware that he was not sufficiently recovered to resume his seat. It was an effective gesture. For over three years, amid all the wrangling and debate in the upper chamber, that empty chair spoke with greater eloquence than the man himself had ever done.

And finally, to round out the troubled national picture, 1856 was a presidential year, and promised to be a crucial one. Smarting from their recent setbacks in the wake of Kansas-Nebraska, their national ranks imperfectly reknit behind the none too solid rampart of popular sovereignty, the Democrats faced a serious challenge. In two short years the infant Republican Party had added enormously to its strength, and in most Northern states it had clearly emerged as the second major party. The Whigs were a scattered remnant, the Know-Nothings in a decline as tumultuous and swift as their rise.

Republican leaders had profited hugely, and calculatedly, from the furor in Kansas and the recent Sumner-Brooks episode. They also began appealing to various Northern interest groups whose goals had been blocked by Southern votes in Congress: agrarians demanding free-homestead legislation, Western merchants desiring river and harbor improvements at federal expense, Pennsylvania ironmasters and New England textile manufacturers in quest of higher tariffs. The Republicans were beginning to make headway in their bid for the support of the foreign-born—especially among the liberal, vocal, fiercely antislavery Germans who had recently fled the Revolution of 1848. Though the pattern for a broad coalition of varied interest groups was thus taking vague shape, the moving spirit of the new party remained, as it had been at the outset, anti-Nebraska: hostility to slavery, and above all to the extension of slavery. Its foremost leaders were prominent antislavery spokesmen like Seward of New York, Chase of Ohio, and Sumner; it had no more than the barest shadow of support in the border slave states, none whatever in the deep South.

Although strictly a sectional party, the Republicans in 1856 stood a fair chance of winning the election: with the free states offering a total of 176 electoral votes and 149 constituting an electoral majority, people were already beginning to search the possible meanings of a Republican victory. On this point the divergent reactions of Abraham Lincoln and Jefferson Davis were highly significant. Unlike too many of his Southern colleagues, Davis did not engage in wild talk during the 1856 campaign, but he was fast becoming convinced that a victorious Republican Party would threaten both the South and the stability of the Union. Lincoln, on the other hand, went over to the new party in the spring of 1856. His hopes of a Whig renascence gone, his alarm mounting at the prospects of a proslavery triumph in Kansas, his original distrust of the radical abolitionist element in the Republican Party fading as more and more moderates joined its ranks, he now concluded that the Republicans offered the only hope of halting the spread of slavery.

Once committed, he threw himself briskly into the task of welding a strong Republican organization in Illinois. His eloquence at the state convention in 1856 was instrumental in unifying and enthusing the ill-assorted throng of erstwhile Whigs, Democrats, Free-Soilers, Know-Nothings, and abolitionists who had assembled in response to a Republican call. Many Illinoisans retained misgivings about the new party, and Lincoln, remembering his own, joined other moderates in pushing through a slate and a platform designed to attract the conservative vote. It was vitally important, he realized, that the Republicans free themselves from the taint of radicalism in the public mind.

The taint was there, ineradicably, and much was made of it during the campaign. Conservative, Union-loving Northerners might accept at face value Republican insistence that the party stood for the containment rather than the abolition of slavery, but they could not help but be alarmed at the threats coming from the South. Many Southern leaders repeatedly announced their determination to take the slave states out of the Union in the event of a Republican victory. A handful of extremists genuinely wanted secession; a much larger group, while not actually wanting it, recognized containment as abolition's entering wedge —which it was—and talked secession in the confident belief that the threat would frighten moderate Northerners away from the Republican ticket. Throughout the border states, and among those elements in the North who feared secession more than slavery, spokesmen for the other parties hammered away at the idea that a vote for the Republicans was a vote for abolitionism and disunion. The effectiveness of this tactic was probably the most important single factor in the Republican defeat.

The race was a three-cornered affair, hotly contested and long in doubt. The Democrats, on a platform that loudly reaffirmed the party's faith in popular sovereignty and the Kansas-Nebraska Act, nominated James Buchanan of Pennsylvania, a canny, cautious political veteran who possessed almost none of the qualities of firm leadership but who, alone of the Democratic aspirants, had adroitly managed to dissociate himself from a vulnerable position on the explosive Kansas-Nebraska issue. (In retrospect, the failure to select Stephen Douglas, who battled for the nomination and had the strength to deadlock the convention but yielded to Buchanan in the interests of party harmony, stands as one of the major blunders of the decade. The known architect of the platform on which the Democrats campaigned and won, Douglas was far better equipped than Buchanan to meet the crises that lay ahead.)

The Republicans met in Philadelphia in an atmosphere of crusading zeal and chose the dynamic Californian, John C. Fremont. Son-in-law of Thomas Hart Benton, widely known for his able and much publicized explorations in the Far West, the youthful Fremont was an ardent Free-Soiler respectably untainted by abolitionism; few seemed worried that his political experience had been limited to a fragmentary Senate term five years before. Fremont's defects in character and political acumen were obscured by his vigor and personal popularity and, like Buchanan, by the supreme asset of acceptability, which disqualified stronger but more radical leaders like Seward and Chase. The Republican platform, of course, revolved almost entirely around the principle of excluding slavery from the territories.

Party platform and candidate once selected, the enthusiastic Illinois delegation put Lincoln's name into nomination for the vice presidency. They had lined up enough delegates elsewhere to give him 110 votes on an informal first ballot, but the support behind New Jersey's William Dayton for second place on the ticket was too great to overcome. Lincoln was, however, beginning to attract mild attention beyond Illinois; several invitations to speak in neighboring states came to him during the campaign.

Meanwhile the Know-Nothings, who had been wrangling for months over what kind of stand to take on the slavery question, hastened their coming demise by breaking completely in half on the issue. The seceding Northern wing was persuaded to endorse the Republican ticket and in effect disappeared into the ranks of that party; the Southern Know-Nothings, mainly border state moderates, teamed up with the thinning ranks of irreconcilably die-hard Whigs in support of Millard Fillmore, the dignified, colorless ex-President whose eminent respectability and lack of identity with cause or controversy were precisely what the coalition wanted. Campaigning without a platform, behind a man who stood vaguely for sectional compromise minus the faintest suggestion of formula or solution, the Know-Nothing–Whig combination aimed itself deliberately at the conservative, Union-loving, plague-on-both-your-houses voter and drove steadfastly up the middle of a road that had already begun to fork.

The real contest was between Buchanan and Fremont, although Fillmore played an important role in the outcome. Fillmore's greatest strength was in the border slave states; if he could carry enough of these, there was a chance of sending the election to the

House of Representatives. Buchanan, however, was able to capture every border state except Maryland, Fillmore's lone electoral triumph. Buchanan also swept the deep South, where the result was never really in doubt.

Fillmore's major influence was in the North. He had not the slightest chance of carrying a Northern state, but in several of them his calculated appeal to conservative Whig voters ate heavily into Fremont's potential strength and may have cost the Republicans the election. Lincoln, among others, had foreseen this. He had hoped that the Republican national convention would abandon Fremont and choose the venerable Justice John McLean of Ohio, a safe, respectable old Whig, every bit as colorless as Buchanan and Fillmore—perfectly designed, as Lincoln saw it, to overcome conservative misgivings about the Republican Party. Once Fremont was selected, however, Lincoln campaigned furiously for the ticket in Illinois. Instead of relying on the party's made-to-order emotional issues, "bleeding Kansas" and "bleeding Sumner," he used every argument and device he could muster to cajole or browbeat unreconstructed Whigs away from Fillmore. Fremont could not carry Illinois without votes from this quarter, Lincoln knew, and Fillmore could not do it in any case. Lincoln constantly reminded the cautious Whigs, whose nervousness about Fremont and inveterate dislike of the Democratic Party were in delicate balance, that a vote for Fillmore was actually a vote for Buchanan.

The results justified Lincoln's fears. In Illinois the Republican candidate for governor, a man acceptable to the old-line Whigs, won by five thousand votes while Fremont lost the state to Buchanan by about nine thousand: the Fillmore minority had been decisive. Altogether Buchanan carried only five of the sixteen Northern states, but this plus his electoral landslide in the South added up to victory: the final tally gave Buchanan 174 electoral votes, Fremont 114, and Fillmore 8. The Democrats also retained comfortable though not overwhelming majorities in both Houses of Congress.

The Republicans, notwithstanding their defeat, had done

extremely well for a brand new party in its first presidential contest. They had carried eleven Northern states, including New
York and all of New England, and they had run strongly in the
other five. The future pointed in their direction, and any jubilant
Democrat who regarded Buchanan's triumph as a repudiation of
extreme sectionalism was making a grievous mistake. In the
popular vote, to be sure, the combined Buchanan-Fillmore total
exceeded Fremont's by a two-to-one margin. This seemed to indicate that a comforting two-thirds of the electorate preferred
one of the national, moderate candidates; how then could the
Union be in danger?

It was, for at least three reasons. First, and most obviously, the
big free-state majority in the electoral college meant that the
presidency could be won in this area alone, without the need for
a single Southern vote. Fremont had come strikingly close to
doing this in 1856: had he wrested Pennsylvania and either Illinois, Indiana, or New Jersey from Buchanan, he would have
won. His popular vote in the North exceeded Buchanan's, and
trailed the Buchanan-Fillmore total by less than 200,000. If the
Republicans could augment their strength in the next four years
with anything like the success of the last two, they would elect
a sectional candidate to the White House in 1860.

Secondly, much of the Northern vote for Buchanan was pred-
icated on two assumptions concerning the future of Kansas, and
if either of them proved wrong the Democrats were going to be in
trouble. The lawlessness and violence in Kansas had been checked
just in time to enable the Democrats, pointing with pride, to make
campaign promises. Buchanan and Douglas could now claim that
genuine popular sovereignty in the troubled area would at last
receive a fair trial. Fair elections, given the pronounced and growing majority of free-soil settlers in Kansas, would inevitably result in a decision against slavery: in other words, Douglas and
other party spokesmen assured anxious Northern Democrats, popular sovereignty would bring Kansas into the Union as a free
state. By and large, the North insisted upon this—Democrats and
Republicans alike. Both opposed the extension of slavery. The

difference, in 1856, boiled down to the fact that most Northern Democrats yet retained their faith in popular sovereignty to do the job. If it failed, the Republicans would profit. If it were to succeed, James Buchanan would have to show much more firmness and impartiality in treating the Kansas situation than Franklin Pierce had done. Yet Buchanan's Southern sympathies were widely known, and at no time in his long political career had he achieved a reputation for firmness.

And finally, any attempt to interpret Buchanan's triumph as a victory for moderation and the Union overlooked the attitude of the deep South. Undoubtedly, a large majority of voters in the cotton states were loyal Unionists in 1856, but neither the tone nor the sentiment of their leaders was exactly moderate, nor did the Southern mood augur well for the future. Southern Unionism was essentially conditional: it went as far as Southern confidence in the security of slavery, and no farther. Support for Buchanan in the deep South was based on a sectionalism as narrow and determined as the Republicans' own; Southern Democrats were voting less for the party of national unity than for the party that would enable them to retain a controlling influence in national affairs and thereby keep the hostile Northern majority at bay. The repeated, vociferous threat to secede rather than accept a Republican victory had influenced thousands of cautious Northern voters away from Fremont, and the South knew it; what worked so well in this election would unfailingly be tried in the next. Although from the Southern standpoint all of this was legitimate self-defense, to less sympathetic observers it was a policy that smacked strongly of rule-or-ruin. It was not, in any case, the tactic of moderation, and if the Republicans should win anyway in 1860, could the South survive without making good on the threat?

In all of the disunion talk that punctuated the 1856 campaign, the exact proportions of bombast, genuine intent, and calculated political effect are hard to determine, but there was no denying the importance of the issue, and many on both sides were convinced that the threat was real. It certainly went well beyond

the customary frothing of the lunatic fringe. Outspoken Robert
Toombs of Georgia, one of the leading battlers for compromise
and Union in 1850, showed how far Southern Unionism had slipped
in recent years. "The election of Fremont would be the end of
the Union, and ought to be," Toombs rumbled. "The object of
Fremont's friends is the conquest of the South. I am content
that they own us when they conquer us, but not before." Howell
Cobb, another prominent Georgian who on earlier occasions had
rallied Southern Unionist sentiment with energy and skill, was
now saying that secession must follow a Republican victory. Even
from moderate Virginia the noises were ominous: Senator Mason
insisted that Fremont's victory would call for "immediate, absolute, eternal separation," and Governor Wise advocated an emer-
gency conference of Southern governors. Similar statements popped
and rattled across the Gulf states like a chain of firecrackers.

Among the variety of Northern reactions to this outburst, nervousness was clearly paramount, but it was a nervousness that
bred defiance no less than fear. Reflecting the fear, typically
enough, was President-elect Buchanan, who insisted afterward
that the Democratic triumph had but narrowly averted disaster.
"We had reached the crisis," he said. "... Republicanism was
sweeping over the North like a tornado. ... Had Pennsylvania
yielded, had she become an abolition State ... we should have
been precipitated into the yawning gulf of dissolution." During
the campaign exultant abolitionists fed Buchanan's fears by wel-
coming the prospect of a Republican victory as the climax in "a
fight between freedom and slavery; between God and the Devil;
between heaven and hell."

But it was Abraham Lincoln who moved to the heart of the
matter. The Union was in no danger, he warned the South. "We
don't want to dissolve it, and if you attempt it, *we won't let you*.
With the purse and the sword, the army and navy and treasury
in our hands and at our command, you couldn't do it. ... All this
talk about the dissolution of the Union is humbug—nothing but
folly. We won't dissolve the Union, and you shan't." The roar of
Northern applause that greeted his response to the secessionist

threat was prophetic. If Southern leaders had sensed, correctly enough, that the threat of disunion would frighten many Northerners away from a sectional party, Lincoln was gauging precisely what the North would do if the threat ever became a reality. In its disunion utterances of 1856 the South was acquiring few permanent allies and one fatal habit.

Jefferson Davis did not add his voice to the Southern clamor for disunion in 1856. He found ample cause for worry in the growing strength of the Republican Party, and in the potential danger to slavery posed by an organization so conceived and so dedicated, but he was not yet sufficiently alarmed to lend himself to Southern saber-rattling. Davis could hardly make secessionist noises from his post as United States Secretary of War, and besides, he reasoned, it was still possible to thwart Republican designs by normal political opposition. Even if Fremont won, the South and her Northern allies would retain effective majorities in both Houses of Congress and on the Supreme Court. In the struggles that lay ahead, loyal Southerners could best defend their principles by putting every talent to work in the great national forum, and with such thoughts in mind Davis again strove to marshal support in Mississippi for a return to the Senate.

This time he succeeded, although not in convincing fashion. Mississippi's Democratic legislature would elect the nominee of the party caucus without a struggle, but Mississippi Democrats in 1856 were evenly divided beween Davis and another favorite son, Jacob Thompson, whose connections, social standing and unswerving allegiance to the Southern cause were on a par with Davis's own. No doctrinal differences were at issue here; Thompson, like Davis, was a Southern-rights nationalist who had fought the Compromise of 1850 and suffered defeat in 1851 at the hands of Mississippi Unionists. Efforts to muster a clear majority for Davis were blocked, in part, by old-fashioned regional rivalry between the Davis bastion around Vicksburg and Thompson's stronghold in northwestern Mississippi. Apparently, too, some of the less radical members tended to regard Thompson as the "safer" candidate, despite the similarity of their records. In any

case, the caucus deadlocked on the first ballot, and Davis won his
Senate seat by the uncomfortably narrow margin of the presiding
officer's tie-breaking vote.

Eighteen fifty-seven dawned in a mingled atmosphere of hope
and tension. The nation had given a mandate of sorts to James
Buchanan and the Democratic Party, and much would depend on
what they did with it. A noted historian once remarked that democracy works best when there is nothing of profound importance
to discuss, which as far as this generation was concerned posed
the problem squarely. In the Buchanan years the agenda was full
—financial panic, corruption in government, tariff bills, homestead
bills, railroad and internal improvement bills, budget questions,
and similar topics. If not unimportant, these items were at least
familiar, and after they had been discussed and voted upon the
minority could accept the verdict of the majority without feeling
that its existence was at stake. Overshadowing these manageable
items, however, and often subverting them, was the slavery question—unsurpassingly important, too explosive to handle, too explosive to ignore. For years the political system had been jabbing
crudely and ineffectually at the peculiar institution, worrying it
into the forefront of national affairs. Now the American experiment faced a showdown. And in confronting slavery—to adapt
the classic comment made, fittingly enough, by an American Negro
prizefighter ninety-odd years later—democracy could run but it
couldn't hide.

More specifically, the Buchanan administration was forced to
make decisions concerning the doctrine of popular sovereignty,
that oft invoked and much abused formula for determining the
status of slavery in the territories. In a sense, popular sovereignty
occupied a precarious middle position in the shifting spectrum
of national attitudes toward slavery. It represented the latest
attempt, however misguided and poorly thought out, to find a
workable compromise amid the clash of pro- and anti-slavery viewpoints. Experience, reinforced in this instance by wishful thinking, suggested that the nation had a genius for this sort of thing.
Popular sovereignty was certainly impressive enough at first

glance. It sounded the way a compromise ought to sound—as vague and flexible, in its small way, as that eminently functional instrument of balance and compromise, the Federal Constitution. It was laudably democratic. It promised to avoid the excesses and conflicts inherent in both the radical Southern approach, which demanded, as the price of Union, permanent guarantees of slavery wherever it sought to go, and in the radical Northern idea, which demanded immediate emancipation of all slaves.

Its one drawback, given the hardening sectional attitudes of the eighteen-fifties, was that it could not possibly work. Popular sovereignty resembled a ten-foot plank laid across a chasm ten feet wide: it would just bridge the gap, but no one dared walk on it. Lincoln had called attention to popular sovereignty's fatal flaw as far back as 1854. How could the system function, Lincoln asked, without specifying *when* the settlers would decide for or against slavery? This ambiguity was present when the idea first appeared in the late forties; it remained there when Congress debated the Kansas-Nebraska Act; and it was still present, essentially, in the popular sovereignty plank of the Democratic platform in 1856. Actually, the platform was explicit enough, calling for the exercise of popular sovereignty in a territory "whenever the number of their inhabitants justifies it to form a constitution"—in others words, not until the area was ready for statehood. But the ambiguity persisted during and after the campaign, because Northern Democratic politicians continued to tell their constituents that a majority could vote to exclude slavery from a territory well before it prepared to enter the Union, while Southerners had insisted all along that no vote could be taken prior to entry.

There was the point. Popular sovereignty could not work while the ambiguity remained—Kansas offered living, scarred proof—and the Democratic Party could not hold its Northern and Southern wings together if the ambiguity were removed. Neither faction had embraced popular sovereignty in the true spirit of compromise, but rather as a convenient, if somewhat makeshift, means to an end—and the ends were diametrically opposed. To Democrats in the North, conscious of their section's growing numerical preponderance, popular sovereignty would enable a free-soil majority to capture every territory. Southerners were even more acutely conscious of the population imbalance, and they had accepted popular sovereignty in the Kansas-Nebraska Act not because they liked the principle—far from it—but because it afforded a chance to destroy the hated Missouri Compromise ban on slavery north of 36°30′. Both sides knew that once slavery took firm root in a region it was difficult to eradicate later on. Lincoln had noted this fact in his first analysis of Kansas-Nebraska, and it explained why Northerners would employ popular sovereignty to vote slavery out of a territory at the earliest possible moment while Southerners would allow slaveholders to migrate without hindrance throughout the territorial stage. The Democrats were totally unable to reconcile these opposing interpretations of their platform.

There was hope, in the early months of 1857, that the Supreme Court might reconcile it for them. Behind popular sovereignty lay an even older and touchier question, more or less at issue ever since John C. Calhoun had begun his intense probing of slavery's Constitutional bulwarks. Did Congress have the power to prohibit slavery in the territories? Northerners, pointing to a host of precedents, argued that it did; Davis and other Southerners, following Calhoun, pointed to the property clauses in the Federal Constitution and argued that it did not. The Democratic platform of 1856, in addition to its reaffirmation of popular sovereignty, had adopted the Southern point of view and denied the power of Congress to exclude slavery from the territories, a plank made possible by the confidence Northern Democrats yet retained in popular sovereignty's ability to register a free-soil triumph in Kansas. In the closing weeks of the Pierce administration the Supreme Court heard the case of a Negro named Dred Scott, who was suing for freedom on the grounds that from 1834 to 1838 he had resided with his former master, an army surgeon from Missouri, in the free state of Illinois and the free territory of Wisconsin. Scott was claiming, quite simply, that residence on free soil had made him a free man.

In December, 1856, after nearly a decade of sporadic litigation in the lower courts, the case came before the Supreme Court.

The Scott case would enable the Court, if it chose, to pass on the constitutionality of Federal laws banning slavery from the territories. James Buchanan, who with other Democratic leaders had kept a close eye on the proceedings—had, in fact, brought something akin to pressure on the justices for a satisfactory ruling—informed the nation in his inaugural address that a forthcoming Supreme Court decision would lay the vexatious territorial question at rest. The new President obviously anticipated a decision favorable to the Democratic platform and the Southern point of view.

Buchanan was supremely confident that the Court's enormous prestige would adhere to the ruling and thus make a closed chapter out of the territorial problem, removing it from politics once and for all. The decision was handed down in March, 1857, two days after the inauguration, and in both the verdict and the response it appeared that the Supreme Court was considerably less remote from politics than Buchanan had thought.

Denying Scott's plea on three separate counts, the Court did in fact comment explicitly on Congressional power over slavery in the territories. As anticipated, the result was a total victory for the Southern viewpoint. Three Justices (with two opposed and four abstaining) pronounced that no slave or slave descendant —in brief, no Negro—could ever be a citizen of a state or of the United States, and hence that Scott had lacked the citizen's right to sue in a Federal court. By a vote of six to two, the Court then dismissed Scott's claim that residence on free soil conferred freedom upon him, on the grounds that his sojourn in Illinois and Wisconsin had been temporary and the laws of Missouri, where his owner had retained permanent domicile during the years in question, continued to govern his status. Since a clear majority so found, the case could have been halted right here, but the Court proceeded, again by a six to two vote, to pass on the territorial question. On this crucial third count, by a variety of reasoning processes, the majority concluded that Congress lacked the power to prohibit slavery in the Federal territories. The Missouri Compromise, true to the Southern contention, had been unconstitutional all along.

The decision immediately touched off a full-fledged uproar, and

Buchanan's pious hope that slavery in the territories would cease to agitate the political scene was quickly dashed. Southern leaders, naturally, were overjoyed, and their triumphant reaction was hardly calculated to soothe the Northern temper. An elated Jefferson Davis apparently shared Buchanan's feeling that the Court had forever silenced Republican clamor against the rights of slaveowners in Kansas. Southern jubilation was understandable. Davis's views, a faithful echo of the late Calhoun's, had been fully and resoundingly vindicated, and the majestic authority of the Federal Constitution now buttressed slavery's power to expand. Even the Republicans, Davis reasoned, could hardly assault so mightily reinforced a citadel as this.

The Republicans could and did. With the Dred Scott decision the Supreme Court had tried to catch the wind in a net. Buchanan and Davis might have known better than to think antislavery sentiment would hold still for such a ruling, and instead of closing, the floodgates of Northern wrath opened wider than ever. In language peculiarly reminiscent of Southern fulminations against another famous Court decision nearly a century later, Republican editors and politicians denounced the majority opinion with hysterical savagery. The six offending Justices were branded tyrants and traitors, their decision "infamous," "atrocious," "a judicial lie." A ruling from a Washington barroom would deserve more respect, snapped Horace Greeley of the influential New York *Tribune*. Paint the flag black, with whip and fetter for devices, railed William Cullen Bryant of the New York *Post*. Many Northern states passed or strengthened "personal liberty" statutes designed to protect colored residents from the operations of the Fugitive Slave Law. Abolitionists preached secession with all the intemperate zeal of a Southern fire-eater, and angry talk of the "slave power conspiracy" was widely heard.

This last point was perhaps the most important. When things go wrong Americans are wont to search for a conspiracy of evildoers, and on the basis of superficial evidence there was much to support the contention that a Machiavellian "slave-power" was subverting the machinery of government to its evil ends. Southerners, so the theory went, dominated the Democratic Party, wrote its platform, controlled the Presidency and both Houses of Congress. They were responsible for the Kansas-Nebraska Act, and for the fraud and violence that had enabled a proslavery minority to usurp power in Kansas territory. They had tried to seize Cuba from Spain, and they were supporting or condoning a host of filibustering activities in the Caribbean—all aimed at adding to slavery's domain. Their answer to a Senate speech was physical assault. With their pliant Northern allies—known contemptuously as "doughfaces," and including such leaders as Pierce and Buchanan—they manipulated the legislative and executive branches of government to thwart the will of the Northern majority on such desired goals as free homesteads, higher tariffs, and federally financed internal improvements. The separate counts in the indictment were true enough. Whether they added up to a conspiracy, or merely to the nervous defensive maneuvers of a conscious minority seeking to protect itself from engulfment and ruin at the hands of an aggressive majority, depended, by this time, on where one lived.

And now, Republican spokesmen shrilled, the United States Supreme Court had convincingly demonstrated its subservience to the slave power. There was reason, certainly, to view the present Court as something less than a stronghold of Olympian detachment. Seven of the nine Justices were Democrats. More important, five were Southerners, and these five, together with the notoriously pro-Southern Robert Grier of Pennsylvania, had written the majority decision in the Scott case. This presumptive evidence of sectional bias was strongly reinforced by the tone and content of the majority arguments, which gave sweeping endorsement to the proslavery viewpoint. Congress could no longer keep slavery out of a territory, notwithstanding the numerous precedents cited by the minority. How long would it be, some were asking, before a proslavery Court struck down *state* laws prohibiting slavery, and permitted the hated institution to invade Massachusetts and Ohio as well as Kansas? The mood of the times, overhung with the anger bred of fear, somehow made the remotest and farthest fetched of contingencies seem imminent.

And the outcry went on. It was bad enough, Northerners argued, that federal judicial districts should be so drawn as to allot five Justices to six million white citizens in the slaveholding states and only four Justices to the sixteen millions in the free states. Even worse were the indications that Democratic leaders, including President Buchanan, had skirted dangerously close to the bounds of judicial propriety in bringing pressure on the Court for a territorial pronouncement in the Scott case. If prominent Democrats and the six majority Justices had avoided actual collusion—which many outraged Northerners refused to believe—there had been enough communication between Court and politicians during the Scott hearings to suggest that most of the Justices knew precisely what was expected of them.

Lack of probity was a false charge. Sectional bias was not. Six Justices of the Supreme Court, speaking in all honesty and out of sincere conviction, had written Southern doctrine into the law of the land. This doctrine went directly against the beliefs of a great majority of citizens, and the beliefs cut deep. Contrary to James Buchanan's wishful thought, the Supreme Court did not "settle" this kind of question. To millions in the North the power to resist slavery—for such seemed at stake—was not an abstract point of law but a matter of principle, inextricably bound up with the heritage and destiny of the republic. The final arbiter in questions like this was not the Supreme Court but the voice of the sovereign people, speaking at the polls. What a sectional Court had done a national Court could undo, and Republicans looked forward eagerly to the day, not much more distant than the next election, when a Northern majority would control the federal government and consign the Scott decision to oblivion. "The remedy is union and action: the ballot box," cried the Chicago *Tribune*. "Let free states be a unit in Congress on the side of freedom. Let the next President be Republican, and 1860 will mark an era kindred with that of 1776."

Twice Lincoln added his voice to the strident chorus of Northern protest over Dred Scott, and the content of his speeches showed that genuine moral concern had not dulled his political instincts. Eighteen fifty-seven was an off year in Illinois politics, and in his first analysis he took the higher ground. The lot of the Negro, he told a Springfield audience in June, was steadily worsening. Far from easing the bonds of slavery, the South was drawing them tighter than ever, consciously sealing off all avenues of escape. State laws prohibited masters from emancipating their slaves, and state constitutions prevented Southern legislatures from abolishing slavery. (As regards the latter the South too, it appears, was on guard against the absurdest of possibilities.) Now the Supreme Court was denying the right of Congress to exclude slavery from the territories, and Chief Justice Taney had gone so far as to maintain that the Founding Fathers had never intended the principles of the Declaration of Independence to apply to the colored man. Lincoln harked to the main theme of his Kansas-Nebraska message three years before: in the process of sanctifying the rights of slavery America was bartering away its heritage of freedom. The Declaration had been intended as a "standard maxim for free society . . . constantly spreading and deepening its influence," ultimately applicable "to all peoples of all colors everywhere."

But now, Lincoln warned, the once-sacred document was being cheapened and diluted and twisted into something unrecognizable —all "to aid in making the bondage of the Negro universal and eternal. . . . All the powers of earth seem rapidly combining against him. Mammon is after him; ambition follows, and philosophy follows, and the theology of the day is fast joining the cry. They have him in his prison house; . . . One after another they have closed the heavy iron doors upon him . . . and they stand musing as to what invention, in all the dominions of mind and matter, can be produced to make the impossibility of his escape more complete than it is." As a capstone to recent trends, the Scott decision had made a travesty of the American experiment.

Lincoln had once again laid bare the heart of the controversy, and his logic was scarcely assailable: if the Declaration of Independence were of limited application, it had no meaning at all. Twelve months later he sounded a less exalted note. In 1858 he was again a candidate for the Senate, battling this time against the redoubtable Stephen A. Douglas himself, and in the heat of political combat Lincoln was unable to resist exploiting the more sensational aspects of the slavery problem. This was the famous speech in which he asserted that a house divided against itself could not stand, undoubtedly the most provocative and least states-manlike of Lincoln's major utterances. Not only did his use of the Biblical quotation imply the coming of open conflict between the sections; the address set forth the slave-conspiracy theory in concrete terms—specifically suggesting that Taney, Douglas, Pierce, and Buchanan were members of a well-laid plot to extend the sway of slavery—and warned that judicial reasoning in the Scott case pointed squarely at the invalidation of state laws pro-hibiting slavery in the near future. It was fallacious to talk of a Union "half slave and half free." The equilibrium was unstable by nature, and one or the other must triumph. Unless the advo-cates of freedom took action to counter the present trend, Lincoln asserted, the national dominion of slavery would soon be complete.

This was strong language, obviously calculated to stir the fears and prey on the emotions of his Northern audience. Other Repub-lican leaders had been harping on this theme for months, and in essence it was no more than a logical extension of the choice Lincoln had posed as early as 1854 between the philosophy of slavery and that of the Declaration of Independence. Yet the words and tone of the House Divided speech were perceptibly less moderate. Gone, for the moment, was the humble confession that with all earthly power he would not know what to do with slavery, gone the gentle acknowledgment that the men of the South "are just what we would be in their situation." The clarion appeal to high principle had taken on a shrill note, edged with fear and undertones of violence. If Lincoln genuinely believed in a "slave conspiracy," his perspective had become clouded by re-cent events—or by senatorial ambition, which he had been nursing since his defeat in 1855.

Warned in advance that his House Divided speech would offend all save the more radical Republicans, Lincoln insisted that he merely wanted to confront the people with the facts; faced after-ward with something of the adverse reaction his friends had pre-dicted, he stoutly denied that an aggressive meaning underlay his words—all of which, for a professional politician, sounds a shade disingenuous. Lincoln wanted the march of slavery halted, and he aimed at rallying public opinion behind his banner. He also wanted to spike a move then under consideration by Republican strategists to unite with Northern Democrats behind the Douglas candidacy. Hence the need to include Douglas in the slave conspiracy, to talk darkly of a Union unable to endure permanently half slave and half free and tending, thanks to Douglas, in the former direction. It was, in short, a campaign speech, and Lincoln was familiar enough with the ways of an audience to know that strong words breed strong inferences, however mild the intent.

That a leader as temperate and fair-minded as Lincoln should let political pressure impel him this close to the brink of demagoguery was symptomatic. By this time, politicians who calculatedly turned the emotional features of the sectional controversy to personal advantage and politicians of a higher stripe who had genuine convictions about the issues at stake were speaking much the same language. The gulf that separated Northern and Southern moderates had widened until no straddle was possible. Senator Jefferson Davis, even less inclined than Lincoln to color his remarks for political effect, was reaffirming the main tenets of the Southern creed before enthusiastic audiences in Mississippi, and nothing Davis said was designed to allay Northern fears. Touring the state in the autumn of 1857 before his departure for the next session of Congress, Davis surveyed the national scene and gave frank support to the very items Lincoln and other Republican leaders saw as evidence of a slave-power conspiracy.

An avowed expansionist, Davis spoke in glowing terms of a future republic that stretched from the Canadian border to the isthmus of Panama—each southerly acquisition, of course, adding slave-state stars to the national flag. It was unfortunate, Davis said, that the various attempts of the Pierce administration to annex Cuba from Spain had failed; further efforts should be made under Buchanan. Davis praised the efforts of William Walker to spread American civilization to the Caribbean, and hoped for the success of Walker's second Nicaraguan venture. (Walker had been ousted from the little republic that spring, and was back in the

United States raising men and money for another go at it.) The
Senator from Mississippi hailed the Dred Scott decision as a cor-
rect and long-needed definition of the Constitutional limits on
Congressional power. And "African slavery, as it exists in the
United States," Davis announced flatly, "is a moral, a social, and
a political blessing."

Davis also explored a new angle. In praising the Dred Scott
decision, he expounded an idea that was about to take its place
at the core of the Southern position. Denying Congress the power
to exclude slavery from the territories was a necessary step forward, Davis said, but it was not enough. Slavery's right to expand
without hindrance required one more bulwark: a federal statute
explicitly guaranteeing that slaveowners and their property would
be unmolested in all federal territories. This was the doctrine of
positive protection, already current in Southern political circles,
designed to prevent a free-soil majority in a territory from taking
hostile action against a slaveholding minority in their midst. Long
before the North had shown the slightest indication of accepting
the idea that Congress could not *exclude* slavery, the South was
preparing to demand that Congress *protect* it.

There was scant room for compromise here. All that Lincoln
had described as parts of a Southern conspiracy—slavery expansion, the Scott decision, a demand for further strengthening of
slavery's legal position—Davis was warmly advocating as no more
than the South's just due. To Davis, the serious threats of the
day came entirely from the North. Democratic institutions were
menaced not by slavery, but by the essential lawlessness contained in abolitionism, in Northern defiance of the Supreme Court,
and in the growing determination of the Northern majority to
enforce its will upon the South. We are not the aggressors, Davis
told the Senate in 1858. "In what have we now, or ever, back to
the earliest period of our history, sought to deprive the North
of any advantage it possessed? . . . You have made it a political
war. We are on the defensive. How far are you to push us?"
Mutual distrust could go no further than this. What one termed
aggression the other insisted was self-defense, and at bottom were
irreconcilable views about the nature of the peculiar institution.

No conceivable brand of statesmanship could find workable middle ground between slavery as a threat to the Declaration of Independence and slavery as a moral, social, and political blessing.

The trouble was that all attempts to find a middle ground, from the Missouri Compromise on, had been frankly expedient, aimed at postponing rather than coming to grips with the situation. Enlightened statesmanship could not begin to operate until some sort of national consensus about the ultimate future of slavery was reached. Clay and Webster, loftiest of compromisers, had steered away from this subject and undercut sectionalism by stirring appeals to the grandeur and glory of the Union. Their chief successor in the search for a middle way was Stephen A. Douglas, who sidestepped the moral aspects of the problem by denying that they existed. Douglas's basic answer to the moral issue was a statement—which his Republican opponents exploited to the full —that he did not care whether slavery was voted up or voted down.

The road between the extremes did not lie in this direction. Lincoln was right in insisting that the problem could not be solved until it was faced. Time would not "take care" of slavery in a peaceful, evolutionary way as long as one section of the country regarded it as a blessing, the other as a curse; and such attitudes would not simply melt away before a man who tried to say it was neither. Statesmanship required that the North recognize slavery as a national problem and cease condemning it in terms the South could not accept; it also required that the South turn away from the moral-blessing idea and agree to enter discussions looking to a gradual, long-range plan for the transition from slavery toward freedom.

Unlike most of his contemporaries, Lincoln understood all of this perfectly. The gradual, long-range approach was exactly what he wanted. Unfortunately, North and South could hardly be persuaded to accept joint responsibility for the problem and work together for its solution until the men who felt this way came to power. Lincoln's talk of conspirators and a house divided against itself had been a response to one of the oldest dilemmas of politics—that of the leader who plans to use the moderate approach when in office but resorts to immoderate language during the campaign in the interests of getting elected. What Lincoln feared, as the decade of the fifties wore to a close, was a weakening of Republican resolve and a surrender to the Douglas type of leadership, which would be a victory for moral indifference and a further erosion of American principles. As Lincoln saw it, only a united Republican majority in control of the national government could halt the twin threats of slavery and disunion—by acting with sufficient firmness to contain the former yet with sufficient moderation and restraint to allay Southern fears and create the atmosphere in which enlightened statesmanship, North and South, could begin working out the pattern for slavery's slow evolution into something better. But this Northern majority had to be roused and made aware of the problem before it could do as Lincoln hoped, and the language that would rouse it might well defeat the ends he had in view.

Jefferson Davis, who just might have responded to a calm atmosphere in the proper spirit had he seen any possibility that the restraint Lincoln advocated would in fact be applied, could only interpret the talk of conspiracy and a Union that must become all slave or all free as further evidence of Northern extremism. His response was unimaginative, but natural; after twenty-five years of stifling all criticism of slavery within its borders the South contained no leader who employed or even contemplated any answer save the continuous demand that slavery be rendered forever secure from attack. Moderation? Davis and Lincoln claimed to be moderates, but their language had taken on an uncompromising quality, and their "moderation" would become operative only when the other side retreated from its present position. Yet neither Lincoln nor Davis could regard a retreat from his particular position as aught but surrender—hence there would be no retreat at all.

The no man's land between these well-entrenched viewpoints was becoming increasingly hard to occupy. Stephen Douglas still camped there, and his eye was not dim nor his natural force abated, but time was running out for him. The Dred Scott decision had cut three ways. While Republican leaders reacted with defiance and invective, exhorting Northern sentiment to rally against the slave power, and Southern leaders stepped up their demands and began asking for federal protection of slavery in the territories, Douglas and his Northern Democrats were nonplussed. They hailed the Court decision—as Democrats they had no choice, since their party platform had affirmed the same principle—but they quickly saw that it put them in a quandary. The Court had made it clear that neither Congress *nor a territorial legislature,* a creature of Congress, could act to exclude slavery. Douglas did not need the Republicans to remind him, although they did so repeatedly and with zest, that this ruling struck a heavy blow at the Northern version of popular sovereignty, well-nigh destroying it.

Under the Scott decision, the people in a territory could not decide against slavery until they drew up a constitution and prepared to enter the Union. This power they had had since the very founding of the republic, which meant that popular sovereignty, under the guise of a great new principle, merely endorsed their possession of a right no one had ever questioned. And meanwhile, true to the Northern fear and the Southern claim, slaveowners and their property could migrate at will throughout the territorial stage. Since slavery once established had a way of clinging tenaciously to a region, the Scott decision had in effect ruined popular sovereignty as a free-soil bulwark.

As usual, Douglas had an answer, although he did not sound overly comfortable. The Scott decision was correct, he said. It upheld his battle-scarred Kansas-Nebraska Act by invalidating what the act had repealed, the tired old Missouri Compromise. It destroyed the Republican contention that Congress had the right to prohibit slavery, and it did not contradict popular sovereignty at all. If a territorial majority were opposed to slavery, Douglas maintained, they could always exclude it by the simple device of refusing to enact protective legislation; without such legislation, slaveowners would shun a territory rather than risk their property in a hostile environment. The will of the majority could always prevail.

In some ways this was typical Douglas reasoning, and as an attempt to stay on the middle ground it constituted a rearguard action. In talking of "protective legislation" he ignored the dilemma that must confront territorial legislators when they refused to exercise the police power in slavery's behalf while sworn to uphold the Federal Constitution, which under the Scott decision obligated them to safeguard the rights of slaveowners. Moreover, Douglas was trying to squeeze through a loophole that Southerners had already spotted and were preparing to plug: the new Southern demand for a federal slave code—positive protection—was specifically designed to prevent a territorial legislature from exercising any choice in the matter of slavery legislation. As it was, Lincoln observed sarcastically, the Scott decision had strained popular sovereignty to the thinness of a soup made by boiling a starved pigeon's shadow. Northern Democrats might accept Douglas's new interpretation, but he could not hope to keep the Southern wing of his party behind him while he clung to any device by which slavery might be barred from a territory. The precarious unity that Democrats had tried to preserve under popular sovereignty's tattered mantle for the past few years was about to evaporate.

The academic debate over the Dred Scott decision was soon overshadowed by developments in Kansas. In the early months of 1857 the proslavery territorial legislature set up the machinery for the election of delegates to a convention that would frame a state constitution. The proslavery forces in Kansas were a minority that grew smaller with each new influx of settlers, but the election, held in June, was so rigged and gerrymandered as to insure a proslavery majority in the convention. In the fall the delegates assembled at the straggling Kansas village of Lecompton and framed a constitution. To no one's surprise, the document was studded with proslavery clauses and consciously paved the way for the admission of Kansas as a slave state.

The swelling uproar from without that accompanied these proceedings was focused primarily on the convention's decision not to submit the entire Lecompton Constitution to the people of Kansas for ratification. Well aware of how quickly the big free-soil majority in Kansas would reject their new document, proslavery extremists had favored not submitting any of it, but a last-minute compromise with proslavery moderates had authorized a partial referendum. Kansas could not pass on the Lecompton Constitution as a whole; they could only choose between the "constitution with slavery" and the "constitution without slavery" —and the vote was to be supervised and tallied by the same legislature that had rigged the convention in June.

Douglas and the Northern Democrats were furious. Until recently they had followed their party in supporting the proslavery Kansas legislature as the lawful government of the territory, but by 1857 the evidence that a large majority of Kansans would repudiate slavery in an honest election was too overwhelming to be ignored, and this brazen attempt to make a slave state out of Kansas inspired huge resentment. Even if the settlers chose the "constitution without slavery"—and control of the referendum by the proslavery forces made this doubtful—they were perforce accepting the balance of the Lecompton document, which fully protected slave property already established in Kansas, forbade any changes in the constitution for six years, and contained other objectionable features. If popular sovereignty meant anything at all, it required that every eligible citizen be allowed to ratify or reject the entire constitution in a fair vote. Instead they were given a fragmentary, meaningless caricature of an alternative that one sardonic Kansan likened to a choice between accepting arsenic with bread and butter or taking it straight.

The ultimate success of the Lecompton maneuver depended on the attitudes and actions of the federal government, custodian of the national territories. James Buchanan was the pivot, and the fateful decision of the Democratic Party to select this man instead of Stephen Douglas in 1856 now came home to roost. In dispatching a new territorial governor to Kansas in the spring of 1857 Buchanan had pledged his full support in behalf of fair elections and the right of the people to decide their institutions freely and without restraint. "On the question of submitting the constitution to the bona fide residents of Kansas," he wrote as late as July, "I am willing to stand or fall. It is the principle of the Kansas-Nebraska Act, the principle of Popular Sovereignty, and the principle at the foundation of all popular government." Now the pledge was coming due. Recent events had indicated that elections in Kansas were unfair and that a packed convention was about to deny the settlers any real choice in their constitution. Honoring the pledge meant requiring a vote on the entire Lecompton document and seeing to it that the referendum was honest.

Instead Buchanan caved in, and with him the papier-maché unity of the Democratic Party. By the time Congress assembled in December, the anxious President had bowed to the pressure that worried him most. Southern leaders were determined to force acceptance of the Lecompton Constitution and admit Kansas as a slave state. They denounced all criticism of the maneuver as Black Republican propaganda, and they openly dangled the secessionist bogey in front of Buchanan as the inevitable sequel to a rejection of Lecompton. Genuinely fearful of this possibility, surrounded by a Cabinet which, like that of his predecessor, was led by men of Southern views and stronger wills than his own, the President went back on his pledge and supported the Lecompton plan to the hilt.

Buchanan now took the line that the forthcoming referendum between the "constitution with slavery" and the "constitution without slavery" would after all be a decision on the crux of the matter, and he announced in his annual message that the vote would provide Kansas citizens a "fair" opportunity to settle the question in a proper way. As for the Northern Democrats, whose outraged cries against Lecompton were mounting at an ominous rate, they would have to be kept in line by administration pressure and party discipline. To Buchanan, secession was the graver threat; the South required appeasement, and the Northern wing would have to bite the bullet. It only remained for Congress to follow the President's lead and vote to approve the Lecompton Constitution, which Buchanan chose to make a test of party loyalty. Kansas would become the sixteenth slave state, the South would rest secure, and the Union would be saved.

The next move was up to Stephen Douglas, pre-eminent spokesman for the Northern Democracy and veteran battler for the cause of popular sovereignty. The Little Giant's response was as thoroughly in character as Buchanan's. Angered beyond measure at the Lecompton scheme, angered even more by the President's acceptance of it, Douglas had not the slightest intention of following the administration. He planned to fight. For the Democratic Party this meant the worst kind of internecine war, possibly an irreparable split, but Douglas neither had a choice nor wanted one. Democratic editors from Maine to Iowa were denouncing the Lecompton Constitution with a virulence unrivaled since Kansas-Nebraska days, and any Democratic leader who ignored this groundswell was going to be in serious trouble—Douglas most of all, with a campaign for re-election to the Senate only a few months away.

Beyond the level of practical consideration, however, was a question of principle. Douglas had fought too long and too hard for popular sovereignty against assaults by Republican foes to give way now that the attack was coming from another quarter. Only the submission of the entire constitution to all eligible Kansans in a fair and impartial canvass would mollify the Northern Democrats and restore the tarnished fortunes of popular sovereignty. Here Douglas would take his stand, and all the fighting spirit that had sustained him in earlier battles was mobilized for the new challenge. "I have taken a through ticket," he announced at the outset of the campaign, "and checked all my baggage." Earlier he had promised to "carry out the principle or fall in the attempt."

Many would fall before the struggle was over, and the Democratic Party would not be the same for a generation. With the President's pro-Lecompton stand already known, the lines were drawn even before Congress assembled, and when Douglas reached the capital a stormy confrontation between the two leaders set the tone for what was to follow. Never overly fond of each other, each convinced that his opponent's stand would ruin the party, the tall, white-haired President and the stocky, pugnacious Senator proceeded bluntly to the heart of the matter. With Andrew Jackson's iron rule in mind, Buchanan reminded Douglas that "no Democrat ever yet differed from an Administration of his own choice without being crushed." Never to be outdone, Douglas pointedly reminded the President that Andrew Jackson was dead.

When the Little Giant stalked out of the White House at the close of this acrimonious exchange the rift was open and final.

Much of the 1857-1858 session of Congress was given over to the Lecompton question, which proved as bitter and relentless a contest as Washington had ever seen. Confusion was added early in the struggle by the news that Kansans had voted twice on their constitution, with diametrically opposed results. The referendum in December under the Lecompton plan resulted, to no one's surprise, in a small turnout and a victory for the "constitution with slavery," free-soilers not actually disfranchised by the voting rules tending to boycott the affair in disgust. But a new territorial legislature had been elected earlier that fall, and when the governor threw out a large portion of the returns on the grounds of incontestable fraud, the free-soilers actually found themselves in control. They quickly arranged for a referendum on the whole constitution, and in early January, 1858, by orderly process, a gigantic majority rejected the Lecompton instrument, root and branch. All this meant in Congress, of course, was that each side could point to one or the other of the Kansas polls and claim that Lecompton had been endorsed or repudiated by a convincing margin.

With a Democratic majority in both Houses, the Buchanan administration did not hesitate to use all the weapons of patronage and pressure at its disposal to force party members into line and obtain approval of the Lecompton Constitution, but the opposing coalition of Republicans, Know-Nothings, and Northern Democrats that rallied behind the indefatigable Douglas proved a shade too strong. The administration had little trouble in the Senate, where Southern leadership was well entrenched and proportionately stronger than in the House, and where the direct pressure of public opinion was less keenly felt; despite the tireless energy and trenchant logic with which Douglas opposed the measure, eight Northern Democrats followed the party line and joined their twenty-five Southern colleagues to give Lecompton a safe majority.

In the Lower House it was different. The big Republican minority was of course a unit in opposition, and all the administration's influence and pressure tactics were unable to hold the Democratic majority. A determined bloc of Northern members held out against every threat and blandishment, and Lecompton stalled.

At the last, desperate for a face-saving measure, administration leaders worked out a compromise which a bare majority in both Houses could accept. What emerged was a bill that allowed Kansas to choose between immediate statehood under the Lecompton Constitution or a delay until the territory reached a population equal to that of a Congressional district (about 90,000, or over twice the number of inhabitants then residing in Kansas). In effect, although it did not say so directly, the compromise bill enabled Kansans to reject the Lecompton Constitution by choosing deferred entry, and in the late summer of 1858 the Kansas voters did precisely that, voting Lecompton down by an enormous majority. For the first time in four years a measure of peace and stability came to the troubled territory. Its role as the violent storm center of national politics was nearly over.

[SIX]

MODERATION
IN ECLIPSE,
1 8 5 8 – 1 8 6 0

Peace in Kansas had been obtained at fearful cost. Southern leaders were bitter and resentful at the failure of their desperate bid to create a new slave state, more determined than ever to resist the rising specter of Northern dominion. The Democratic Party was hopelessly divided, and its prospects for victory in 1860 were darkening steadily. The administration's frank pro-Southern stand during the Lecompton battle had damaged the party beyond measure in the free states. The fall elections in 1858 saw Democrats toppled from office by the score across the North, and those who survived entertained few doubts about the folly of continued acquiescence to Southern leadership. The only important Democrat with the slightest chance of carrying any Northern states in 1860 was Stephen A. Douglas, whose battle for fair play in Kansas and defiant refusal to knuckle under to the administration had greatly enhanced his popularity. Yet this was the man whom James Buchanan and the Southern leaders had marked for destruction. These Southern leaders would never follow Douglas again. Many were determined to ruin him if they could, and a small minority could face with equanimity, even enthusiasm, the thought that this might ruin the party and divide the country as well.

For Douglas, exhausted and unwell after his prolonged exertions at the head of the anti-Lecompton forces, the battle in Washington was only one phase in a larger contest. With the adjournment of Congress in June, 1858, Douglas was off for Illinois to open his campaign for re-election to the Senate. He had no illusions about the difficulties that lay ahead of him. The national administration of his own party was going all-out to destroy him, and had already started wielding the patronage to harass his lieutenants, oust his followers, and build an anti-Douglas Democratic machine in Illinois. Before leaving Washington he learned that his Republican opponent in the Senate race would be Abraham Lincoln, for whose political abilities Douglas had the highest respect. It was hardly a pleasant prospect, and for all that he throve on combat he could be excused the wish that his troubles would stop coming in battalions.

Douglas must have thought more than once about the ironic twists of political fortune. Four years ago he had been on a similar journey, returning to Illinois at the end of a hard-fought Congressional session with fences to mend and a host of enemies mobilizing to defeat him. In 1854, as in 1858, Kansas and popular sovereignty lay at the heart of the controversy. On the first occasion his devotion to popular sovereignty had won the support of his administration and the Southern wing of the Democracy, while Northerners burned him in effigy and formed a new party whose sole basis was opposition to Douglas and his ideas.

Now the situation was reversed. Northern crowds cheered him at every stop. Douglas effigies were burning in the South; a Democratic administration was working openly to drive him from power, and the Republicans were so delighted with his recent labors during the Lecompton struggle that some of their leaders spoke frankly of endorsing his Senate candidacy in 1858 and even supporting him for the Presidency in 1860. And all because he had hewed through thick and thin to the principle of popular sovereignty!

The Republican organization in Illinois was annoyed by the growing disposition of Eastern party leaders to look upon Douglas with such unwonted favor. For Illinois Republicans Douglas had always been the archenemy, destroyer of the Missouri Compromise and defender of the Dred Scott doctrine that Congress had no power to exclude slavery from the territories. His recent alliance with Congressional Republicans in opposition to Lecompton did not right these earlier wrongs; it merely indicated, as Lincoln remarked, that Buchanan was "a little farther wrong of the two." To Lincoln and his supporters a formal Douglas-Republican coalition, now openly talked of by such eminent party spokesmen as Seward of New York and Horace Greeley of the New York *Tribune,* would ruin the organization in Illinois and fatally undercut the basic principle on which the national party had been founded. The Illinois contingent thought its chances of unseating Douglas in 1858 better than fair—but only if their ranks held firm, only so long as the thousands of Illinois Republicans who subscribed to Mr. Greeley's famous *Tribune* ignored his newfound effusions in praise of Douglas.

It was to counter such praise that Lincoln made Douglas a major architect of the "slave-power conspiracy" in his House Divided speech before the Republican state convention in June. Lincoln reminded waverers that popular sovereignty had proved its ineffectiveness as a device for justice and peace, that Douglas, with his oft-expressed moral indifference to the institution of slavery, was unfit to be a leader in the antislavery cause, that only Republican leadership could ensure the triumph of Republican principles.

Unless the Eastern dalliance with Douglas proved contagious in Illinois, Lincoln felt that his own senatorial prospects were favorable. His position within the party had never been stronger. State and county leaders were overwhelmingly in favor of his candidacy, and Senator Lyman Trumbull, the Democrat-turned-Republican for whom Lincoln had stepped aside in 1855, was bringing his influence to bear in Lincoln's behalf. By any test—ability, party loyalty, previous sacrifice, known effectiveness as campaigner and orator—Lincoln deserved the prize, and the Republican high command in Illinois was determined to resist the pro-Douglas blandishments of Seward and Greeley and hold its following in line. The state convention gave Lincoln a ringing endorsement, and in the face of this local display of unity the

New York *Tribune* abandoned its flirtation with Douglas and moved to the support of the dedicated lawyer-politician whose days of timeserving obscurity were about over.

Douglas reached Chicago on July 9, greeted like a conquering hero by enthusiastic crowds, and the stage was set for the most famous political debates in American history. On his first night in town Douglas launched his campaign by attacking Lincoln's recent House Divided speech, denouncing it as inflammatory, conducive to sectional conflict, and a denial of that local autonomy in domestic institutions on which the nation's strength rested. Our government, Douglas added, was "made by the white man, for the white man, to be administered by the white man," and popular sovereignty was the essence of the democratic way.

On the following day another huge Chicago audience heard Lincoln open fire in reply. Denying that he favored or predicted a sectional conflict, Lincoln reaffirmed the Republican doctrine: his party would leave slavery alone where it now existed, but was unalterably opposed to letting it expand. This meant containing the institution, which Douglas's oft-invoked formula of popular sovereignty was powerless to do because the Dred Scott decision forbade any legislative action against slavery in the territories. As before, an invocation of the Declaration of Independence lay at the core of Lincoln's appeal. A white man's government? "Let us discard all this quibbling about this man and the other man— this race and that race and the other race being inferior ... and unite as one people throughout this land, until we shall once more stand up declaring that all men are created equal."

Although these twin Chicago speeches set the tone and general content for the entire campaign, the formal Lincoln-Douglas debates did not begin until later. Douglas started on a downstate speaking tour with Lincoln close behind him, Republican strategy being to follow the Democratic candidate wherever he went and take advantage of his crowds. The Douglas press immediately taunted Lincoln with the charge that he lacked sufficient popularity to draw crowds of his own, and Lincoln's managers suggested that he challenge his opponent to a series of debates. The Douglas forces consented reluctantly, hardly daring to refuse,

yet quite aware that this merely formalized the Republican intention of profiting by the Little Giant's popularity. A schedule of
seven debates was duly arranged, to take place between August
21 and October 15 at one major town in each of the seven Congressional districts as yet unvisited by the candidates. Both men
planned to intersperse among the formal confrontations a full
campaign agenda of lesser speeches, huddles with local political
managers, handshaking, and the other assorted hallmarks of a bid
for public office. Reporters converged from afar, and Illinois
girded itself for a struggle that no one doubted would be absorbing, close, and sternly fought.

Few more picturesque ways of dramatizing the political habits,
social currents, and economic sinews of a people in transition
could possibly have been staged. The American landscape stood
sharply etched in the afternoon sunlight, every feature brought
into bold relief by the storm clouds that darkened the far horizon.
The setting was Illinois, whose flat, fertile prairies and bustling
small-town streets were product and symbol of the nation's westward growth. It was late summertime in Illinois, and late summertime, too, for the rural America that had fathered these people
and given them their hopes and brought them face to face with
problems too great to be solved without pain and torment. Rural
America was in retreat, and the mark of its conqueror was also
present among the stage props for the Lincoln-Douglas debates:
in this campaign the candidates came and went by the railroad,
whose stark iron tangents already laced the level countryside and
bound it forever to smoking chimneys and crowded docksides far
away to the eastward and beyond the sea.

Across the length and breadth of Illinois, while golden summer
drifted lazily into golden fall, and the eastward-pointing shadows
in the golden cornfields stretched imperceptibly farther each afternoon, while the locomotive whistle slanted its shrill summons
across the tasseled farmland, rural America converged by wagon
and carriage and horse and foot along slow dusty roads toward
the towns where two men would debate the nation's destiny. They
came toward Ottawa and Freeport and Jonesboro, Charleston and

Galesburg, Quincy and Alton, names altogether American and totally unromantic, like the names of those Virginia hamlets on the other side of the Blue Ridge—all soon to find their modest place in the history books and to evoke memories whenever men ponder the events by which America stumbled toward her own peculiar tragedy.

As electorates go the people who flocked to hear Lincoln and Douglas were well informed on political issues and they did not take these issues lightly. They came, primarily, to affirm or re-examine party loyalties, to hear and weigh the opposing sides of a question that genuinely troubled them, to see for themselves which of these able, forceful, oddly-matched contestants had the better case. They came, too, out of plain curiosity, reflecting a measure of grass-roots interest in politics for its own sake that no succeeding generation would equal.

And not least important, they came to be entertained. A red-hot political campaign in this unjaded era was festival, circus, and bank holiday rolled into one. To a disordered society in the grip of change, the spread-eagle democracy of log-cabin campaigning and professional party organizations was vitally important. Politics was church and country club, intellectual stimulant, mass entertainment, and prime emotional outlet for this generation, and every facet of the American experiment—rough edges, partisan enthusiasm, ballyhoo, and all—was on exhibit during the Lincoln-Douglas debates.

The two candidates did not disappoint their constituents. It would have been worth the trip just to go and look at them. Few could fail to take delight at the contrast: the short, broad-chested Douglas, energy incarnate, a commanding presence in linen and broadcloth, dark eyes snapping and long locks tossing as he drove his points home, vigorous words and imperious gestures so many shock troops hurled into combat, a bristling, thickset bulldog of a man, tenacious and powerful in debate; and Lincoln, taller, thinner, and more angular than ever beside his stocky opponent, ill-fitting clothes and ill-coordinated gestures accentuating his awkward appearance, sallow of skin and large of feature, punctuating his shrill-voiced delivery with wild swings of his long

arms and sudden knee-dips followed by spasmodic upward jerks
to full height, earnest and full of conviction, keen eyes and firm
chin suggesting a latent intellectual power that emerged with
increasing force as he warmed to his subject, like a tall clipper
crowding on sail and gathering way before a stiff breeze.

In the course of their seven debates Lincoln and Douglas explored every angle of the complex slavery question. They gave
it the full treatment—high and low, abstract and personal, logical
and emotional, lofty and partisan. These two were not academic
theorists but professional politicians thirsting after high office,
and each, accordingly, was as quick to score his opponent by the
use of smear and innuendo as he was to enunciate high principle.
Neither candidate broke new ground; most of their points were
restatements and refinements of positions they had held for some
time. But by the end of the campaign none who heard or read
the various speeches could have many doubts about where the
two men stood or where they differed. The Northern versions of
the questions at issue were being reviewed by a pair of experts.

The chaff in these debates—and there was much of it, this being
a bare-knuckles political contest—included the usual hackneyed
accusations. Douglas made much of the charge that the Republicans were abolitionists, that Lincoln had been trying for years
to "abolitionize" the Illinois Whigs, and that Lincoln's defense
of Negro rights under the Declaration of Independence amounted
to a plea for racial equality. Lincoln repeatedly and at times
exasperatedly denied all of this. The Republicans, he insisted,
stood for the containment rather than the abolition of slavery;
they had no intention of disturbing the institution in the South.
As for racial equality, Lincoln firmly repudiated any thought of
it in the political or social areas; he held fast, however, to the
idea that the Negro shared with the rest of humanity a natural
right to life, liberty, and the pursuit of happiness. There was
ambiguity here, and hedging: Douglas wryly observed that Lincoln's views changed color noticeably as he moved from the
Yankee strongholds in northern Illinois to the Southern-oriented
population in the central and lower parts of the state. On the
race question Lincoln was no radical, and as an Illinois politician

he dared not be, but he steadfastly refused to make the white man's antipathy to the colored man a justification for slavery—and whether he realized it or not, this was the crack in the racial facade that would ultimately collapse the whole of it.

As a counterattack on the same level Lincoln steadily accused Douglas of participating in a "slave-power conspiracy" that sought to force slavery on the entire country, territories and free states alike. To Douglas this charge was beneath contempt, but his opponent hammered away at it whenever he could. In an attempt to reopen old sores Douglas appealed to Western expansionist sentiment by reminding his listeners that Lincoln had opposed the Mexican War in Congress ten years before. This kind of shadow-boxing was a feature of each debate.

A great deal was said, naturally, about popular sovereignty. At Freeport Lincoln purposefully asked Douglas for a restatement of his attempt to reconcile popular sovereignty with the Dred Scott decision. Unflinchingly Douglas repeated what he had said before: the Scott decision was a correct limitation on Congressional power to exclude slavery, but a free-soil majority in any territory could always refuse to enact protective legislation. Lincoln insisted, and Douglas as vehemently denied, that a correct reading of the Scott decision would prevent any such action by a territorial majority. Regardless of the Court, Douglas said flatly, under popular sovereignty "the right of the people to make a slave Territory or a free Territory is perfect and complete . . ."

This view, though no more than a repetition of what he had long maintained, passed into political currency as the Freeport doctrine, and Douglas was fully prepared to stand or fall by it. Both men knew that the local Buchanan followers, and the South generally, disagreed strongly with the Douglas position. Lincoln had asked the question, in fact, with an eye to underscoring the cleavage between the Douglas and Buchanan wings of the Democratic party, both in Illinois and in the country at large. Douglas recognized the maneuver and swerved not an inch from his principles. Whatever happened, he would hold fast to his claim that a territorial majority could never be deprived of the right to decide its institutions. When Lincoln pointedly asked him how he would react to a Southern-sponsored federal slave code for the territories, Douglas proclaimed his emphatic opposition to any such measure. Anything that contradicted or curtailed popular sovereignty was wrong.

In this vein, Douglas was able to counter with the charge that Lincoln favored enforced conformity and opposed local autonomy in domestic institutions: the Republican determination to exclude slavery from the territories by federal statute was undemocratic. Variety of local institutions and freedom of choice in selecting them were among the sources of the nation's strength, Douglas said, and had been recognized as such by the Founding Fathers. In answer, Lincoln reminded his opponent that the whole people had a stake in the federal territories and a legitimate concern with the institutions established there. He added that he approved of variety and local autonomy with no less fervor than Senator Douglas, but that slavery was no such desirable variation—and had been recognized as an exception by the framers of the Constitution, who had put limitations on slavery with a view to its ultimate extinction. Douglas disagreed: freedom and slavery had existed side by side in 1789 and had done so ever since, and if the Republican party would cease agitating the question there was no reason why they could not coexist indefinitely; talk of a "house divided against itself" was demagogic, dangerous, inaccurate, and inflammatory.

In their various appeals to the wisdom and intent of the Founding Fathers both men were stretching things a bit. The Fathers had by no means accepted slavery as blithely as Douglas would have it, but they had had much less certainty about slavery's ultimate extinction than Lincoln claimed for them. For both candidates exact historical accuracy was less important than an appealing argument. And as Southern theorists of the Calhoun-Davis school could testify, the Founding Fathers had left enough ambiguous wisdom lying about to provide posterity with any number of conflicting interpretations.

When the campaign finally ended, two or three features of the Lincoln and Douglas positions were clear. Both men, obviously, were staunch Unionists. They had the highest regard for the heritage and beneficent meaning of the American experiment, and if they traced heritage and meaning along different paths there was no mistaking the faith in democracy that underlay their position. The Union was the ark of democracy's covenant, and the Northern Democrats for whom Douglas spoke would rise no less quickly than Lincoln's Republicans to beat down any attempts to rend the national fabric. Disagreement over slavery was submerged in this broader consensus, and Southern leaders who encouraged their people to rely upon secession as a last resort should have read the Northern mind more carefully.

On all save the one crucial point the Douglas brand of democracy coincided fairly well with Lincoln's. Douglas perhaps came closer than any leader of his generation to embodying the old Jacksonian position, with its fierce Unionism, its expansionist zeal, its respect for the rights of states and its distrust—in theory more than in practice—of a strong central government, its belief in a properly balanced federal system, and its devout faith in the not always reconcilable principles of equality, individualism, and majority rule. Save for his distrust of Douglas's aggressive expansionism, Lincoln could endorse all of this with equal sincerity.

The only vital area of disagreement concerned the place of the Negro in the American system. Neither man wanted full racial equality and both opposed slavery extension—the North was almost a unit on these points—yet at bottom was a moral issue that found Douglas indifferent and Lincoln firmly committed. As Douglas saw it, the birthright of democracy and the Declaration of Independence belonged solely to the white man, and the expansion or contraction of slavery's domain was entirely a matter for the white majority in any given area to decide; outside interference with this decision posed a far greater threat to democracy than did slavery. And Negro slavery itself was in no way inconsonant with American principles rightly understood.

For four years Lincoln had been hammering away at just this point. In the debates, before what amounted to a national audience, he merely took occasion to restate his long-held convictions about the true meaning of the controversy. The quarrel over slavery was part of a world-wide struggle between right and wrong, with the "common right of humanity" arrayed against the advocates of slavery expansion.

"I do think," Lincoln said at Galesburg, in one of the more eloquent passages of the debates, "that Judge Douglas and whoever, like him, teaches that the Negro has no share, humble though it may be, in the Declaration of Independence, is going back to the era of our liberty and independence, and, in so far as in him lies, muzzling the cannon that thunders its annual joyous return; that he is blowing out the moral lights around us, when he contends that whoever wants slaves has a right to hold them; that he is penetrating, so far as lies in his power, the human soul, and eradicating the light of reason and the love of liberty, when he is in every way possible preparing the public mind, by his vast influence, for making the institution of slavery perpetual and national."

Lincoln was here enunciating the very keystone of his political philosophy, and he would accept partisan strife, disunion, and civil war itself before he abandoned it. His belief in the cause of human freedom—*universal* human freedom, applicable everywhere, to all men—attested to his nineteenth-century faith in man, but there was no facile optimism in Lincoln's outlook. Progress was never automatic. The forces of evil were always present, and could as easily triumph as the forces of right. If freedom's impulse was natural, it was also reversible, in danger everywhere when denied to anyone. What appalled Lincoln about the Douglas approach was its exclusiveness, its frank assertion that freedom and equality belonged only to the fortunate. Once admit that slavery was right (denying that it was wrong amounted to the same thing), and no man was safe; any argument that justified enslaving the Negro as easily justified enslaving the factory worker, or the immigrant, or whatever group might now or later be denied membership in the ruling elite. Popular sovereignty, and the moral standard behind it, were a fatal snare; the nation could not follow Stephen A. Douglas and preserve its heritage. Freedom, in short, was indivisible. And until he grasped this fact, man's destiny lay elsewhere.

This basic disagreement suggested, certainly, that Americans had scarcely begun to examine the deeper meaning of their own political ideals. They had not begun soon enough. Symptomatic of the lateness of the hour was the fact that neither Lincoln nor Douglas could envisage a solution to the problem along lines much different from his own; yet the section whose domestic institution lay at the core of their earnest debates was denouncing the utterances of both with fine impartiality. The prevailing Southern attitude reduced long arguments about popular sovereignty and the meaning of the principles of 1776 to the level of academic hair-splitting, and whichever man the North chose to follow would meet only hostility and obstruction on the other side of the line. The outlook was dim. If Southerners saw a threat in the Douglas philosophy, they would inevitably resort to violence before abiding Lincoln's.

Though a nation and its children's children might sit in judgment, Lincoln and Douglas were not speaking primarily to the country at large, nor to posterity, and whatever verdict these would render mattered less at the moment than the reaction of the people of Illinois. Knowing that the result would be close, both men campaigned with furious energy right down to election day. Illinois was actually voting to elect a new legislature, by whom the contested Senate seat would be filled early next January. There were three legislative tickets in the field—the Republicans, the Douglas Democrats, and the Buchanan Democrats, the last a party machine thrown together early in the campaign by a vengeful administration in the frank hope of unseating Douglas even at the cost of a Republican victory.

The Buchanan forces were a constant headache to the embattled Douglas, provoking him to wrathful outbreaks more than once, but they barely dented his strength. They could use the patronage to fire his supporters from Federal office and create their own machine, and they could disrupt his stump speeches by putting brass bands and other hecklers into action while he spoke, but such tactics merely underscored the bankruptcy of the administration position and probably lost more ground than they gained; the Illinois Democracy was almost a unit in support of its favorite son. From first to last the only real struggle was between Douglas and his Republican opponent.

Douglas finally won, by a margin every bit as narrow as the experts had predicted. The Republican legislative candidates obtained a slight plurality in the total popular vote, polling 125,000 against 121,000 for the Douglas Democrats and a minuscule 5,000 for the hapless Buchananites. Despite this Republican edge, apportionment in Illinois underrepresented the fast-growing Republican counties in the northern part of the state and gave the Democrats a bare majority in the new legislature, which duly re-elected Douglas to the Senate in January by a vote of 54 to 46 over the disappointed Lincoln. For the second time in four years the lanky attorney had lost a senatorial race by a handful of votes.

Drawing the right conclusion from the Lincoln-Douglas contest was none too difficult. The Little Giant had won the battle, but he and his party might well have lost the war. The split between Douglas and the national administration was wider and deeper than ever. The South could take no comfort from the Senator's vigorous, uncompromising defense of popular sovereignty, which was bound to collide with the Southern plan for a Congressional slave code in the territories. The dominant group among the Southern leadership was strengthened to the point of inflexibility in its resolve to keep the Democratic presidential nomination away from Douglas in 1860. Yet Douglas by his victory had convincingly dramatized the prevailing temper among Northern Democrats. The renewal of his mandate in Illinois stood in sharp contrast to the extended roll call of party defeats elsewhere in the free states that autumn—defeats traceable, beyond question, to the administration's pro-Southern stand on the Lecompton issue. Only a Democrat of the Douglas persuasion could anticipate Northern support in months ahead; leadership of the Northern wing of the party could only come from Douglas himself.

For Lincoln and the Republicans the picture was correspondingly bright. The party could hardly help exulting at its prospects in the next election, with the opposition grievously split and exhibiting from both factions a spirit that promised to make the breach irreparable. As for Lincoln himself, his stock within the party had risen even in defeat. Those who followed the campaign closely—and they were numerous—came away impressed. They had seen political skill, vote-getting ability, and recurrent flashes of keen insight and hard eloquence. Thoughtful Republicans kept this prairie orator in mind. Party leaders from other states began corresponding with him, seeking his advice on a variety of political matters, inviting him to speak at rallies and conventions, virtually admitting him to informal membership in the loose aggregation that constituted the Republican high command. Though he disclaimed future ambition after his loss to Douglas and turned aside suggestions that he became an active candidate for the presidential nomination in 1860, the talk would not down. Whether he fully realized it or not, Lincoln's national career had begun.

During the summer and fall of 1858, while Lincoln and Douglas exchanged their historic broadsides in the long, running battle for an Illinois Senate seat, Jefferson Davis also had occasion to express himself on the overriding issue of the day. For Davis no political contest was involved, although in their way his remarks were as carefully attuned to political reality as anything Lincoln or Douglas said in Illinois. Davis was on vacation in New England that summer—the last look the North would ever have at this poised, urbane Mississippian whose gray and butternut columns would so soon issue forth to do battle with Northern sons, the last genuine relaxation he would know until long after his cause had gone the way of dead dreams, dissolved forever in the smoke and fire of war—and here amid the busy towns and rugged landscape of America's oldest frontier a Senator from Mississippi could speak with earnest politeness to an earnest, polite New England audience and try to bridge the yawning sectional gulf with one final appeal to sweet reason.

The calm appeal to reason was thoroughly characteristic of Jefferson Davis. So too, in the home of William Lloyd Garrison and Charles Sumner, where hostility to the South smoldered sullenly in many a Yankee heart, was his refusal to temper his convictions or veer by so much as a hair's breadth from what he regarded as the truth. Earnest conviction was bedrock for this man, at once his greatest strength and greatest weakness. Conviction invested his every utterance with an unimpeachable quality; it was the basis for the imposing dignity that he wore like a tailored uniform wherever he went; it underwrote the steadfast, unflinching courage and the quiet self-assurance that made him a natural leader of men. Even his enemies could not fail to be impressed by all of this, as the militantly antislavery editor Horace Greeley was quick to recognize in the columns of the *Tribune*. "Mr. Davis is unquestionably the foremost man of the South today," Greeley wrote. "Every Northern Senator will admit that from the Southern side of the floor the most formidable to meet in debate is the thin, polished, intellectual-looking Mississippian with the unimpassioned demeanour, the habitual courtesy and the occasional unintentional arrogance, which reveals his consciousness of the great commanding power."

Sincere conviction was also, at bottom, the man's fatal flaw. It was responsible for the unyielding attitude that lay at the core of the Southern temperament. This innate refusal to yield was what made the Lost Cause a cause and insured that it would be lost, sustaining it amid amounting wartime adversity long after defeat was certain, serving as a built-in guarantee that the South would break before it learned how to bend. Davis's conviction was impenetrable by any brand of logic that ran counter to his own; it amounted, in practice, to a well-reasoned, patient, fatal narrowness of mind. On the slavery question it brooked no answer save the one his Northern countrymen must ultimately reject. It made every difference of opinion the basis for a wasteful running argument, couched on Davis's part in tones of querulous patience that could not conceal an inner amazement at his opponent's wrong-headedness—the unfailing tendency of such tactics being, of course, that his opponents clung to their views the more tenaciously as Davis laboriously explained the nature of their error. Such controversies, acrimonious and unresolved, would later form a recurrent *leitmotiv* in the Confederate theme, diverting the attention and the energies of the Southern president from more important matters and contributing no little to the divided, fractious quality that permeated much of the Southern war effort. The very patience and tact with which the courteous, unruffled Davis defended his views, the fact that during the war, at least, he was more often right than not—to the Confederacy's fiercely independent spirits these merely served as extra irritants. For good or ill, Jefferson Davis was fundamentally incapable of speaking or acting in any way contrary to his basic convictions. On occasion— rare occasion—the man could admit a mistake; he could never trim, or hedge, or alter his views for effect.

This patent sincerity was amusingly revealed in the early spring of 1858, a few weeks before he left with his family for the vacation in New England. During the long, rancorous debate in Congress over the Lecompton Constitution Davis had become seriously ill. Exhausted and run-down from his exertions in the Senate, he suffered increasingly that winter from the facial neuralgia that had troubled him off and on since his bout with pneumonia in frontier Wisconsin many years ago. In February a cold developed into laryngitis and the neuralgia grew much worse, paralyzing the right side of his face and inflaming his right eye so severely that the pupil nearly burst. For weeks he lay in a darkened room, wracked with pain and barely able to see or speak.

Visitors came frequently to lighten the tedium of his confinement, and among the most loyal of these was the affable, kind-hearted William Seward, Senator from New York and a leading candidate for the Republican presidential nomination in 1860. It was a surprising friendship. The two men were archfoes on the floor of Congress, diametrically opposed in their views of slavery and the sectional controversy, totally unlike in temperament and philosophy. The dapper Seward was a politician to the very depth of his soul, resourceful and devious, never happier than in the proverbial smoke-filled rooms where intrigues are hatched and deals are made—thoroughly at home, in other words, in an atmosphere utterly strange and distasteful to the high-minded Davis. Yet the two liked each other: both had an abundance of charm, Seward the politician's knack of staying on good personal terms with his bitterest opponents, and both were intelligent enough to derive a certain fascination from the relationship.

During one visit to Davis's sickbed Seward frankly admitted that many of his antislavery utterances were expedient, calculated for their effect on the Northern voter. Davis was genuinely aghast. "But, Mr. Seward," he husked, "do you never speak from conviction?" "Ne-ver," Seward replied cheerfully. Davis was so astounded that he tried to sit up in bed, and his reaction came straight from the heart: "As God is my judge, I never speak from any other motive." His friend nodded sympathetically. Even the cynical Seward could recognize a fundamental truth when he heard one.

Davis had mended sufficiently by late spring to resume a portion of his legislative activities and spend a few hours each day in the Senate, but his doctor was emphatically prescribing a complete rest, and when Congress adjourned in June the Davis family—Jefferson, Varina, and the two small children, Maggie and Jeff Jr.—took ship from Baltimore for a leisurely convalescent summer in Massachusetts and Maine. Numerous friends awaited their arrival, and under the tonic effects of freedom from tension and the cool Atlantic breezes Senator Davis found health and strength returning rapidly. From Boston the family sailed to Portland, going thence by rail to Bangor and on by stage and oxcart into the remote mountains of northern Maine, where crisp clean air and utter quiet were a healing contrast to the pressure-laden atmosphere of Washington. By the time they returned to Portland and Boston in the early fall the Senator's recovery seemed complete.

Several times on that leisurely tour the Senator responded to invitations and addressed small New England audiences—trying, in his dignified, courteous way, far from the pressures of the stump, to find the tone that might restore harmony between the sections without compromising the essence of the Southern view. His words, moderate and reassuring, were carefully chosen and effectively delivered. His hearers could not fail to be impressed; in so far as they shared the prevailing New England sentiment, however, they remained politely unconvinced.

Much that Davis said, to be sure, they could applaud with genuine enthusiasm. In Portland they warmed to his deft praise and keen analysis of the agricultural and industrial progress on display in the state of Maine. Wherever he spoke he stressed his reverence for the national Union and its benefits, gently touching on the variety of local institutions that thrived side by side within the broad national framework. Reviewing his own labors on behalf of a Pacific railroad while United States Secretary of War, Davis urged that the building of transcontinental rail lines—not one but several, crossing the northern, central, and southern portions of the Great West—would effectively bind the vast nation together and insure its continued progress in the years ahead. The underlying note in all his utterances was patriotism, a tactful, eloquent plea for a harmonious Union that would remain true to its heritage by safeguarding individual freedom and the rights of states. To none of these principles could New England take exception, as Davis well knew.

Homeward bound, the Davises passed through Boston again in October, and the Senator accepted an invitation to address a large gathering. The date was set for October 11, two days before Lincoln and Douglas met on the Mississippi River bluffs at Quincy for the sixth of their seven debates, and like those western encounters the farewell appearance of Jefferson Davis in downtown Boston provided another clear study of the moods and contrasts of ante-bellum America—another vivid, poignant, daguerrotype of the nation's past and future captured briefly together on a single stage.

The setting this time was Faneuil Hall, a far cry from the prosaic courthouses and bunting-draped public squares of Lincoln's Illinois—Faneuil Hall, Boston's celebrated "cradle of liberty," historic emblem of the struggle for independence, a name that gave off echoes, conjuring up shadowy heroic visions of Boston's massacre and Boston's tea party, of Paul Revere and Bunker Hill and the minutemen assembled on Lexington Green.

There were ghosts hovering about the speaker's stand in Faneuil Hall on that cool October evening when Jefferson Davis addressed a Yankee audience for the last time, and most of the assemblage— the speaker included—knew enough American history to be aware of their presence. Here James Otis and the Adamses had exhorted town meetings and fanned a revolutionary spirit nearly a century before. A short time later, while Washington's militia dotted the heights outside Boston with their campfires and kept a British army under siege, Faneuil Hall became a theater where Tory audiences applauded plays written and acted by the debonair British general, Gentleman Johnny Burgoyne. In 1811 Faneuil Hall had been host to an angry meeting of New England Federalists, who gathered to pass resolutions denouncing a recent Federal statute as "ex-post facto, and void, unjust and tyrannical," in direct forecast of the nullifying spirit of John C. Calhoun. Yet here again, in 1832, New Englanders cheered the great Daniel Webster while he castigated South Carolina's ordinance of nullification and endorsed President Jackson's affirmation of an indivisible Union.

More important on this October night in 1858 were the old building's echoes of a cause still very much alive. For the past two decades Faneuil Hall had resounded to the arguments of the anti-slavery spokesmen. Here the thorny, emotional issues of the sectional controversy—the murder of abolitionist Elijah Lovejoy in Illinois and the right of free speech, the Fugitive Slave Law and the recapture of runaways, the Mexican War, the Kansas-Nebraska Act, and all the rest—had come under the eloquent scrutiny of men whose parts in the national drama had some distance yet to run: Wendell Phillips, Charles Sumner, Theodore Parker, and William Lloyd Garrison, pouring their acid indictments on the institution of slavery.

Now the poised, cultured Senator from Mississippi was speaking within the historic walls that had rung to fervent appeals in behalf of liberty and Union since before the nation was born.

Keenly aware that any man who sought a hearing for his cause in Faneuil Hall was encompassed about with so great a cloud of witnesses, Davis did not shrink from his assignment, nor was he conscious of the slightest incongruity between the subject of his address and the weight of what had gone before. The profound conviction that prompted his every move had assured him that his views were not merely reconcilable with the American dream but vital to it.

This was, to be sure, a conservative audience, already nine-tenths persuaded of Davis's brand of truth. The Democratic Party of Massachusetts had invited him to speak, and it had become an impotent minority in the Bay State because it tended toward a pro-Southern position in national politics and stood in frank and horrified opposition to the antislavery leanings of the Republican Party. (Massachusetts Republicans leaned unusually hard in this direction; though not without their moderate element they were, by and large, the most radical of the state organizations.) Introducing Davis this evening was Caleb Cushing, old friend and one-time colleague in the Pierce cabinet, a man of pronounced Southern sympathies. Seated on the stand behind Davis were two eminent, respectable pillars of Bay State politics, Edward Everett and Robert C. Winthrop, dignified Whig aristocrats whose party had withered away beneath them, displaced leaders who had never fully adjusted to the fact that they were without a following, still earnestly advocating an end to sectional agitation and a policy of compromise and moderation.

Abolitionism was totally repugnant to such men. Among the hundreds who jammed Faneuil Hall to hear the distinguished Senator from Mississippi there were doubtless many who had misgivings about the beneficence of slavery, but the prevailing tone of the gathering was set by respectables of the Cushing-Everett-Winthrop caliber, men far less offended by slavery than by attacks on it, men thoroughly inclined to meet the distinguished Senator more than halfway.

Davis acquitted himself handsomely. From his tactful salutation—"Countrymen, brethren, and Democrats"—to his closing plea for a renewal of the ties that had bound the colonies together in their struggle for independence, he handled his delicate theme with restraint, honesty, and persuasive eloquence. Adroitly he quoted sound New England scripture of an earlier day to buttress his defense of strict construction and state rights, yet made no allusions to the touchy subject of Bay State nullifiers during the War of 1812. Instead, he appealed to "the proud spirit of independence, manifested in your colonial history . . . fit foundation for a monument to state rights!" It was well done, and the audience was captivated. "A better, fairer, a more thoughtful or earnest speech he never made," one observer remembered. "He was the last great slaveholder that ever stood on that historic platform and talked out of his heart to the people of Boston."

Davis minced no words on the subject of slavery. It was a benevolent institution, he repeated firmly—a positive good. "Why then," he asked earnestly, "in the absence of all control over the subject of African slavery, are you so agitated in relation to it? With pharisaical pretension it is sometimes said it is a moral obligation to agitate. . . . Who gave them the right to decide that it is a sin? By what standard do they measure it?" And the usual sanctions were invoked: "Not the Constitution; the Constitution recognizes the property in many forms, and imposes obligations in connection with that recognition. Not the Bible: that justifies it. Not the good of society; for if they go where it exists, they find that society recognizes it as good. Is it in the cause of Christianity? It cannot be, for servitude is the only agency through which Christianity has reached the Negro race."

It was an impressive performance, applauded enthusiastically by genteel Bostonians who liked being told that there was no real cause for sectional strife, no need to attack so worthy an institution, no serpent in the American Eden after all. They were applauding, too, a distinguished guest whose intellectual power and dignified charm could hardly fail to elicit a warm response. There was a compelling quality about this man, and his very sincerity added a dimension to anything he said. But for all the statesmanship and high principle in the Faneuil Hall speech Davis's reasoned defense of slavery was, as the tall lawyer from Illinois had expressed it in Galesburg just four days earlier, an attempt at "muzzling the cannon that thunders its annual joyous return ... [at] blowing out the moral lights around us." The heritage symbolized by Faneuil Hall did not point in this direction.

No single spot in all the continent etched more sharply the contrast between what the South wanted to be and what the nation was in fact becoming than did Boston, even if the Boston that gave Jefferson Davis a last ovation in Faneuil Hall was not quite ready to admit it. A few rods from the hall the great wharves thrust their rows of brick and granite counting-houses thousands of feet into Boston harbor, their very names—Long Wharf, India Wharf, Central Wharf—redolent of the exotic seaborne cargoes that had underwritten Yankee fortunes for over half a century and given Boston its immodest title of The Hub of the Universe. Across the harbor was East Boston, where the shipyards of Samuel Hall and Donald McKay and other master builders had just completed a decade of turning out the mightiest sailing ships ever built. By 1858 the Yankee clipper was already in the twilight of its brief golden day, but neither Boston nor the ocean-sea beyond had yet seen the last of the tall ships with the clean graceful lines and sky-sweeping canvas towers and names as hauntingly musical as the craft that bore them—*Surprise, Winged Racer, Stag Hound, Witchcraft, White Swallow, Morning Light, Flying Cloud, Lightning, Sovereign of the Seas.*

The wharves were still lined with a forest of black spars and a vinelike tangle of cordage; Boston was still The Hub. In recent years, however, The Hub's most important spokes were of finance and industry rather than commerce. The fortunes based on trade with Canton and the Levant, Java and Sydney, Malaga and Halifax, Rio and San Francisco and the Baltic were now creating railroad empires in eastern Pennsylvania and southern Michigan and northern Illinois and beyond the Mississippi, or paying new dividends in the busy textile mills and shoe factories and locomotive works that drew a tight cordon of smoking chimneys around suburban Boston and flecked the rural landscape of New England with growing clusters of industrial towns.

The surge of a McKay clipper before the wind, the whir of spindles from the cotton mills that lined the Merrimac, and the clank of hammers in William Mason's grimy locomotive shops in Taunton were odd heralds of freedom; there was truth enough in the Southern claim that few fieldhands encountered the brutality meted out to clipper-ship crews by bucko mates and hard-driving captains, or toiled under conditions as harsh as those inflicted on the ragged millhands and sweating shop mechanics of industrial New England.

Yet freedom for these varied engines of Yankee progress lay not in the manner of their going but in the destination they sought —material profit, to be sure, but something more besides, a general lifting of the narrow horizons that had circumscribed the living standard of all save a tiny minority of mankind since time began. The road that led ultimately to Freedom from Want was unbelievably cruel, its wayside littered for miles by the worn-out human wreckage cast aside in the building. Northern wage slavery existed, as its critics claimed. But the antidote was built into the system; from chattel slavery there was no appeal, no chance to rise, no deliverance save by the incredible violence that was an unstable democracy's last resort. Countless thousands of Boston's Irish immigrants lived in squalid rabbit-warren slums beside which the tidy slave cabins on Senator Davis's Mississippi plantation were palatial indeed, but no Irishmen had yet been observed volunteering to trade places with the Southern Negro, and the "underground railroad" that led a few dozen runaway slaves into free soil each year had never been known to run in the opposite direction. There was an inherent magic in the idea of freedom that none of its drawbacks could render less potent.

And anyway, Boston in the eighteen-fifties was more than shoes and ships and sealing wax; American democracy had not hitched all its energies to the bank draft or the combustion engine. In recent decades a great burst of intellectual and cultural activity had enriched the pattern of American life. For a generation and more New England had been the most fertile seedbed for this cultural flowering—the operative word had first been applied to the region by a New England Adams—and Boston, to mix the metaphor, could lay fair claim to being The Hub of this activity as well. The shadows that fell across Faneuil Hall while Davis spoke were not alone those of the factory chimney and the yard-arm and the banking houses on State Street; they included the Athenaeum, the church spire, the Public Library, and the dignified mansions of Beacon Street, whence Lowells, Lawrences, Prescotts, and other first families had converted wealth and leisure into an intensive cultivation of literature and scholarship, law and theology, humanitarian reform, education, and philosophy. Intellectual curiosity, moral fervor, patriotism, and a firm belief in progress and human dignity underlay this cultural flowering, reinforced as it was by a rich and varicolored heritage that included Puritan zeal and the humane warmth of Unitarianism, the rational faith of the Enlightenment and the emotional faith of the Romantic Movement, with seasoning touches of English utilitarianism, German idealism, and Oriental thought.

Americans had taken this mélange and stirred it thoroughly, suffusing it with an energy and a pragmatic flavor peculiarly their own, and the results were impressive enough for so young a people. If American thought was more imitative than original, it nonetheless belied the long-standing claims that democracy and the dollar sign would forever stifle cultural or intellectual achievement. Boston had reason to be proud of its crowded lecture halls and its thriving bookstores, its new *Atlantic Monthly* and other periodicals, its energetic press, its glittering array of historical scholars—Hildreth, Prescott, Motley, Parkman. Boston could not help reflecting the soaring humanitarian spirit of its great Unitarian ministers, William Ellery Channing, George Ripley, Theodore Parker, James Freeman Clarke; or the reforming zeal of Garrison's editorials and Wendell Phillips' oratory, Whittier's poems and the crusades of Dorothea Dix in behalf of society's outcasts; it felt the innovating touch of Horace Mann in its public schools, and responded to the brooding introspective Hawthorne in his grapples with original sin and human depravity.

Boston's radius included Cambridge, where Harvard was already a tradition and a pioneer, humming in the fifties to the scholarly efforts of George Ticknor, the elder Holmes, Longfellow, Louis

Agassiz, Asa Gray, young Charles W. Eliot, and James Russell Lowell. It extended beyond to Concord, host to a bright galaxy of restless intellects, where Thoreau cut cleanly to the essence of things and found individual freedom, where Ralph Waldo Emerson found a touch of the divine in every human soul.

The American mind was hard at work in a bewildering multiplicity of directions—asking questions, calling itself names, criticizing, advancing tentative answers with scholarly caution or affirming self-evident truths with all the assurance of a zealot. For all its imperfections and contradictions, this variegated activity laid unmistakable stress on rational free inquiry, individual initiative, human betterment, innovation, and social reform. The institution of slavery was as out of place here as an Egyptian galley in a convoy of clipper ships.

Davis also found time to make a speech in New York on his way home. He warned this Northern audience that the growing, aggressive Republican Party might soon constitute a tyrannical majority to which the freedom-loving South could not in honor submit. After pointing out the inaccuracy of abolitionist descriptions of slavery, he took strong issue with Senator Seward's oft-quoted "higher law" doctrine (in which, some years before, the New Yorker had gone beyond the Constitution and the Bible to find an ultimate moral authority that justified the antislavery crusade). Davis so far forgot himself in this impromptu speech that he ended with an angry tirade against all believers in the "higher law," specifically advocating lynch law as the ideal mode of dealing with such depraved and criminal enemies of society. It was probably the most intemperate remark he ever made.

Notwithstanding his repeated defenses of slavery in the very citadels of Charles Sumner and William Seward, Davis found upon reaching Mississippi that his own people were more than a little dissatisfied with what they had read of his Northern tour. To the more extreme Southerner—of whom Mississippi had a full quota—there had been too much appeasement in the Senator's New England utterances, too much praise for the North, not enough angry defiance, no ringing secessionist manifestoes. Some were unkind enough to accuse him of tempering his Southern convictions in a conscious attempt to win Northern support for the Democratic presidential nomination in 1860. (This charge, surely, was wide of the mark; whatever vague thoughts of the White House Davis might have permitted himself, he was too realistic to give it serious consideration at this particular time and far too sincere to angle for it in the manner suggested by his critics.) If possible, Davis's homeland was less receptive to the unimpassioned approach than the North had been, and the Senator found it necessary to address the Mississippi state legislature in November in an attempt to keep the record straight and explain the true meaning of his Northern speeches.

It was perfectly true, Davis said calmly, that he had not gone about New England advocating a dissolution of the Union—for such, apparently, was the only language his more vocal constituents would have found acceptable. Unblinkingly he told the restive Mississippi lawmakers that he favored preserving the Union and defending the Southern position within the national framework until every recourse had been exhausted. With no less pride and far more high-flown rhetoric than he had displayed in the North, he reviewed his own long career in the nation's service. "I love the flag of my country with even more than a filial affection," he intoned. "For many of the best years of my life, I have followed it, and upheld it on fields where, if I had fallen, it might have been claimed as my winding sheet. . . . I glory in the position which Mississippi's star holds in the group. . . ."

Then, however, the Senator proceeded to give ringing endorsement to the idea of secession, long a respected doctrine in the deep South and now exercising a well-nigh hypnotic appeal on all too many Southern politicians. For Davis secession was a last resort, "the final alternative," about which, however gently, he had tried to warn his Northern audiences that summer and fall. Quoting Calhoun, Davis admitted that there was one greater calamity than the disruption of the Union: secession was preferable to submission. What he had seen and heard of Republican activity

in the North had about convinced him that the time for a choice
between just these alternatives was fast approaching. If it came,
he left no doubt as to what his own decision would be.

The Republicans, he said, brought by such intemperate and
misguided leaders as Seward to an unjust view of slavery and
the Constitution, were organizing to gain control of the Federal
government in order to "attempt legislation both injurious and
offensive to the South." To counter this threat, to be ready for
"whatever contingency may befall us," Mississippi should begin
making specific preparations right away. The military-minded
Davis was speaking here not of defiant resolutions but of martial
activity, a careful mobilizing of men and resources for the possibility of conflict. Preparedness was a good thing in itself, but Davis
was also advocating it as a deliberate warning signal, unmistakable
token of Southern intentions: it "will give to our conduct the
character of earnestness of which mere paper declarations have
somewhat deprived us." As Davis saw it, Republican depravity
had by no means infected everyone in the free states; Mississippi's
physical preparations would weaken the Republican threat by re-
inforcing the efforts of the untold thousands of Southern sympa-
thizers in the North. (Davis had been led to believe by old friends
like Franklin Pierce and Caleb Cushing that there were vast
legions of such folk, "sound" Northerners who would actually
rise to do battle with any abolitionist army that assembled to
subjugate the South. This fatal misconception may have played
its part in the Confederate decision to bring matters to a head
on that gray April dawn in 1861.)

And if the worst should happen anyway, an armed and watchful Mississippi would then be ready to do what had to be done.
In 1860, Davis concluded, "if an abolitionist [in Southern parlance,
any Republican] be chosen President of the United States, you
will have presented to you the question of whether you will permit
the government to pass into the hands of your avowed and im-
placable enemies." Then came the manifesto his volatile audience
had been waiting for: "Without pausing for your answer, I will
state my own position to be that such a result would be a species
of revolution by which the purposes of the Government would be

destroyed and the observance of its mere forms entitled to no respect. In that event, in such manner as should be most expedient, I should deem it your duty to provide for your safety outside of the Union of those who have already shown the will, and would have acquired the power, to deprive you of your birthright and reduce you to worse than the Colonial dependence of your fathers." Jefferson Davis had spoken. Secession must be the answer to a Republican victory. Here the Southern moderate and the Southern extremist stood hand in hand, and retreat from a position assumed thus dogmatically so far in advance would be inordinately difficult.

For nearly a year after Davis's return from New England and Lincoln's loss to Douglas in Illinois the offstage drumbeats of sectional discord mounted tempo slowly, until another lurid, dramatic episode occurred to summon forth a loud tattoo and propel the nation another giant step toward its rendezvous with violence.

For Abraham Lincoln, the months that preceded John Brown's bizarre reappearance on the national stage in the fall of 1859 were busy but unspectacular, combining sustained legal activity with a steady round of letters, trips, and speeches devoted to political fence mending and the fortunes of the Republican Party. Whatever his innermost ambitions, he refused to lend himself to the Lincoln-for-President enthusiasm that some of his friends and political associates began trying to kindle after the narrow defeat by Douglas. All he wanted, Lincoln said, was another try for the Senate in 1864; his efforts in the interim would be aimed at keeping this prospect alive. Despite his demurrals—which were never exactly vehement—a handful of Illinois Republicans kept right on booming the presidential idea and laying their plans accordingly. By the end of 1859 he had acceded so far to their requests as to compile a short autobiographical sketch for use as campaign material. ("There is not much of it, for the reason, I suppose, that there is not much of me," he commented ruefully in submitting the sketch.)

At the same time the chairman of the Illinois state central committee, with an eye to Lincoln's candidacy, helped convince the national Republican organization that Chicago would be a good site for the nominating convention in 1860. Lincoln soon concluded that a favorite-son nomination by the Illinois delegation would augment his senatorial chances in 1864. Thenceforth, though ostensibly for this reason only, he was an avowed presidential candidate. Joseph Medill put the energetic Chicago *Tribune* to work on Lincoln's behalf, and the party hierarchy in Illinois eyed him with growing enthusiasm and began pointing in his direction. Outside Illinois there was mention of Lincoln as a possible dark horse—ever since James K. Polk had come from nowhere to capture the Democratic nomination in 1844 politicians had been alive to this device—and while prominent national chieftains like Seward and Chase commanded the most support in preconvention months, a deadlock in Chicago could easily result in the search for an acceptable compromise candidate. Republican state and national headquarters buzzed with this kind of talk in the feverish preparation for the 1860 campaign.

While Lincoln's presidential prospects gradually took shape, Jefferson Davis returned to Washington in December, 1858, for the short session of the Thirty-Fifth Congress. It was a barren session, almost completely deadlocked by sectional antagonism and serving chiefly to widen the grievous North-South split in the Democratic Party. The recent elections had dealt a sharp rebuke to the administration and heightened the mutual hostility of the Douglas and Southern factions, neither of whom entertained the slightest thought of accommodation or compromise. Republicans naturally worked to exploit this schism, and the arid debates produced little save extra dividends of bitterness and futility.

Measure after measure went aground and broke to pieces on the unyielding sectional reef. Believers in an evil conspiracy, whether Northern or Southern, had a field day mustering evidence to support their claim. Buchanan's annual message, looking feebly to an issue around which the torn party could unite in 1860, was decidedly expansionist in tone. It called for the purchase of Cuba from Spain and an aggressive stance toward Mexico and the Central American republics that could hardly fail to plant the Stars and Stripes around the Caribbean. Northern Congressmen blocked the Cuban appropriation bill and cast angry scorn on a belligerent foreign policy that seemed a mere cloak to Southern schemes for slavery expansion; each side could call the other aggressor here. Buchanan angered the North by vetoing a bill to provide land grants for agricultural colleges; the perennial Pacific Railroad bill failed for perennial lack of agreement over location of the route. Southern votes in the Senate blocked Northern bills for free homesteads, internal improvements, and upward tariff revision —measures which would help the Republicans assemble a winning coalition in 1860. Few topics of legislation or debate did not lend themselves to subversion by the sectional controversy.

In the Senate, the split between Douglas and the Southern wing of the party was hardened and codified. Davis took the lead in a series of acrid debates with the Little Giant concerning that tiresome old chestnut, the status of slavery in the territories. Nearly thirteen years had passed since David Wilmot first attached his troublesome proviso to a Mexican War appropriation bill, and no Congressional session since 1846 had been entirely free of the subject; some had talked of little else. His resolve strengthened by the recent triumph over Lincoln, Douglas would not budge from his so-called Freeport Doctrine, the modernized version of popular sovereignty aimed at getting around the Dred Scott decision: Congress might not exclude slavery, but a territorial majority could always do so, either by passing hostile legislation or by refusing to enact protective legislation; in either case, the right of a majority to prohibit slavery was in no way curtailed by the Scott decision.

Davis and other Southern leaders had freely admitted this in months past; Davis had even enunciated something very like it in his recent tour of New England. Now the South would have none of it. Their new response to the Freeport Doctrine was a measure that had been advanced some time ago and was now raised to the level of dogma: a federal slave code for the territories, specifically and absolutely protecting slaveowners and their property against any action by a free-soil majority. Determined to keep leadership away from Douglas in 1860, Southern Democratic leaders made the slave code a principle from which no compromise or retreat was allowed. They knew Douglas could not accede to the slave code without surrendering all he stood for, and they now began to make it clear that they would back no candidate or platform that did not support it. Extremists frankly hoped that such a stand would ruin the party, ensure a Republican victory, and precipitate secession. Moderates, among whom Davis and most of the other Southern leaders still numbered themselves, apparently hoped that a slave-code ultimatum would persuade the Northern Democrats to abandon Douglas and close ranks with the South in time to beat back the Republican threat, keep the Union intact, and render slavery secure behind a triumphant Democratic majority.

It was bad reasoning, fatally bad, and in charting such a course the South was closing its eyes to almost every development in Northern politics since 1854. The battle over Kansas-Nebraska had hurt the Democracy and led to the rise of the Republican Party; the battle over Lecompton had hurt the Democracy even more, strengthened the Republicans, and provided an unforgettable object lesson for Northern Democrats; it was now apparent that an overwhelming majority of Northern voters, whether Democrat or Republican, would acquiesce in no measure whereby slavery would be permitted to expand. To Douglas and his followers the demand for a slave code smacked of a deliberate plot to wreck the party and hand the election of 1860 to the Republicans. They could only remember that until the present session of Congress most Southern spokesmen, including Alexander Stephens and Davis himself, had agreed with the Douglas position; they apparently forgot that Davis had spoken of the need for a slave code as early as 1850 and had mentioned it again in a speech in Mississippi in 1857, during the aftermath of the Scott case. Davis and his Southern colleagues were not plotting to wreck the party, as the indignant Douglasites claimed, but they did want to rule it, which by this time perhaps amounted to the same thing.

To the practical-minded Douglas this talk of a slave code was completely out of tune with reality. It was already apparent to most men—indeed to most Southerners, in their more rational moments—that nearly all of the unsettled territories were unsuited to slavery and had no attraction for slaveholders. Why insist upon this pernicious idea, Douglas asked, when demanding a slave code would split the party and obtaining it would yield slavery no tangible benefits? In taking this line Douglas was over-looking, no doubt conveniently, what neither Lincoln nor Davis had forgotten for a moment. Slavery might have no future in the present territories, but it could certainly prosper in those Latin American areas that expansion-minded Democrats—among whom Douglas himself had always been prominent—still talked of add-ing to the national domain. The North was in no mood for such adventures at the moment, to be sure, but deft leadership and the proper circumstances could evoke a change in sentiment. There would be nothing abstract about the slave code if Manifest Des-tiny turned southward.

In any event, when Congress adjourned in the early spring of 1859 it was evident that the Freeport Doctrine and the federal slave code would be the battle lines in the Democratic Party's search for a candidate and a platform one year hence. Frustrated lawmakers took their rancor back home and cultivated it. From April till October, the sectional quarrel gave forth spasmodic rumbles of distant thunder. Few communities lacked a militant ed-itor or two and a handful of zealous politicians and other earnest spokesmen, each pointing with alarm and reminding the people of wrongs that cried out for justice and a crisis that lay at hand. There were enough leftover shreds of violence in Kansas to keep tempers ruffled and nerves on edge. Southern leaders boiled with indignation at the efforts of Republican Congressmen to circulate cheap editions of a recent book by that angry North Carolinian, Hinton R. Helper, who urged poor whites to band together for the immediate abolition of slavery and an end to planter domina-tion of the South. Northerners were infuriated by the vociferous Southern demand for a renewal of the African slave trade, and by evidence that Southern juries were systematically acquitting cap-tains who had actually landed illegal cargoes of African Negroes on American shores. Southerners objected more strenuously than ever to the defiant manner in which Northern states and Northern mobs obstructed the Fugitive Slave Law and interfered with the recapture of runaways.

And yet there was abundant evidence, as 1859 wore to a close, that a large majority in all parts of the country would prefer a moderate way around the controversy if one could be found. Eighteen fifty-nine was a prosperous year. An expanding economy had shown its resilience by climbing rapidly out of the depression that had come in the wake of financial panic in 1857. The westward movement continued as empty farmlands in Wisconsin and beyond the Mississippi continued to lure the homesteader and the speculator. War in Italy created new demands for American meat and grain. Rail and river traffic flourished. In every state new rail lines were being projected and laid down with boundless optimism, while large integrated systems took shape in the minds of ambitious Eastern financiers. The recent discovery of oil in western Pennsylvania generated a rush in this direction; gold and rumors of gold drew an even larger swarm to Colorado. In Nevada the Comstock Lode began yielding up its incredible treasure, and elsewhere in the western mountains the quest for mineral wealth had started in earnest. Ore boats were coming down from the Soo in larger numbers each year. Everywhere, cities grew and wealth multiplied and opportunity beckoned, and the voices of trade and commerce were almost a unit in their demand that such enterprise be allowed to develop the nation without restraint, free from the dampening effects of political conflict.

In politics, too, the voice of moderation gathered strength. It was true that the fall elections registered Republican gains in nearly every Northern state, but this was largely due to the steadily waxing unpopularity of the Buchanan administration. The Republican Party contained a large moderate element that decried the radical utterances of Seward and Chase and looked with increasing hopefulness to the possibility of nominating someone like Edward Bates of Missouri, a dignified ex-judge of irreproachably conservative views and respectable Whig antecedents who might well attract moderates from all parties and sections on a sound, conservative platform in 1860.

Equally hopeful were the signs of resurgent compromise sentiment in the border states. From Maryland and North Carolina to Missouri a new party took shape and showed signs of vigor in the summer and fall of 1859. Condemning the extremists on both sides, standing rather vaguely on a platform whose only planks were the Constitution and the Union, much of its following based on the Whig–Know-Nothing combination that had supported Fillmore in 1856, this border-state group hoped to wean large numbers of moderate, conservative voters from both parties in the North and from the Democracy's ever more intransigent Southern wing. The prospects were encouraging. Radicalism was distasteful to millions in the North, and from many parts of the South came signs that Union-loving elements were taking alarm at the secessionist leanings of the dominant political faction. Rising steadily, as summer blended into fall, was the hope that moderation reflected the true national sentiment, that a party based on compromise and love of Union contained enough appeal to keep the extremists at bay in 1860.

The moderates were probably right about national sentiment, but their hopes depended upon a continued absence of those inflammatory, sensational episodes which enabled the bitter-enders on either side to exploit sectional fear and hysteria. That a small, earnest group had been concocting just such an episode for over two years is hardly surprising. The nation contained more than a few men who thirsted to force the quarrel over slavery to a climax, and violence as the ultimate means of coping with an insupportable problem was as time-honored an American tradition as the ballot box. October came, and on a cool Sunday evening history pointed its long finger at the sleepy Virginia town where the Shenandoah and Potomac rivers converge amid scenic hills. Moderation was about to receive a body blow. The country awoke on Monday, October 17, to learn that John Brown and his little band had descended on Harper's Ferry.

Brown's raid, spearhead of a fantastic plan to use Harper's Ferry and its federal arsenal as a base for fomenting a slave insurrection, was speedily contained by local militia, then crushed by a detachment of United States regulars sent up from Washington. Brown himself received a fair trial and was found guilty of murder, insurrectionism, and treason to the Commonwealth of Vir-

ginia. On December 2 he was hanged, stepping erectly to his place
on the scaffold while Virginia troops stood impassively rank on
rank in the forty-acre field outside of Charles Town and the distant Blue Ridge shimmered grandly in the noonday sun.

Extremists could not have managed this better if they had been
permitted to write a script for it. No conceivable appeal to moderation possessed one-tenth the cumulative emotional impact of
the John Brown affair, and what had been an abortive, foolish,
ill-conceived, and totally insane gesture quickly took on the proportions of historic drama. In gaunt John Brown—whether as
mad incendiary at the head of an army of fanatic conspirators
or as glorious martyr dying in the furtherance of a just and
righteous cause—the nation had found all the symbol of irrepressible conflict it needed. His grave would molder in solitude
for a bare eighteen months.

Reactions, of course, were wholly predictable. Fear of a slave
insurrection had always lurked in the back of the Southern mind,
and the fact that a handful of respectable abolitionists had
demonstrably consorted with Brown in planning the raid confirmed the Southerner's worst suspicions. As rumors of similar
abolitionist plots flashed wildly across the slave states, shock and
fear gave way to outrage. The rabid fringe had a field day, exult-
antly aware that their hopes for secession had been materially
advanced by the Brown affair. Even the more temperate Southern
leaders gave vent to expressions of wrath and warning. Harper's
Ferry was the logical fruit of Northern agitation on the slavery
question!

The South was quick to blame not merely the abolitionists,
whose culpability, direct and indirect, was hard to gainsay, but
also the entire Republican Party. Republican leaders were prompt
and on the whole sincere in their repudiation of Brown, but the
South needed no further proof of Republican intentions. Useless,
now, for party spokesmen to proclaim noninterference with slavery where it already existed. John Brown had dramatized the
arrant falsity of this claim, and even if the Northern party had
avoided direct complicity, what happened at Harper's Ferry was
no more than the natural result of Republican attacks on slavery.

More and more Southerners were now convinced that their institution could not survive a Republican victory in 1860. The Federal Union itself, as a few secessionists had long maintained, now
seemed a menace rather than a safeguard to Southern rights.

If further confirmation of what the South could only regard as
Northern depravity on this question were needed, the North was
quick to provide it in the weeks that followed Harper's Ferry.
Northern moderates were properly horrified, to be sure—a reaction in which genuine shock was strongly infused with the realiza-
tion by Douglas Democrats that an effective means of discrediting
their Republican opponents had just been presented them. But
Northern condemnation of the deed was less vocal and far less
impressive than the fervent, abiding, deeply religious wave of
sympathy for John Brown that swept across the free states. Brown
living was a half-pathetic, half-mad failure, his raid a crazy, senseless exploit to which only his quiet eloquence during trial and
execution lent dignity; Brown dead was martyr and battle-cry
and enduring legend, his cause now indissolubly linked with that
of human freedom. Abolitionist exaltation of Brown was to be
expected, but the image of the gallows on Charles Town field was
graven far beyond the haunts of abolitionism. The spectacle of
devout Yankee women actually praying for John Brown, not as
sinner but as saint, of respectable thinkers like Thoreau and
Emerson and Longfellow glorifying his martyrdom in Biblical
language—this could not fail to appall the most temperate Southern observer. By the end of 1859 the two sections had essentially
lost the power to communicate.

What Davis and Lincoln had to say about John Brown showed
how wide the gulf had become between men who still called themselves moderates. In Congress, which unfortunately convened
within four days of Brown's death, when emotional reaction to the
raid and the trial was reaching a peak, Davis made it perfectly
clear that he regarded the Republican Party as John Brown's ac-
complice. Attacks on slavery, Davis snapped, had proceeded from
political through social to revolutionary agitation. He spoke of a
vast conspiracy, active throughout the North and extending clear
to England, to stir servile insurrection and overturn the institu-

tion of slavery by violence. The Republicans, he asserted angrily, were "organized on the basis of making war" against Virginia and the South. Davis was strongly implying what other Southern spokesmen had said outright: the South and the North could not live peaceably together until the Republican Party changed its ways or disbanded, preferably the latter.

Almost simultaneously, Lincoln was presenting the Republican view of the matter. In a New York speech in February, 1860, he flatly denied any connection between his party and John Brown. He also reminded the South that using Brown as a club to break up the Republican Party was both futile and dangerous: "There is a judgment and a feeling against slavery in this nation, which cast at least a million and a half of votes. You cannot destroy the judgment and feeling—that sentiment—by breaking up the political organization which rallies around it. . . . But if you could, how much would you gain by forcing the sentiment which created it out of the peaceful channel of the ballot-box . . . ! Would the number of John Browns be lessened or enlarged by the operation?"

Earlier, speaking in Kansas only a day or two after the execution, Lincoln had firmly denounced the lawlessness of Brown's act and as firmly endorsed the justice of his punishment. Violence and bloodshed were wrong, even in a just cause—and so, he added significantly, was treason. On these counts Brown had been guilty, beyond peradventure, yet here again Lincoln warned the South to learn the real lesson of Harper's Ferry: treason was wrong in whatever guise it appeared, and if the Southern states should ever attempt to break up the Union, "it will be our duty to deal with you as old John Brown has been dealt with." Moderate or no, Lincoln and Davis could not have been farther apart had they spoken from different planets.

And so the presidential year dawned in an atmosphere of renewed tension and acerbity. From the Republicans came exultant prediction of victory in the fall, from the deep South much gasconade and no little serious planning on the imminence of secession. The new Congress took up where the old had left off—its work constantly impeded by partisan bitterness and emotional outbreaks that repeatedly threatened to take the form of physical violence. Many lawmakers acquired the habit of taking weapons to the daily sessions and wondered uneasily in the course of hot-tempered debates how long the weapons would go unused. No party had a majority in the Lower House. The Republicans slightly outnumbered the Democrats, who were grievously split along North-South lines, while the balance of power was held by a small group of Know-Nothings and Whigs. Under these dis-organized conditions, sectional animosity was such that forty-four dreary ballots and nearly eight quarrelsome weeks were required to elect a Speaker. Slavery once again had virtually de-prived the federal government of its power to function.

In those early months of 1860 politicians in and out of Congress operated with an eye on the forthcoming national conventions. As seldom before or since, the future of the republic depended in no small part on what these conventions would do, and well be-fore the Democrats assembled in Charleston or the Republicans in Chicago, it was not overly difficult to gauge the direction of the wind. The identity of the party nominees was still an open question, but the various stands which the major political factions would take at convention time were hardly in doubt, leading spokesmen having made their respective positions almost painfully clear as early as February. The outstanding conclusion to be drawn from such statements was a grim one: they admitted al-most no possibility of compromise or harmony.

Though their parties did not lack other spokesmen, Lincoln and Davis enunciated in February what were perhaps the clearest assertions of the moderate Republican and moderate Southern points of view. The other bands on the spectrum were equally distinct. On either flank stood the extremists, North and South, whose language and tone had altered little in the past decade unless it was to acquire added frenzy. Between Lincoln and Davis stood the Whig–Know-Nothing–Conservative element on the one hand, talking vaguely of a Constitutional Union party whose only visible program for a fast-changing society was the *status quo,* and the Douglas Democrats on the other. Douglas and his fol-lowers could only repeat what they had been saying for the past six years and invoke the formula of popular sovereignty, together with its latest refinement, the Freeport Doctrine. It remained for Lincoln and Davis to make the pattern of rigidity complete.

Jefferson Davis spoke first, and his message was defiantly inflexible. In the Senate, on February 2, he introduced a set of resolutions which amounted to a Southern manifesto, stating in unequivocal terms the full price of Southern security within the Federal Union. States must never interfere with either the recovery of runaways or the domestic institutions of other states, and any attack on slavery within the slave states was a violation of the Constitution. (John Brown's shadow was daily growing longer.) Not only were Congress and territorial legislatures powerless to *impair* the rights of slaveholders in all federal territories, but the national government was duty bound to provide such slaveholders "all needful protection"—i.e., the slave code. In order to hammer his point home, Davis included as one resolution the long-standing Southern claim that no territory could decide on the subject of slavery until it was admitted to the Union.

In tone and philosophy, and no doubt consciously, this was pure John C. Calhoun. For years Davis had more or less fancied himself the heir apparent to the illustrious South Carolinian, and he was now bringing Calhoun's demands up to date in the light of more recent and more extreme Northern attacks on the institution of slavery. Rigid enforcement of the Fugitive Slave Law, an end to any sort of interference by one state or any of its citizens in the domestic affairs of another, complete protection for the rights of slaveholders in the territories—these were restatements of the Calhoun position in the late eighteen-forties, a repetition of the old Calhoun warning that the slave states would find their position within the Union intolerable unless every power of law and government were employed in behalf of the peculiar institution. All the South really wanted was security, and her leading spokesman in 1860, as in 1850, was putting the desire in the form of a demand—actually, an ultimatum.

In the abstract, and on the surface, these demands were not unreasonable. Nor would meeting them have changed anything much. Southern nerves might have been soothed by obtaining complete security in the territories, by the prompt return of all runaways and by an end to John Brown raids (although it is difficult to imagine how similar incursions could have been crushed more efficiently or punished more thoroughly than the attack on Harper's Ferry). Even with all of this, however, the continental territories would inexorably become free states sooner or later, and in point of fact the South—the cotton South in particular, where all the noise was coming from—had never lost enough runaway slaves to constitute a genuine grievance.

The specific planks in the Davis Manifesto were not issues but symbols; Southerners were really asking for far more than legal protection. They wanted the North to change its mind (or remain forever silent) on the subject of slavery, to cease agitating the question, to accept it as a permanent feature of the American way of life. This was a manifest impossibility in 1860 and always had been, yet under the tutelage of Calhoun and Davis the South had been convincing itself for a generation that it could tolerate no less. In terms of practical politics, the Davis resolutions asked the Republicans to disband and the Douglas Democrats to surrender; Davis was consciously maneuvering to unite the South on a platform that Douglas could not accept in order to spike the Little Giant's presidential prospects at the forthcoming Charleston convention.

Davis did not seem to realize how perfectly this tactic played into the hands of the secessionists. Demanding the Union on Southern terms or not at all did not really pose a choice for the North. A few Southern leaders knew this, and deliberately pushed the demand in full confidence that secession must follow when the demand was unmet. But a majority, Davis perhaps above all, apparently retained until the very outbreak of hostilities the wild notion that Northern antislavery sentiment and delusions about popular sovereignty would melt away in the face of determined Southern opposition, that Northerners had embraced these heresies under the false impression that the South did not mean what it said. This latter impression existed, but it did not govern; the Northern majority would meet defiance with defiance, and they would preserve the Union by other means before they accepted either the letter or the spirit of the Davis resolutions. In demanding that the North change its mind or suffer the consequences the South was asking not one impossibility, but two.

In any case Davis had spoken, and the content of his resolutions left little hope for a restoration of Democratic unity at Charleston. At the end of February it was Lincoln's turn. As with Davis in the Senate, practical politics was involved. In the fall of 1859 Lincoln had been invited to give a lecture in New York, and had accepted on condition that his subject be political. Sponsorship of his address quickly passed into the hands of a group of New York Republicans, including Horace Greeley and William Cullen Bryant, whose primary motive in cultivating Lincoln was to block Senator Seward's bid for the presidential nomination in Chicago that spring. Aware that his own political caliber would be on exhibit for the first time in the East, without whose support no Republican candidate could expect to win, Lincoln prepared as painstakingly for this speech as he had for the Springfield address that brought him out of retirement back in 1854, and his eastern plans included a trip through New England by way of extending his political impact. He spoke in New York on the evening of February 27, and an estimated fifteen hundred people braved a snowstorm to pack the new Cooper Union building and take his measure.

Lincoln responded magnificently. Even in the more sophisticated East his impassioned eloquence and clear argument soon had the audience with him, overcoming whatever initial impression his lanky awkwardness might have created. His speech was a forceful, reasoned statement of the Republican attitude towards slavery. Both Stephen A. Douglas and the Southern leaders, Lincoln said, entertained misconceptions about this attitude which ought to be corrected. Turning first to Douglas, who had recently written a widely discussed article on the subject, Lincoln quoted an impressive array of facts to show that a majority of the Founding Fathers had done everything they could to prevent the expansion of slavery, that nowhere had they sought to limit or forbid federal authority over slavery in the territories, and that the modern Republican Party was not revolutionary but conservative in its attempt to carry out the expressed desire of the Fathers with regard to slavery. The ruling idea, then and now, was to tolerate and even protect the institution where it already existed, but to employ the powers of government with equal vigor to circumscribe and contain what was—then and now—a necessary evil. It had all been said before, many times, but never with greater attention to historical fact or keener understanding of the meaning of the American past.

Lincoln then addressed himself to the South. None of the stock Southern accusations against the Republican Party, he said, was true. George Washington himself had called for the restriction of slavery; how then, in calling for the same thing, were the Republicans radical, destructive, or revolutionary? They were only a sectional party in so far as the South forced them to be, not by design. They were not insurrectionists—here Lincoln emphatically repudiated John Brown, and cautioned that breaking up the Republican Party would produce more Browns rather than less—and the party had had no connection with the Harper's Ferry episode nor any influence, real or attempted, on the slave population. The Republicans were not unconstitutional. A correct reading of that document would show that the Court majority in the Dred Scott decision was wrong in its contention that the Constitution "distinctly and expressly affirmed" the right of property in a slave. The contrary was true: the refusal by the framers to mention slavery explicitly "was employed on purpose to exclude from the Constitution the idea that there could be property in man." Under these circumstances how could the South claim that its interpretation of the Constitution was the only correct one, and must prevail? Nothing the Republican Party wanted to do was in any way inconsonant with legality or the American tradition, yet the South was threatening to secede rather than abide the election of a Republican president. This, Lincoln said, was tantamount to extorting the Northern vote at gunpoint.

In the end, he insisted, it came down to a matter of principle, and here he was answering Jefferson Davis as directly as though they had been in actual debate. In the interests of peace and harmony the Republicans ought to yield to the South as much as their sense of duty would allow, but what after all would truly satisfy the Southern people? Neither opening all the territories to slavery nor returning all escaped fugitives nor abstaining from all "invasions and insurrections" would suffice, alone or together. "What will convince them? This, and this only: cease to call slavery *wrong,* and join them in calling it *right.* And this must be done thoroughly—done in *acts* as well as in *words.* Silence will not be tolerated—we must place ourselves avowedly with them. ... The whole atmosphere must be disinfected from all taint of opposition to slavery, before they will cease to believe that all their troubles proceed from us."

He had read the Southern mind precisely. There was only one answer, and he gave it in terms that summoned forth a roaring ovation from the packed audience in Peter Cooper's new hall. "All they ask," Lincoln said, "we could readily grant, if we thought slavery right; all we ask, they could as readily grant, if they thought it wrong. Their thinking it right, and our thinking it wrong, is the precise fact upon which depends the whole controversy. ... Thinking it wrong, as we do, can we yield to them? Can we cast our votes with their view, and against our own? In view of our moral, social, and political responsibilities, can we do this? ... If our sense of duty forbids this, then let us stand by our duty, fearlessly and effectively. ... Neither let us be slandered from our duty by false accusations against us, nor frightened from it by menaces of destruction to the Government nor of dungeons to ourselves. *Let us have faith that right makes might, and in that faith, let us, to the end, dare to do our duty as we understand it.*"

Lincoln's first appearance before an Eastern audience was an unqualified success, and in the Cooper Union he took a long stride closer to the Republican nomination. The implications of his speech were unmistakable. Both he and Senator Davis had called upon their respective followers to do their duty as they understood it, and neither could possibly grant what the other asked. American society's tragic, compounded, centuries-old debt to the Negro bondsman was coming due at last, and the hardened, resolute attitudes expressed by America's foremost leaders in 1860 were ample guarantee that it would be paid in full, every drop of blood drawn with the lash paid for by another drawn with the sword.

Winter gave way to April, and across the lower South the land blazed into springtime. Cotton ripened in its bolls and flecked the fields with touches of white, and in South Carolina delegates from all over the country were converging on Charleston for the Democratic national convention. The next twelvemonth, so laden with final acts in the prewar drama, would begin and end with a scene in the proud, tradition-laden city on the Carolina coast. The year of decisions had begun.

[SEVEN]

THE CAMPAIGN OF 1860

Another springtime: vibrant as always with its unfailing promise of warmth and growth, of hope and renewal and dappled sunlight on green fields, a time to be born, the time for planting. This particular springtime came softly as usual, unattended by portents or lurid warnings in the sky for men to read and foretell that disaster lay so near ahead, that the time to tear down and to mourn—a time for war—would follow next year's thaw. The signs were there, of course. They lay not in the stars but in the people themselves, and men could read the message if they would. In the next twelvemonth much would be decided. Not inevitably, perhaps, but ever so logically, each decision led to the next, and by the spring of 1860 there were a few at least who saw, hopefully or fearfully according to their wont, that the republic was striding almost purposefully into disunion and civil conflict.

The stage for the year of decisions was set, the varied backdrops ready to be shifted with the scenes: Charleston in April, where fractious Democrats began tearing their party asunder; Baltimore two months later, where they completed the task; Chicago in May, where jubilant Republicans applauded their new presidential candidate and whooped in anticipation of victory ahead; the scattered polling places of the nation at large in the fall; Charleston again in December, where a defiant convention unanimously approved the ordinance that proclaimed South Carolina's withdrawal from the Union; the faithful echoes of this ordinance in half a dozen Gulf state capitals during midwinter; tiny Montgomery witnessing the inauguration of the new president of a new nation in the mild warmth of an Alabama February; the sullen skies of Washington in March, where a tall figure on the Capitol steps read a message whose soothing words did not hide the warning couched in tones of steel; and finally Charleston again in April, 1861, with flame and gunsmoke over the fort at the harbor entrance signaling an end and a beginning.

And the major actors were standing in the wings—some already famous, accustomed to the center spotlight, striding about impatiently waiting for their cue; others lesser known or totally obscure, expecting bit parts or no cue at all; not one in his wildest dreams capable of imagining how the lead roles would finally be cast or the lines written, or by what grim turns the script would veer toward its final curtain in Appomattox Court House five years hence.

Some were already hard at work behind the scenes, confident that they would soon be needed onstage: among these were the stocky, combative Senator from Illinois and the adroit, genial Senator from New York; among them, also, were the inimitable Charles Sumner and the dignified, ambitious Salmon P. Chase; fiery William L. Yancey of Alabama; bluff, harsh-tongued Ben Wade of Ohio; the artful Louisianians, smiling Judah Benjamin and devious John Slidell; Pennsylvania's able, grim-visaged Thaddeus Stevens; and the flamboyant, talented, unstable Georgian, Robert Toombs.

Some waited fearfully, dreading what might come: Breckinridge and Crittenden of Kentucky; mild-mannered Bell of Tennessee; pale Alexander Stephens, alert mind burning restlessly in a wasted body; and the aging, earnest, white-haired President himself, fussy and well-intentioned and afraid.

Others waited quietly, hardly knowing that they waited: the courtly, handsome officer from Virginia who would ride like a romantic legend at the head of his columns for four unbelievable years, all that was noblest in a doomed quixotic dream wrapped about him like a flowing mantle; the taciturn professor at the Virginia Military Institute, who would be the other Virginian's terrible right arm until it was time to rest in the shade of the trees after Chancellorsville; the one-time West Pointer of reddish hair and beard, high strung and mercurial and fiercely energetic, now an obscure principal at a remote boys' academy in Louisiana, soon to write his signature indelibly across Georgia and the annals of war; and that other quondam West Pointer, unobtrusive Sam Grant, the firm-jawed little ex-army captain with no luck and no prospects, as unlikely a candidate for the loftiest pinnacle of fame and success, probably, as any American then living. With all of these, impatient or indifferent or unknowing, waited the other captains and politicians and strange mixtures of both who would have parts to play as the unwieldy drama unfolded.

Waiting also, ambitious and ready to serve but hardly expecting the full nature or extent of the leadership so soon to be thrust upon them, were the two men from Kentucky whose diverse careers, characters, and intellects came close to symbolizing all that was at issue in this tragic conflict: Abraham Lincoln and Jefferson Davis, both devout patriots, believers in versions of the American dream that differed only on the single point which had given birth to the dream in the first place—the true definition of freedom. Each, like respective millions of his countrymen, believed strongly enough in his particular version of the dream to wage unrelenting war for it; and even as their prewar utterances best underscored the causes and nature of the controversy, the peculiar tone and talent with which each man conducted his half of the war would go far in explaining its course, outcome, and ultimate meaning. In more ways than one, the divided country was about to select the leaders it deserved.

Scattered among and behind this odd stellar assortment were the extras—thirty-two million of them, North and South, black and white, now routinely absorbed in their daily humdrum tasks, for the most part blissfully unaware that the play was about to begin, or that there would be a play at all. When it started, however, legions of them would come forward, many knowing well, in the words of the old ballad, that it might be for years and it might be forever, and perhaps dimly conscious, too, that they were not really extras but principals, playwrights, and producers all in one, without whose will and response the curtain could not rise, nor the acts unfold, nor the final ending be written.

Scene One belonged to Charleston and the Democrats, and the party's efforts to unite behind a candidate and a platform provided a sad commentary on the stricken, well-nigh paralytic condition to which the quarrel over slavery had reduced the American political process. All attempts at unity, carried on as they were amid vexatious conditions in the distinctly unneutral, highly charged atmosphere of Charleston, collapsed under the weight of sectional discord and egregious miscalculation. The end product of the Charleston convention, and of the adjourned session which met in Baltimore a few weeks later, was an irreparably divided party that stumbled into the momentous election of 1860 with two candidates, no confidence, vast seething reservoirs of ill feeling on all sides, and not the remotest chance of a meaningful victory.

The Democratic convention of 1860 was neither the first nor the last episode in this unhappy era to suggest that fate or blind circumstance or the momentum of impersonal forces had removed all control of the situation from the hands of the men involved, or to point up the alarming disparity between what actually happened and what people wanted to happen. It is no more than a dodge, perhaps, to say that the whole of the Civil War and its causes was greater than the sum of the parts; certainly the whole appears greater than the sum of the infinite multitude of human decisions that went into the making of it. An open party rupture was foreseen and desired by the barest handful of Democratic delegates at Charleston and Baltimore. None of the important party leaders wanted it, and most of them were fully, if a little tardily, conscious of the disaster that it portended. The thing was atrociously handled, to be sure, but the disruption in no way reflected the intent of those who fondly imagined at the outset that they were going to manage the affair. They failed, dismally.

Only the extremists on the Southern secessionist fringe were happy at the result, and the red trail toward which their efforts and the blunders of their fellow delegates were propelling the distracted republic would all too quickly mark the hollowness of their triumph.

Actually, of course, Democratic unity had been little more than a façade for months before the delegates converged on Charleston. Kansas-Nebraska had undermined the party's foundations, Lecompton had shivered the superstructure; and the long, bitter feud between Stephen A. Douglas and the Buchanan administration had virtually completed the wrecking process. There was also a cluster of lesser weaknesses: an ineffectual, corrupt administration that had managed to make itself unpopular in all parts of the country; a bitter factionalism within many of the state organizations, notably in the East and South; a large quota of self-seeking party hacks and insecure placemen, whose fear of losing office rendered them susceptible to any kind of deal and encouraged them to put local above national considerations; and the absence of any conceivable candidate who could command both support and enthusiasm from the country as a whole. It was a tired, confused, essentially bankrupt organization even before it put itself on display in Charleston, and anyone who sought to crumple what was left had merely to watch, and wait, and apply modest pressure at the right moment.

And yet, even under such circumstances, a break was by no means inevitable. The Democracy was in the doldrums, a normal occurrence for a party too long in office, largely discredited, devoid of strong issues or strong candidates, and confronted by the challenge of a new, dynamic, virile organization that had clearly put together a winning combination and knew how to exploit every advantage. Even united, the Democrats figured to lose in 1860. The usual tactic is to trim sails, ride out the storm, regroup, and plan to regain power next time around. The party's wounds were deep but not necessarily mortal, and the factional and sectional animosities that divided it were endemic rather than unique, even though the proportions had become rather alarming.

In general, at least, everyone knew the proper formula. Whenever a party faced internal disagreement, it worked out a compromise. There was always a compromise; that was the way politics worked. Thus reassured by long experience, party managers in 1860 seemed to forget that the process was never automatic, and that the heightened problems of this particular epoch would require far more give and less take than compromise normally entailed. From first to last, none of the would-be powers who sought to make the Democracy respond to their various strategies in 1860 gave the problem the kind of sober, realistic appraisal it demanded, and the tiny, far from influential band of deliberate party-wreckers found to their glee that most of their work was being done for them—unwittingly, but well.

Nearly everyone wanted compromise, but by the time the convention assembled nearly everyone had convinced himself that compromise had to be on his terms. The one ingredient that was missing, tragically, from the calculations of even the more sagacious and statesmanlike of the Democratic chieftains, was a truly national or party-wide viewpoint. Instead, fear and insecurity had replaced clear vision with the myopic conviction that only what was good for the South—or the Northwest, or the East—was good for party and country alike. When these views hardened, there was nothing meaningful left to compromise. The only alternative was debacle.

It is still difficult, notwithstanding the magnitude of the roadblocks in their path, to see any gray pall of inevitable doom hovering over the Democratic deliberations in Charleston and Baltimore that spring. So much that happened was traceable to whim, or accident, or spur-of-the-moment decisions that could easily have been made another way. It was certainly blind chance that had dictated the choice of Charleston for convention headquarters—a careless move made four years previously, with no thought of its possible effect. What Charleston provided, in addition to heat and overcrowding, was a demonstrative partisan throng in the galleries that gave the Gulf state delegations the worst possible encouragement to take the dramatic, extreme, pro-Southern stand, whereas the moderate atmosphere of a more neutral city (almost *any* other city) could well have had a different

effect. And many of the decisions that turned out to be momentous were not the result of plot or plan or careful calculation, and
can hardly be placed in the category of things that were bound
to happen.

Although the long roster of possible Democratic candidates was
crowded with the customary dark horses and favorite sons, the
clear front runner was always Stephen Douglas. By every standard
—party record, national stature, general ability, breadth of support, vote-getting strength, winning prospects—Douglas towered
far above the motley gaggle of other contenders, and a simple
majority of the delegates, though not the necessary two-thirds,
were more or less committed to him throughout the dreary proceedings. Despite the administration's unremitting efforts to break
his ranks before convention time, the Northwest was virtually a
solid bloc in his behalf; a majority of the Eastern delegates also
favored him, albeit less unswervingly; and he was not without
scattered support in the South. Under normal circumstances, his
simple majority on the first or second ballot would have produced
the usual flurry of withdrawals and shifts and quickly swelled
his total past the requisite two-thirds. Throwing together a platform with a suitably equivocal plank on slavery in the territories
would then have been well within the grasp of the political skills
assembled at Charleston, and the party could have gone into the
campaign with its best foot forward, however shakily, and its
one real chance for victory at the head of the ticket.

Instead, the Gulf state delegations and administration leaders
redoubled their sworn efforts to keep the nomination away
from Douglas. The result was a matching display of stubbornness
on the part of Douglas's managers and, in due course, an open
party rupture. Neither side played its hand very well; the Douglas
men were overconfident and his opponents did not realize until
too late that their threats to bolt the convention rather than
accept Douglas would be allowed to succeed.

At the outset, leading strategists in both camps faced the possibility of a split with equanimity, based on the kind of faulty
reasoning that typified nearly everything the Democrats had done

since 1854. A split would probably be avoided, but if it came each side could see certain advantages accruing. Already counting on a simple majority of the delegates, the Douglas group believed, first, that a Gulf state walkout would make it that much easier for their man to reach two-thirds of the reduced total, and, secondly, that a Southern bolt would create a new wave of sympathy and support for Douglas in the Northern states, where victories were essential to a Democratic triumph in the fall. If this brand of logic contained flaws, that employed by the anti-Douglas forces belonged in the realm of fantasy. A party split, they reasoned, would produce a three-sided presidential race and prevent any one candidate from achieving a clear majority. This would throw the election into the House of Representatives, where no party could claim control; the result would either be a compromise choice favorable to the South, or a permanent deadlock—which would enable the safely Democratic Senate to choose from among the vice-presidential candidates and, in the absence of a decision by the House, elevate their choice to the presidency. Political wisdom of this caliber was hardly designed to steer the troubled party through the reefs and shoals confronting it in 1860.

Inextricably tied to the battle over Douglas's nomination was the territorial plank in the party platform. Douglas and his followers were committed, as they had been for years, to some version of popular sovereignty that would leave ultimate control over slavery to the will of a territorial majority. Although he would accept watered-down statements of this concept, Douglas would run on no platform that did not at least make room for his interpretation, and everybody knew it. Armed with this knowledge, the Southern leaders—excepting that small minority of secessionists who worked all along for a party split—figured to force the Little Giant's withdrawal by holding out for a platform that included the slave code; Douglas could not accept this nullification of popular sovereignty.

While a few Southern leaders had apparently persuaded themselves that a slave code was absolutely vital to Southern security, for most of them the maneuver was political, designed to block the nomination of Douglas. With Douglas out of the way and a

safe man at the head of the ticket most Southerners would be
ready to retract the slave code and accept a sufficiently innocuous
territorial plank. By threatening to bolt unless the slave code were
written into the platform, Southern strategists reasoned that many
Eastern delegates, frankly opportunistic and ready for any kind
of deal, would desert Douglas in the interests of party unity
and combine with the South to adopt an anti-Douglas platform.

The convention reached the area of multiple miscalculation at
about this point. Sublimely confident that they could retain control, the Douglas forces played into their opponents' hands by
agreeing to reverse the customary order of business and consider
the platform before choosing the candidate. This was not only
unnecessary but foolish, since it brought the most divisive single
issue into the open right at the beginning, where it could do the
most damage, and gave the obstructionists vast opportunities for
mischief that they would not otherwise have had. In planning this
tactic, meanwhile, the anti-Douglas people made three miscal-
culations of their own. They seemed to forget that a substantial
number among the Gulf state delegations actually *wanted* to bolt
unless they got their slave code, and might carry the maneuver
too far; they ignored the essential unreliability of the Easterners,
whose rank opportunism could easily cut both ways; and they
never appreciated the uncompromising determination of the Douglas forces to stand by their man at any cost.

These Northwestern Democrats who had closed ranks so firmly
behind the Senator from Illinois were convinced that their very
survival depended on getting what they wanted at this convention.
They could no longer remain a tail to the Southern kite. For
years they had seen the issues closest to the heart of the expanding, dynamic Northwest—popular sovereignty, free homesteads,
internal improvements, a Pacific railroad—blocked by Southern
Democratic votes in Congress or vetoed by Southern-oriented
Democratic presidents, and they had seen their strength dwindle
steadily at home as a result. Now it was about gone, and whatever
happened to the Southern wing, Northwestern Democrats were determined to reorient the party in their direction. In this matter
they were more royalist than the king; Douglas would probably

have withdrawn before letting the party break in half, but in his absence his followers ignored all such suggestions, even when they came from Douglas himself, and pushed his candidacy with blind zeal until they got him nominated—at the irredeemable cost of Democratic unity. To the Douglasites this was secondary: if properly handled the Southern bolters would probably return soon enough, and the fact of their leaving made the party's chances in the North all the stronger. And the party's chances in one's home district, to these as to nearly all of the hapless men at Charleston, counted for more than the party as a whole.

Without quite intending it that way, the Southerners saw their cherished weapon of a bolt transform itself with dismaying rapidity from a threat to a gesture, and from a gesture to an accomplished fact. After due deliberation, the platform committee not surprisingly put forth a slave code (or Southern) and a popular sovereignty (or Douglas) platform. The confident Douglasites outmaneuvered their opponents in parliamentary tactics, forced the platform to a vote, held their majority in line—the hoped-for Eastern switch away from Douglas did not occur—and voted approval of the popular sovereignty version.

For a few moments everything hung in the balance. The Alabama delegation, in particular, had been instructed by the state legislature to withdraw from the convention if a slave-code plank were not adopted, and other Gulf state delegations were poised to follow Alabama, but some of the leaders hesitated. Only the extremists really wanted to bolt; the majority of the anti-Douglas group, including a few Democratic Senators actually on hand and others, notably Jefferson Davis, who were keeping in touch with the Charleston proceedings by telegraph from Washington, now realized that a bolt would merely ensure Douglas's nomination. Alarmed, they tried to persuade the wavering Alabamians that only by remaining in the convention could the South hope to keep the Little Giant away from the necessary two-thirds.

It appeared for a time that the logic of this argument was not altogether lost on the men from the cotton states. Then the city of Charleston, aided by another outbreak of overconfidence from the Douglas bloc, fanned Southern intransigence back into full flame. In the discussion that followed the crucial platform vote, the staunch Douglas lieutenant from Michigan, former Senator Charles Stuart, delivered a speech insulting to the South in tone and content, while the partisan galleries continued to applaud every gesture of defiance or opposition from the Southern side of the floor. Stuart's remarks may have been deliberate—the Douglas forces were still partially persuaded that a Southern bolt would help their prospects in the North—and in any case the delegates from the lower South were not going to give way before the eyes of Charleston. While the galleries cheered, Leroy Walker of Alabama rose to announce that his delegation could not remain a part of the convention if Southern demands for a slave code were not met. The Alabamians forthwith left the hall, followed in turn, with appropriate rounds of oratory and applause, by the delegations of Mississippi, Louisiana, South Carolina, Florida, and Texas. The first positive step on the road to secession had been taken.

From then on all plans went awry. With the bolters gone, the Douglas group proceeded confidently to the balloting, only to see their hopes for a two-thirds majority vanish. The New York delegation—switching just a trifle too late—joined the remaining anti-Douglas forces to pass a resolution requiring the candidate to receive two-thirds of the *total* convention vote, not merely, as the Douglasites had planned, two-thirds of those still present. This effectively stymied the Douglas bandwagon; through dozens of dreary ballots his total hovered slightly above a simple majority but never approached two-thirds, with the remainder scattering. Thus deadlocked, the frustrated delegates finally voted to adjourn and reassemble in Baltimore in June. The bolters, meanwhile, were sitting discreetly and with growing dismay a few blocks distant, making perfunctory speeches and waiting for the offer of an olive branch that never came. The Douglasites had counted on victory after the bolt; many of the bolters had counted on being asked to return on some sort of acceptable compromise terms; when the convention finally left Charleston no one but the exultant secessionists had achieved what he wanted.

In the interim between sessions, both sides worked feverishly to improve their position. While laboring to keep their own ranks intact, the Douglas forces tried to enlist moderate opinion in the South for the appointment of new, pro-Douglas delegates to the Baltimore convention, using the argument that the original Gulf state delegations had disqualified themselves by their bolt. The opposition, of course, attempted to counter this move, thoroughly convinced by now that Douglas would win at Baltimore if the seceders did not return. Loyal Southern Democrats who opposed Douglas were now fighting, in effect, a two-front war—against the secessionists who wanted to preserve the party rupture intact, and against the effort by the Little Giant's Southern lieutenants to replace the bolters with pro-Douglas delegates. The loyal opposition won most of these battles; when the adjourned session convened in Baltimore nearly all of the bolters were there to seek readmission and block Douglas from within. In two or three of the Gulf states, however, by more or less irregular processes, the Douglas men had put together rival delegations who went to Baltimore to contest the bolters' seats and seek admission for themselves.

Within a few days at Baltimore everything fell apart once and for all. The Douglas group still had a workable majority, and although they readmitted some of the original Gulf state delegations as a compromise gesture, they also voted to seat the new, pro-Douglas men from Alabama and Louisiana. This the angry Southerners refused to accept. They resented the tactics employed by the Douglas forces, both in gathering and in seating the rival Southern delegations, and they suspected that the new alignment would nullify any further attempts to block Douglas's nomination. When it became obvious that the maneuver with regard to Alabama and Louisiana was going to succeed, nearly all of the delegates from the upper South joined the rebellious cotton states in staging a second walkout. Joined by scattered anti-Douglas delegates from the North and Far West, the Southerners paraded solemnly out of the crowded Front Street Theater in Baltimore to form a convention of their own. They would not be back; this time the rupture was final.

A gloomy Douglas, in touch with the proceedings by telegraph from Washington, tried at the eleventh hour to withdraw his name and throw his support to an acceptable compromise candidate, but the determined Northwestern phalanx refused to heed him. They had gone too far to turn back. Convinced that no other Democrat could carry their states, they ignored his instructions and pounded home their triumph, such as it was. By now there was virtually no one left in the hall except Douglas men, who proceeded without further ado to nominate their hero by an enormous majority. Still hopeful of support from moderate voters in the slave states, the Douglasites then sought a respectable Southern Unionist for second place on the ticket. When the honor was declined by their first choice, the venerable Senator Fitzpatrick of Alabama, they turned to Herschel V. Johnson of Georgia, who accepted. The seceders, meanwhile, stayed in Baltimore long enough to draw up a platform containing a slave-code plank and nominate John C. Breckinridge of Kentucky for president. As his running mate the Southern Democrats chose the affable, ambitious Joseph Lane of Oregon.

With few hopes and fewer prospects, each wing of the splintered party turned to the task, now rendered almost insuperable by conditions they themselves had made, of staving off disaster in the coming campaign.

No group or faction could escape a share of the responsibility for what had happened. Certainly an important role must be assigned the small, energetic battalion of Southern die-hards, who alone thought they had achieved what they wanted, who had used every obstructive device possible to bring about a split. But the extremists could never have succeeded without great quantities of unwitting support from other quarters.

A contribution was assuredly made by the undistinguished Eastern delegations—generally representing, as one historian has aptly put it, the rotten boroughs of the Democratic organization, faction-ridden, unprincipled, and afraid. These Easterners were often in position to mediate the entire quarrel, had they but known how to do it. Astute leadership and conscious sense of direction from the East could have produced the necessary strength to defeat

Douglas before the first rupture took place, or to nominate him before it became irreparable, or to apply the kind of pressure that might have created a workable compromise. But insight and talent of the proper dimensions were in short supply among Eastern Democrats, and what leadership the convention possessed came from abler but less flexible sources.

Douglas and his followers, too, contributed heavily. Douglas himself, who had a grasp of the situation and a statesmanlike, party-wide viewpoint that his cohorts conspicuously lacked, failed repeatedly to employ his qualities to good advantage. His health grievously impaired and his fighting spirit somewhat dulled by years of the most strenuous political combat, the shadow of his untimely death a year hence already upon him, Stephen Douglas was ineffectual that spring for the only time in his energetic career. His presence at Charleston might have averted many of the difficulties created by his overzealous lieutenants in the early stages, and his presence at Baltimore—assuming that the last-minute attempt to withdraw was seriously intended and not a mere gesture —would probably have forced his managers to obey orders and thus, presumably, avert the final Southern walkout. If Douglas faltered, his unyielding supporters from the Northwest were blinded throughout the convention to anything save considerations of personal survival; they would return home to campaign beneath the banner of Stephen Arnold Douglas even if they had to smash the national organization in order to do it. Correct in their belief that they could not win at home with any candidate save Douglas, they refused even to consider the notion that there might be truths present other than their own, and of greater import.

One truth, at least, remained beyond the grasp of almost everyone. A species of monomania afflicted both the Southern and Northwestern leaders, blinding them to the fact that the Democracy did face a workable alternative between Douglas and disruption. It was true enough, as his followers never tired of pointing out, that only behind Douglas did the party have any real hope of victory in the fall. It was equally true, and totally ignored until too late, that for both party and country a Democratic victory in the short run was less important than Democratic unity in the long. Preserving the one remaining national party would not only be an effective bulwark against the possibility of secession and civil war, but from the political standpoint it offered the party minions much greater chances of ultimate survival.

The old saw about hanging together or hanging separately was never more applicable. If a party's primary goal is victory, its overriding concern is survival, out of office as well as in, and such was quite within the range of possibility in 1860. A united Democracy behind some uninspiring compromise candidate would probably have lost the presidency to the vigorous Republicans that fall, to be sure. But with its ranks closed, even in defeat, the Democratic party would have served as a rallying-point, a focus for effective opposition; and it would have offered the uneasy South a degree of security far greater and more tangible than that actually obtaining after Lincoln's election.

The South. Always it came back to the South, angry and insecure in the grip of a reality it refused to face. Southern leaders simply could not see that they were demanding the impossible. Absolute security for the highly sensitive institution of slavery was not merely something the rest of society did not choose to grant. In a nation such as the United States was rapidly becoming, well before the political events of 1860-1861, such security was not to be had. And the search for it was bound to be illusory; even victory on the battlefield would not have provided it for long, nor solved the basic dilemma that must remain as long as Negro slavery existed, and for an unconscionable time thereafter.

As for slavery itself, of course, guilt was nationwide rather than Southern, and the entire nation, even unto the third and fourth generation, would be called upon to render payment. Now that the first installment was coming due, Southerners were understandably appalled at the size of their portion, and they can perhaps the more readily be excused for seeking any road save the one they must sooner or later follow. But in the closing months of peace the South was truly hastening the one solution it most dreaded, virtually guaranteeing by its own confused tactics what was by no means inevitable, even in the spring of 1860: that when slavery died it would die quickly, and soon, and by violence, and at incalculable cost.

Primary responsibility for the Democratic split in 1860—the act that ensured a Republican triumph and left the South no cohesive national institution through which it could hope to share or regain political power—belongs to those respectable Southern leaders who used threats of party rupture and secession as political tactics, in the vain hope that a majority in the party and the nation would fall in behind them before the tactic got out of hand. Because they would not adjust to circumstances they were engulfed by them—all without understanding that they were the leading architects of their own disaster.

Blame, in other words, must rest in large measure at the door of men like Jefferson Davis, who stands as the pre-eminent representative of the dominant faction in Southern politics. These men —Davis, Cobb and Toombs of Georgia, Hunter and Mason of Virginia, Slidell and Benjamin of Louisiana, Hammond of South Carolina, and a few others—were the recognized, self-conscious inheritors of the old Southern tradition of leadership by a well-knit plantation oligarchy (Benjamin alone, a city lawyer of humble origins and a foreign-born Jew besides, was something of an oddity here, in, but never quite of, the group). This upper stratum of Southern society, always open to the self-made man but usually insistent that he conform as nearly as possible to the planter-statesman model, had furnished the nation with most of its leaders, including many of its best, since the days of the Revolution. In the eyes of the men composing this Southern elite in 1860—men who read their history far more carefully than they gauged current events—this was the way it had been in the beginning, was now, and ever ought to be; and their greatest single failure was an inability to understand that what Mount Vernon and Monticello had been to the nation in 1790, or The Hermitage in 1830, Brierfield could not possibly be in 1860, or ever again. They were not the first group, nor the last, who so desperately wanted time to stand still that they convinced themselves it actually had.

The fatal strategy of these Southern leaders—moderate men threatening extreme measures they did not really want—begins to make more sense as the extra dimensions of their predicament emerge. They were facing a challenge not merely from the North but from their home districts, which were by no means private preserves whose support could be taken for granted. Local opposition to the Southern ruling clique was of two varieties, often overlapping but fairly distinct. On one hand were the professional fire-eaters—the Yanceys, Rhetts, Ruffins and related types, a small but vocal faction in almost every Southern state, men who had been preaching and plotting secession for a decade and now sensed that their hour was at hand. (To this extent, at least, these sincere advocates of disunion were more realistic than the Davis element: the former had at least realized that slavery within the Union was doomed, sooner or later, and frankly sought independence as the only means of preserving the institution. Their departure from reality came with the belief that independence would succeed, or that slavery would endure permanently even then.)

The other local challenge to the ruling oligarchy was primarily social and economic; it came from a new group of politicians who championed the cause of the poorer, nonslaveholding Southern whites. The criticism of the existing order symbolized by the very existence of these new leaders gave a prophetic ring to the class-struggle diatribe of Hinton R. Helper, the irate Southern author whose recent book called for an overthrow of plantation rule. Each Southern state had its share of this small-farmer, lower-class leadership: men like Albert G. Brown of Mississippi, Joseph E. Brown of Georgia, Andrew Johnson of Tennessee, and others, from some of whom more would be heard. Some, like the Browns, talked secession in their bid for support; others, like Andrew Johnson, were staunch Unionists. But all were critical of the present leadership, and all were building their support upon the vague aspirations and discontents of a large and increasingly restive segment of Southern society. It was a large enough segment, if sufficiently roused and capably led, to unseat the establishment and revolutionize the scope and orientation of Southern politics, and the establishment understood this perfectly.

In these factional contests on the state and local level, issues became weapons in a naked struggle for power, and the uneasy planter oligarchs responded not as statesmen but as politicians. They quickly decided that the only effective means of retaining support was to outbid their less responsible opponents in the defiant, saber-rattling language of Southern rights. This was primarily for home consumption, and it did not accurately represent a certain willingness to compromise on national issues which these basically moderate leaders yet retained. Only by using extreme language on the slavery issue, they reasoned, could they avoid being branded appeasers by their local rivals, which seemed a sure road to defeat at the polls. It had become easier, in the South as elsewhere, to prey upon the fears and excite the prejudices of the electorate than to take the higher ground. The fears and prejudices were there, and if the moderate did not make his bow to them someone else would. Union sentiment was present in the South, but it could hardly assert itself when most political contenders vied with one another in assuming postures of defiance or doom. Unionism's appeal was one of calm and reason, of common sense and responsibility and the long view; it had too few forthright spokesmen, and its voice was drowned by the more strident accents and more stirring arguments of the other factions.

Whether they realized it or not, the respectable Southern leaders who resorted to extremism in self-defense were making commitments and fostering a public mood which could hardly be ignored at their convenience later on. But it is difficult for a politician to reason with scholarly dispassion when he is under fire from several quarters at once, and the old order feared nothing so much as disestablishment: wherever the South went, they wanted to remain out in front.

Hence Jefferson Davis went on record in the early months of 1860 with his defiant Senate resolutions, couched in the form of an ultimatum that demanded an impossible set of guarantees for the security of slavery. Davis and his Southern colleagues pushed these resolutions hard, persuading first a majority in the Senate party caucus, then a majority in the Democratic Senate itself, to approve the substance of Davis's demands. They did all of this just before and during the Democratic convention, with a calculated eye to its effect. And while the delegates maneuvered clumsily toward their unhappy denouement in Charleston, Davis deliberately engaged Douglas in a series of Senate exchanges concerning the slave code and related matters, designed primarily to convince the nation—and above all the people back home—that Southern leadership required no stiffening, that the South would not submit to Northern rule. Small wonder that the last-minute efforts by Davis and others to keep the lower South from bolting the convention ended in failure, when all they had just said and done in the Senate contributed so heavily to the defiant mood that made a bolt possible.

In national terms, all Davis and his Southern colleagues wanted to do was block Douglas. The slave code figured to accomplish this. As for the code itself—the Southern leaders would have liked one, to be sure, but they were not so removed from political reality as to think they could actually obtain it. (When speaking off the record most Southern leaders would frankly admit that slavery had no future in the federal territories.) And they certainly did not intend to take their final stand on this issue, or make it the permanent price of Southern cooperation with the Democratic Party or the nation itself.

The trouble was that in effect they *had* so made it—at least in the eyes of thousands, North and South, who took their pronouncements at face value. This was not the year to bend Northern Democrats to the Southern will. ("Gentlemen of the South," Senator Pugh of Ohio cried fervently during a debate on the slave code at the Charleston convention, "you mistake us—you mistake us! We will not do it!") When it came to national issues, the Southern leaders retained the politician's faith in compromise and mutual concession. But the Davis faction was also speaking for local effect. Their gravest blunder, and in retrospect the least excusable, was the notion that they could participate— even lead—in whipping up the most extreme and uncompromising attitudes among their constituents and local party delegations, then restrain these attitudes in time to avert misfortune.

It was not necessity, really, but weakness, that dictated such a policy. Most of the established leaders—Davis above all—would have been indignant at the charge of political opportunism; these men did not take honor lightly, and in theory they would welcome defeat and retirement in a just cause rather than take the expedient course. They regarded their policy as both shrewd and statesmanlike. Shrewd it most emphatically was not; and preservation of all these men held dear—nation, party, plantation slavery—required a hugely different brand of statesmanship from the one they employed. It required an earnest, sustained, impassioned appeal to the Southern people in behalf of moderation, patience, restraint, principle, unity, compromise, patriotism, and common sense. The South was not without its quota of these items, even though too many of their spokesmen had been trying to hammer it out of them for the better part of a decade.

It is an unfathomable might-have-been, and an intriguing one. These were the men—Jefferson Davis, Robert Toombs, Howell Cobb, and the rest of their order—who possessed the stature and prestige to do the job, if it could be done at all. Perhaps scorn, contumely and political oblivion would have been their reward; certainly the eager opposition would have made the most of their opportunity, and the Southern temperament was possibly too tormented by fear and uncertainty to produce a favorable response. Later events would show that moderation was in fact present in the slave states; in 1860 it could merely have been waiting for the appeal. Even the visible stakes seemed to make failure worth the gamble: party unity preserved, the Union intact, slavery secure for the breathing-space that might have permitted cooler heads to consider its future. And unseen in the background, just incidentally, hung six hundred thousand lives.

Instead, by going so dramatically and forcefully on record in favor of the extreme position, Davis and his colleagues encouraged, if they did not ensure, the political result they did not really want, and gave immeasurable aid and comfort to their most inveterate foes. Rightly or wrongly, they were convinced that they would be in trouble at home if they did anything else, yet in retrospect their policy smacks of bankrupt wisdom and abject surrender. The moderate Southern-rights leadership so perfectly exemplified by Jefferson Davis was simply moving to join and lead a radical movement that it felt unable to oppose.

Now it was the Republicans' turn, and the mood of the drama shifted as tangibly as the scene. No two cities in all the country stood farther apart, symbolically or in essence, than Charleston and Chicago. As America measured such things Charleston was a venerable town, consciously aristocratic, with tradition and pride and grace, dignity and gentle manners, unsurpassable charm, the leisured tempo of humid summers and sub-tropic heat. There was an aura about Charleston, uniquely its own—a soft blend of sun-baked waterfront and cool shaded streets, of church bells and stately town houses and brilliant foliage, of tall palmettos stirring gently in the evening breeze, of birth and breeding, elegant courtesy, and mannered pride, of cotillions and iced drinks and easy laughter, of soft Negro voices, and cotton bales stacked along the quay, and all the pretension and beauty and lost magic of the Southland shrouding the city like the blue haze of a summer afternoon. Present, too, beneath the veneer of genteel tradition and palpable charm, was a faint but undeniable whiff of decay, for in every contour, line, and accent Charleston embodied the tender grace of a day that was very nearly dead.

Jump then to Chicago, a noisy, vigorous beehive clustering along the marshy southwestern shore of Lake Michigan. Scarcely a generation ago Chicago had been an unlovely swamp at the mouth of a narrow, crooked river, with little save a log fort and a handful of shacks in a clearing beside the stream to show that men knew the place existed. As a city it had no tradition at all, less than no elegance, the easiest of manners, and nothing whatever that by normal definition could be called charm. It did have, in 1860, over 100,000 inhabitants—more than twice the population of Charleston—superabundant energy, an exhilarating variety of opportunities that came, literally, by the carload, and a boisterous, brash, firmly grounded confidence that this city and and its people were the wave of the future. They were. Chicago was a boom town, new and raw and not very pretty, but bursting with all the promise and vitality of a young nation on the move.

The city presented a crude kaleidoscope of unfinished buildings, unpainted storefronts, crowded hotels, packed warehouses, rows of schooners loading and discharging along the docks, laden barges in the river, redolent woodyards, whirring factories, neat frame houses, undulating board sidewalks, dust-coated streets thronged with bulky drays and jolting high-wheeled wagons, and an irregular pattern of railroad tracks that sliced and crisscrossed their uncompromising way toward the heart of town, carving the city into iron-bound sectors. Chicago smelled like fresh-cut pine lumber and hogs and harbor water; it echoed to the clank of hammers and the rasp of saws, the shouts of teamsters and the cough of steam locomotives, all accompanied by the restless, unceasing murmur of high-pitched human voices, the urgent voices of men in a hurry—making plans, placing orders, concluding deals, hatching projects, buying, selling, cajoling, searching, arguing, bragging. Everything was movement, confusion, optimism, growth, bustle. Already visible, in spirit and embryo, was the smoky, sprawling giant that would be hog-butcher for the world, toolmaker, stacker of wheat, player with railroads and the nation's freight handler. By 1860 Chicago was tomorrow incarnate, and none who stopped to savor its turbulent energy could fail to catch a glimpse of what lay ahead.

And Chicago, from the massive new auditorium at Market and Lake streets that the Republicans had built especially for their convention, was about to launch Abraham Lincoln on his journey to the White House.

Few among the packed trainloads of eager delegates who swarmed into the city in the early weeks of May could have anticipated this particular outcome. They had heard of Lincoln, of course; and some had seen and heard enough to be impressed; they knew that Illinois Republicans were enthusiastically behind their favorite son. But Lincoln was merely one among a sizable clutch of favorite sons, by no means the best known of them, and in the busy preconvention months more than one name had been mentioned far more frequently than his.

Besides, like the Democrats before Charleston, the Republicans had a distinct front runner, a nationally prominent and widely respected figure with impressive support, a commanding lead, and better than odds-on chances of securing the nomination on an early ballot—the astute, ambitious William H. Seward. Seward enjoyed numerous advantages. Well liked and able, a tried political veteran of wide experience, worthy record, and considerable skill, the affable Senator from New York was far and away the best known Republican in the country, and he had been in avowed and efficient pursuit of the presidential nomination since 1856. Working and voting as a unit in his behalf was the powerful New York delegation, headed by his resourceful manager and long-time political ally, the adroit Thurlow Weed. Seward could also count on the support of several Northwestern states and much of New England, and his total strength was such that a bandwagon could easily start moving in his direction on the first or second ballot. A large and enthusiastic (if somewhat disreputable) crowd of Seward followers had come to Chicago to demonstrate noisily in the galleries for their champion. The busy Seward headquarters exuded confidence as the convention opened; all seemed ripe for their candidate's success.

It was Seward against the field, and the field was crowded, with none of the other contenders possessing more than scattered or provisional support outside his home state. Yet Seward's very primacy made him vulnerable. Of necessity, everyone outside his camp thought in terms of combinations against him. If his enemies were divided, they were both skillful and determined, and they were numerous enough to pose a serious challenge should the right combination take shape amid the welter of deals, bargains, and promises that began to offer as the party chieftains and delegates assembled.

The Republicans had reason to be confident of victory in the fall, especially now that the Democrats had split, but the politicians in Chicago were inclined toward caution. Success would not be automatic. Like all major political organizations, the Republicans were supported by a loose congeries of ill-assorted interests, and the dislike of slavery expansion that had brought the party together in the first place would not be enough to hold them together unless delicately handled. Their ranks included reformers and machine politicians, staunch abolitionists and equally staunch conservatives who detested abolitionism, urban capitalists and yeomen farmers, immigrants and nativists, high-tariff men and free traders. Moreover, all save the youngest party members had been something else before they became Republicans —Free-Soilers, anti-Nebraska Democrats, oldline Whigs, Know-Nothings—and veterans who had not forgotten older party ties retained all their former distrust of new bedfellows who had once been enemies. Anything that gave offense to one or more of these diverse, overlapping groups could easily cost the Republicans the election.

Though better organized and stronger than ever before, with a divided opposition and a discredited, corrupt administration presenting ideal targets, the Republicans never forgot their gravest single handicap. Except for Missouri, where the party enjoyed considerable support in the St. Louis area and entertained some slight hope of victory, Republican strength lay entirely in the free states. Electoral arithmetic was impossible to misread: the eighteen free states offered 180 votes, and it took 152 to win. This was not much leeway; the loss of New York alone would prevent a Republican triumph, as would the loss of Pennsylvania and any other state, or a variety of other two- and three-state combinations. With such calculations in mind the party managers were determined to step softly, and to avoid any candidate or issue that might shift the delicate balance against them.

Although his followers would deny it, Senator Seward had certain liabilities that offset his strength. Too many important elements in the party distrusted the man. An inescapable taint of machine politics and backroom bargaining clung to him, and this gravely offended the large number of dedicated reformers and idealists who swelled the Republican ranks and gave its campaigns and conventions their crusading tone. Who could crusade for political honesty and clean government behind a devious, faintly unsavory manipulator like Thurlow Weed, Seward's manager and alter ego? Anti-Seward professionals were not about to gloss over this problem. They did not use the term then, but what a later generation would call a candidate's "image" was very much on the minds of the men at Chicago. They were bothered not so much by any real corruption or irregularity in the Seward-Weed record as by the fact that Seward had acquired this kind of reputation, however vague—and in a year when one of the party's best campaign issues was the corruption and dishonesty that had characterized the Buchanan administration.

There were other strikes against Seward. Out of all his many utterances, two phrases were etched indelibly across his name. Earlier in the decade he had identified and invoked a "higher law" than the Constitution, one which fully sanctioned otherwise illegal acts against slavery; and in 1858 he had called the sectional controversy an "irrepressible conflict" between freedom and slavery that could not end until one or the other were crushed. In the minds of many, North and South, these doctrines stamped Seward as far more of an antislavery radical than he really was, and the professionals were seriously concerned that dislike of abolitionism would frighten away thousands of conservative Northern voters; many were convinced that this issue had beaten the party in 1856. If on the slavery question Seward seemed too radical to the conservatives, he had also managed to impress some of the hard-core abolitionists as too expedient, too "soft" on the subject, too likely to compromise—a reasonably accurate judgment. Seward's attempts to please both sides had backfired twice; his radical speeches had frightened many who might have taken comfort from his political adroitness, and the adroitness had created distrust among those who were supposed to like the speeches. In addition, there were Westerners who simply disliked him because he was from the East, and many Republican leaders from key areas where the electoral results were most uncertain—Illinois,

Indiana, New Jersey, Pennsylvania—were saying frankly that Seward could not carry their states.

Reason enough, then, for those who were not for him to be against him. But where could the opposition unite? Few of the other candidates could inspire much enthusiasm outside their own orbits. Salmon Chase of Ohio had certain assets—dignity and good looks, vigor, ability, a long and creditable record in the antislavery cause, vote-getting prowess in his native Ohio, an unimpeachably upright quality that Seward somehow lacked— but this was hardly enough. Chase was ill equipped with charm or warmth or personal magnetism or political skill; he was too ambitious, by half, and there was a streak of opportunism in his political career that had offended several. He had not picked his friends well or put together an efficient machine; even the Ohio delegation was neither unanimously nor unswervingly committed to him. And on the slavery question, conservatives were as frightened of Chase as they were of Seward.

Many aspirants could be dismissed almost out of hand. Jacob Collamer was a stolid, honest, public-spirited Senator from Vermont, and very little else. William Dayton of New Jersey, Fremont's running mate in 1856, had little to recommend him save lack of identity with any controversial issue; more than this was clearly needed. Simon Cameron of Pennsylvania, a canny, unprincipled leader who had done much to create a Republican machine in his home state from among a variety of dissident, anti-Democratic elements, pursued a dual career in business and politics with no known philosophy save that each field should serve the other in any way possible; if the reformers balked at Seward, they would bolt before they swallowed Cameron. N. P. Banks of Massachusetts was several sizes too small, by any measurement. Ben Wade of Ohio—able, forceful, outspoken, and receptive—had far too many rough edges, even for this epoch. Justice John McLean of Ohio was respectable, colorless, superannuated, and impossible.

One contender who drew much favorable notice from the anti-

Seward forces was Edward Bates of Missouri, an old Henry Clay Whig with a long record of opposition to the spread of slavery and a sound Republican attitude toward such important goals as tariff revision, internal improvements, homestead legislation, and the admission of Kansas. His backers argued that Bates would cement the allegiance of the Whig-conservative element in the North far more effectively than any other candidate; they also maintained that, as a Missourian and a known moderate, Bates might well swing some of the uncertain border slave states into the Republican column. These were effective talking points, but Bates's very strength was his greatest weakness: a man who could hold the Northern conservatives and carry the border states was almost bound to be suspect in the strong antislavery regions of New England, upstate New York, and the upper Northwest. Furthermore, Bates had endorsed Millard Fillmore on the Whig–Know-Nothing ticket in 1856, and even this rather tenuous connection with political nativism was enough to incite hostility among the liberal German-American element, whose support in more than one Northwestern state was deemed essential to Republican hopes.

And then there was Lincoln, waiting discreetly at his home in Springfield while his lieutenants in the Illinois delegation labored in Chicago to further his cause. His prospects were much better than they appeared at the first glance. Along with his ability, which had registered firmly with the more observant Republican leaders, Lincoln had three valuable assets that ultimately proved decisive. To begin with, Chicago was an ideal spot for booming the candidacy of a local favorite, and Lincoln's backers, who had angled for this convention site months ago with just such thoughts in mind, were making sure that an easily recruited throng of native support would be on hand to make the galleries ring whenever Lincoln's name was mentioned. The talents of his managers, on display at every stage of the proceedings, were a matchless asset. These Illinois Republican leaders were able and well organized—skilled in the art of politics, unswervingly devoted to their candidate, adept at the earnest, endless, backstage maneuvering by which a political convention gets its work done, tireless and persuasive in exploiting the tangled assortment of fears, ambitions, and prejudices that motivated the men from rival camps. Not even Seward was better represented at Chicago, no other candidate half so well.

Finally, Lincoln's record was composed of the ideal ingredients for a compromise choice. Unlike Seward and most of the other contenders, Lincoln had no sworn political enemies, no important factions that might defect rather than support him. He had avoided making enemies not by avoiding controversy but by taking stands that were at once firm, clear, moderate, and reasonably consistent. With Lincoln alone, his supporters could argue, it was possible for all of the dissident groups within the party to make common cause. The touchiest matter for any candidate was his position on the slavery question, and here the Illinoisans could point out that Lincoln's position was well-nigh perfect: forthright enough to mollify the radicals and sufficiently remote from abolitionism to soothe the conservatives.

Other merits could be added, point by point. Lincoln's years of faithful service in the Whig party were well calculated to attract that element, yet he had joined the Republican ranks early enough and labored in them devotedly enough to avoid the charge of opportunism, and his record of political allegiance lacked the note of backing and filling that weighed against Chase. His managers had little trouble in demonstrating that their man was better known and stronger than Dayton, younger and more attractive than McLean, superior on all counts to such as Banks and Wade, of sounder principle and firmer record than Cameron, and so on. As a moderate Illinoisan of Kentucky background, Lincoln would be almost as strong as Bates in the border area, far stronger everywhere else.

On the matter of log-cabin birthplaces and humble origins, still a powerful asset in the country at large and above all in the Northwest, Lincoln was obviously made to order. Well before the convention his managers had begun to exploit the rail-splitter theme and present their candidate as an honest, rugged, self-made Man of the Plain People. In the course of marketing their product in Chicago the Lincoln strategists were materially aided by the

fact that most of the delegations included men who had seen
and heard enough of Lincoln—at the Cooper Union last February,
for instance, or in Illinois, or during his visits to New England
and the Northwestern states—to retain a favorable impression of
the man and even, in some instances, to push actively for his
nomination.

Thus systematically the men from Illinois went about their work.
As the time for balloting approached, a vague but tangible Lincoln
combination had taken shape, its ultimate strength and cohesive-
ness yet to be tested. His backers knew better, of course, than
to think that all of the sharply calculating spokesmen from other
camps could be persuaded by logic and reasoned argument alone,
and in the course of their manifold negotiations the Lincoln
group made tentative bargains and promises whenever it seemed
necessary.

So completely did the Lincoln movement gather momentum
behind the scenes, and at such a late hour during the last sleep-
less night were most of the final arrangements made, that few
experienced observers outside Lincoln's headquarters had much
inkling of what was afoot. The Seward camp remained sublimely
confident right to the last, and many of his opponents were correspondingly glum. It was hard to believe that the fragmented
opposition could possibly muster enough strength to stop the powerful Senator from New York. Even the weary Lincoln men were
nervous. They had done their work well, but they were quite
aware that any number of developments, not least the notorious
unreliability of most political bargains in the face of a moving
bandwagon, could destroy their hopes.

And yet the thing was done, neatly and efficiently. It was
Lincoln on the third ballot, while the galleries resounded with
ecstatic cheering and the Sewardites sat in stunned disappointment. Taking advantage of the Seward organization's penchant for
parading about outdoors, the Illinoisans had seen to it that the
hall was packed with leather-lunged Lincoln supporters on the
day of the balloting, and the delegates were treated to a sustained,
impressive roar with each mention of Lincoln's name. Enough
Seward men were on hand to make considerable noise in behalf

of their champion, but they were thoroughly outshouted by the exuberant homefolks, and the mood of the convention could hardly avoid responding to the enthusiastic, stampeding atmosphere that Lincoln's following created.

With 233 votes constituting a majority, Seward—as expected—led with 173½ on the first ballot, followed by Lincoln with 102, Cameron of Pennsylvania with 50½, Chase with 49, Bates with 48, and scattered votes elsewhere. The Seward people exchanged confident glances; their man would probably go over on the next roll call. But the second ballot showed the effects of Illinois' handiwork. Seward's total advanced only to 184½, while Lincoln leaped to 181—Pennsylvania's dramatic switch of 47-odd votes from Cameron to Lincoln bringing consternation to the Seward camp—and Chase and Bates lost strength. The tide was clearly running, each new swing to Lincoln greeted by joyous thunder from the galleries. On the third ballot it became a flood almost immediately, as state after state announced switches in favor of Lincoln until a change of four votes in Ohio pushed him over the necessary 233. After a moment's hush the crowded hall, and soon much of Chicago, gave way to uproarious bedlam—cannon booming, boats whistling, churchbells pealing, men shouting as loudly as strained throats would permit. A smiling Lincoln received the news at the Springfield telegraph office, shook every hand that offered, and went home to tell his wife and receive congratulations while the town staged a celebration of its own.

It was obvious, from almost every angle, that the party had put together an excellent combination. The platform, drawn up with no more than a modicum of friction just before the nominations, was a neat blend of idealism and realism, perfectly designed to sustain the moral fervor that had marched briskly in the Republican center and van from the very beginning, while at the same time making a distinct nod to each of the self-conscious material interests that would provide diversity and recruits if properly cultivated.

In language forthright enough, but milder and less inflammatory than the ringing phrases of 1856, the new platform endorsed the egalitarian and natural-rights clauses of the Declaration of Independence, called for the preservation of the Union, insisted that slavery could have no legal existence in the federal territories, upheld the principle of noninterference in the rights and domestic institutions of the states, criticized the Democrats, denounced the recent attempts to reopen the African slave trade, called popular sovereignty a fraud, and asked for the admission of Kansas. In its final clauses, bidding frankly for the support of every major interest group in the Northern states, the document advocated higher tariff duties, river and harbor improvements, free homestead legislation, a Pacific railroad, and full protection of the rights of immigrants against any discriminatory changes in the naturalization laws.

The platform contained something for everyone, and the party was moving from convention to campaign in the best possible spirit—confident, full of energy, and reasonably united. The exceptions here, of course, were the downcast followers of William H. Seward, who had just suffered the cruelest sort of defeat. But this threatened breach in the party ranks was soon covered over by the magnanimous Seward himself. As heartsick as only a keenly ambitious man can be who had begun to savor in advance the fruits of an expected victory that never came, Seward indulged in a pardonable bit of tent-sulking, then came out loyally in support of the party ticket and agreed to campaign wholeheartedly in its behalf. (There was much solid gold in the uneven alloy that was William Henry Seward, and this ability to employ his many talents in the capacity of follower when leadership was denied him augured well for the future of the Lincoln administration.) With Seward and his legions back in step, the party could breathe easier. For second place on the ticket, in the further interests of balance and harmony, the convention had nominated the reliable, sober Hannibal Hamlin of Maine.

In their choice of standard-bearer, even on the face of it, the Republicans had done extremely well. No one could possibly foresee the fullness of the disaster that impended, nor the fullness of the talent that would emerge from the White House to meet it, but on the basis of what was actually known, Abraham Lincoln was a good candidate—the best they had. It went well beyond the fact that he combined depth of intellect, firmness of principle, and political skill more effectively than any other Republican leader; this was hardly self-evident in 1860, and those beyond the small inner circle of his staunchest supporters were understandably waiting to be convinced.

What mattered most, for the future of both the Republican Party and the slavery controversy—the war aside—was that Lincoln uniquely embodied the unshakable core of his party's collective attitude toward the peculiar institution. This attitude was discordant and diffuse: it ranged from rank abolitionism all the way to the mildest and most dilute antislavery sentiments, and between these extremes the area of tactical and philosophic disagreement was enormous. But at the heart of the general attitude was a principle that Lincoln had been enunciating almost without letup since 1854, one which summed up everything that millions in the North really felt about slavery, however vaguely, and one which, as far as it went, both abolitionist and Northern conservative could honestly endorse: slavery was a moral wrong that should not be permitted to expand. On the higher level this conviction stemmed from a belief that the spread of slavery jeopardized the nation's future and blotted its heritage; on the lower, it simply reflected a widespread popular aversion to sharing a single square inch of the national domain with a system so wholly uncongenial to the wants and tastes of free men.

But in any case, slavery must be contained. If the Republicans had a unifying theme and purpose above those of power, pelf, and the diverse goals of faction and section, this was it. And if they were going to translate their anticipated victory into anything meaningful, it would have to be on such a basis, and behind a leader thus dedicated; the alternative would simply be a newer version of the squabbling, drifting, faction-ridden, corrupt administration they sought to displace. (After Lincoln's death his party recast itself into such a mold quickly enough; the components had been there all along.)

It was also true, if yet to be demonstrated, that Lincoln not only mirrored the prevailing Northern attitude but transcended it.

Unlike too many of his countrymen, Lincoln possessed the requisite patience and maturity to resist what he thought wrong without actually fighting a war over it, or, if war should come anyway, to fight without hating. These were not idle considerations. It was still barely possible in 1860 that civil conflict might be averted, allowing time for proper leadership to begin the slow, painful process of steering national sentiment toward the gradual eradication of slavery by peaceful means; for such a solution, Lincolnesque wisdom and restraint were indispensable.

They would be indispensable, in fact, whatever happened. True to its temperament, the nation would try the quick solution before it realized that this particular problem could never be solved quickly. The quick solution was not merely futile but dangerous. This none too patient people, once committed to a war, might give itself over so completely to hatred and destruction that all higher purpose would be distorted or forgotten, all values crushed. A war could destroy slavery, to be sure—and at the same time destroy the spirit that alone could make emancipation mean anything, the spirit that would embrace the full implications of freedom for all and devote itself systematically to preparing both races for the process of adjustment to a nation of equal, first-class citizens.

And more would be at stake than the institution of slavery and the place of the Negro in America. The very nature of the federal Union, the shape of its future, its chances of survival, and the extent of its authority, were all tied to the sectional controversy. The North was determined to block the expansion of slavery, but this sentiment included no desire whatever to fight a war against slavery where it now existed. All the North demanded, in short, was that the South acquiesce in the decision of a national majority and keep their slaves at home. But the demand carried no option. If the South preferred to quit the game rather than accept the decision, the rest of the nation would define this— quite accurately—as rebellion, and move to crush it. The Union was sacred to the great majority of Northerners, and they were more fortunate than they knew in having summoned a man who not only shared their reverence but appreciated, more keenly than they, exactly why the Union mattered.

It mattered, as Lincoln saw it, because it embodied the principle of human freedom and provided a framework for an experiment in popular government and individual opportunity. The war posed its own challenge to these concepts, and when the test came Lincoln's unwavering concern for the Union included a firm awareness that democratic government could as easily fail to survive a victorious war as a lost one. If he could, he would save both the form and the substance of the American experiment, even while stretching it into new and unaccustomed shapes to fit the demands of war.

Nor was he blind to the inescapable logic of interpreting a battle for the Union as a battle for freedom. (Re-enter, at this point, the slavery question; liberty and Union, as the great Daniel Webster had observed thirty years before, were truly one and inseparable.) That the war finally succeeded in both preserving and enlarging the fundamental promise of American life, making possible its eventual fulfillment, was due in large measure to the character and purpose of the man from Springfield, selected for the unimaginable task ahead for no better reason, really, than that a group of hardheaded politicians coldly calculated their prospects of winning an election and came up with his name.

There would, of course, have to be an election before any of these larger events came to pass. As presidential contests go, this one had the normal quota of sound and fury, spectacular demonstrations and impassioned oratory and all the customary trappings, but it generated a different kind of excitement. The immediate outcome, once the various nominating conventions had done their work, was hardly in doubt. Everything pointed to a Republican triumph, and what lent the campaign of 1860 its peculiar and unforgettable tension was the widespread degree of uncertainty about the aftermath. Would all parts of the country accept the will of the sovereign people in November, expressed as best it might through the indelicate machinery of the electoral college? More to the point, would the South in fact go through with its vaunted threat to secede rather than accept a Republican president? Fear stalked this campaign like a tiger on the prowl, its dread scent and soft footfall intruding tangibly on the consciousness of thoughtful Americans, and much of the political oratory—including the reasoned and the statesmanlike as well as the wild and the irresponsible—was directed not toward the election itself but toward what might happen later.

Four parties had entered the contest: the Republicans, the Northern and Southern segments of the broken Democracy, and a new organization that had adopted the impressive title of Constitutional Unionist. This fourth party was a direct outgrowth of the compromise movement that had showed considerable strength in the border states in 1858-1859. Conservative in tone, largely old-line Whig and displaced Know-Nothing in composition, staffed principally by respectable, elderly citizens whose only formula for solving the sectional problem was to stop talking about it, the Constitutional Unionists met in Baltimore in May and nominated John Bell of Tennessee for president and Edward Everett of Massachusetts for vice president, on a platform that went no further than advocating "the Constitution, the Union, and the enforcement of the laws." Bell and Everett were thoroughly typical of the new party: distinguished, respected, veteran public servants utterly lacking in the kind of forceful personality, vigor, or intellectual depth that might capture public imagination or make an impact on the campaign. Predictably enough, the only real support for the Bell-Everett ticket came from the border slave states, where the people yearned desperately for any formula that might lay the specter of disunion. Elsewhere the Constitutional Union Party was little more than a series of earnest gestures.

By midsummer the results appeared so foregone that no one outside the Republican Party could summon much real enthusiasm for the campaign. Sensing that their hour had come, the Republicans grew more and more exultant. They treated the cities and towns across the North to the customary ballyhoo on a lavish scale—volunteer marching companies, transparencies, torchlight parades, campaign songs, and all the rest of it. The other parties also tried to put on a show. The Douglasites in the Northwest organized companies of "minutemen" to rival the Republican "Wide Awakes"; volunteer drill teams of pointedly martial mien paraded endlessly for Breckinridge in the South. The Constitutional Unionists were sufficiently inspired by their candidate's surname to announce and punctuate their rallies by ringing huge bells. But the zeal that goes with high expectations was clearly lacking, and about all the opposition orators could do to counter Republican enthusiasm was point with varying degrees of alarm.

Everyone agreed that the Republicans were going to win, and nearly everyone in the three other parties felt that the results of such a victory would range from unfortunate to catastrophic, but the one hope of stemming the Republican tide was never seriously considered. This hope, faint enough at best, called for uniting the three opposition groups behind a single candidate. Jefferson Davis, the one leader of national prominence who made an active attempt to form such a coalition, recorded in his memoirs long afterward that both Bell and Breckinridge, when he approached them, had agreed to withdraw in favor of a fusion candidate, but that Douglas, on the familiar (and unassailable) ground that no other man could hope to stop Lincoln in the North, would have none of it. After much labor and bickering the Bell, Breckinridge, and Douglas forces did achieve partial fusion of electoral and local tickets in three or four Northern states. But voters and politicians alike were generally opposed to the idea, and it never took hold with sufficient force to accomplish anything.

Sectional ill feeling, reinforced by partisan bitterness, had grown too strong for a coalition; members of the opposition disliked and distrusted one another as much as they feared the Republicans. Each of the other parties had wide support in a single area—Bell-Everett in the border states, Breckinridge in the South, Douglas in the North—and the very reasons for their strength in one region explained their weakness in the others. While the Constitutional Unionists, vulnerable to charges of appeasement and double-talk in North and South alike, were neither broad enough nor strong enough to bridge the sectional gulf, the sundered wings of the Democratic Party were too full of mutual hatred to reunite on any terms or behind any candidate.

The Breckinridge Democrats included a Northern fringe, mostly administration stalwarts and "doughfaces" of the Pierce-Buchanan stripe, whose only discernible motive was to crush Stephen A. Douglas; and a solid core of Southern-rights men and secessionists, the former hoping to frighten voters away from Lincoln and the latter frankly working for disunion. The Douglas wing of the party, though not without scattered backing in the South, relied mainly on the support of the vast majority of Northern Democrats, who had had enough of Southern leadership and wanted above all else to reshape their party along Northern lines. These men would make no deal or bargain whatever with the South. Their reaction to a proposed compromise maneuver that aimed at depriving any candidate of an electoral majority, thus sending the election to Congress, was succinctly answered by Douglas himself. "By God, sir," the Little Giant exploded, "the election shall never go into the House: before it shall go into the House, I will throw it to Lincoln."

Douglas had put his finger on something important. A few years ago he and his supporters had been Democrats first and Northerners second; now it was the other way around. The main theme of the Breckinridge forces, echoing the tactic used so successfully by Southern spokesmen in 1856, was the threat of disunion. The South, it was repeated over and over in all parts of the country, would secede before it abided a Republican president. Not all who used such language meant what they said, but Douglas was among those who took this talk seriously. He had seen enough of Southern maneuvering during the past few years to form a profound distrust of Southern intentions, and he became convinced early in the campaign that a definite plot to disrupt the Union was actually afoot in the cotton states.

Once convinced, his reaction was thoroughly in character— prompt, vigorous, outspoken, and courageous. To Douglas, keeping the Union intact was far more important than who might win the election, and when he realized that his own chances of victory were hopeless, he threw every remaining ounce of his magnificent

energy into warning the electorate that the Union must be preserved at all costs. His dislike of the Republican Party was as
strong as ever, but should Lincoln triumph in a fair and legal
canvass, Douglas vowed to support the new President unswervingly against any who refused to accept the popular verdict.

He then proceeded, in all parts of the country, to make this
abundantly clear. The final months of his life were a blaze of
glory for the Little Giant, and the greatness that had always
hovered above his dogged trail descended fully upon him at the
last. Of all the varied courses pursued by America's leaders in the
loud, uneasy campaign of 1860, his alone was that of the statesman. Not only grasping but squarely confronting the probable
course of events that would follow a Republican victory, Douglas
made the Union his sole platform.

His purpose was simply to remind the electorate, and especially
the Democrats, that defeat at the polls in a fair election was no
valid cause for destroying the government, that duty to the
nation and its legally chosen officers came ahead of allegiance
to place or party, and that secession would not be allowed to succeed. Douglas even carried his message to the deep South, where
it took real courage to glorify the Union and repudiate secession
at this late date. Abuse, rotten eggs, and detailed threats of physical assault attended his swing through the cotton states, none of
it, as might be imagined, deterring him by so much as a hair. The
vocal segments of these Southern audiences were in angry opposition to everything Douglas said, but countless others heard him
in uneasy doubt or silent approval, and would find his message
hard to forget in the terrible days ahead.

It was a splendid performance—the first real stump campaign
by a major presidential candidate, and one whose ultimate success
transcended his own defeat in November and the temporary defeat
of his cause in the weeks that followed. For Douglas, through no
final fault of his own, vindication was forced to wait upon violence, but in the end it came: the North would hardly have
closed ranks behind Lincoln so firmly after Fort Sumter had
not the best-known Northern leader played thus effectively upon
the theme of Union in the closing months of peace.

While Douglas pleaded eloquently for unity and obedience to the popular will, the other national leaders of comparable stature addressed themselves to this crucial question in far different terms or ignored it altogether, displaying, on the whole, a tendency to drift with the current rather than join Douglas in a valiant last effort to stem it. Breckinridge himself said very little. That little was couched in moderate terms, but the Kentuckian was totally obscured by his party's other spokesmen, including President Buchanan and most of the Southern leaders, who could only play endless variations on the theme of disaster that must follow a Republican victory. In warning the people not to vote Republican, these men did not hesitate to threaten secession, and most of them either implied or said outright that such a course, should the electorate fail to take heed, was not merely inevitable but just. The timid, ostrichlike posture of the Bell-Everett party offered no counter to this grim approach; though vaguely sharing his sentiment, the Constitutional Unionists lacked the type of will and boldness that would have enabled them to take their stand alongside Stephen A. Douglas.

Among the Republicans, Seward was busy trying to tone down his earlier radical statements and assure Northern audiences that he had never really called for an irrepressible conflict, that his party was in fact moderate and responsible in its approach to the slavery problem. This reasoned, restrained approach was probably quite helpful in the North, but it had no effectiveness whatsoever as a message of reassurance elsewhere, partly because the South had long since made up its mind about Seward and would listen to no eleventh-hour recantations from this quarter, and partly because all such moderate Republican utterances were more than offset by the aggressive, intemperate blasts against slavery that issued from more radical spokesmen like Sumner and the liberal German-American, Carl Schurz.

There remained Davis and Lincoln, both of whom, despite a mutually keen awareness of the impending crisis, declined to take an active part in the campaign. Their attitudes were oddly similar, and if each could adduce much solid evidence to justify his position, it is Stephen Douglas who gains in stature by comparison. Early in the campaign, for different reasons and in varying degree, both Lincoln and Davis seem to have concluded that they could no longer alter the course of events and that it was senseless to try. Resignation rather than complacency prompted such a view, and as fatalism it came close to reflecting the dominant national mood in 1860, but more should have been forthcoming from leaders of their caliber. Surrender to impersonal events was in fact a surrender to those activists who still sought to influence them, and the tragedy was that in this camp there were a dozen Yanceys and Sumners for every Douglas.

Jefferson Davis began to relinquish an active role in the early summer, as soon as he became convinced that Douglas could neither be forced nor persuaded to withdraw from the campaign. To Davis this had seemed the only hope. All of his Senate maneuvering before and during the Democratic conventions had been aimed at uniting the party behind someone other than Douglas. His later efforts to persuade Bell, Breckinridge, and Douglas to step aside and combine forces behind a single anti-Republican candidate were aimed at saving the country by eliminating first Douglas and then Lincoln. When this last effort failed Davis apparently resigned himself to the inevitability of a Republican triumph, and his spirits drooped accordingly. They had been dropping, in fact, since before the Democratic debacle at Baltimore. As Davis viewed the situation, Douglas had ruined everything by his refusal to withdraw. "If one little grog-drinking, electioneering Demagogue can destroy our hopes," Davis wrote in a bitter reference to the Little Giant, "it must be that we have been doomed to destruction."

To Davis, statesmanship accrued only to those acts which gave the South what it wanted, and since the day for such acts was palpably over, his gloom was understandable. Thereafter, as summer lengthened into fall and the portents of Republican triumph mounted, he contented himself with writing letters from the seclusion of Brierfield and commenting sadly on the imminence of disaster. Although he did not, in these letters, countenance the immediate secession of individual states as soon as Lincoln's elec-

tion became official, he both favored and predicted a united front
on the part of the cotton states—before the election, in order to
rally Constitution-loving Northerners in their battle against the
Republicans, and afterward, in order to afford the best possible
protection against a Republican assault on slavery that was bound
to come. This was not the extreme language of the fire-eater, but
it looked in the identical direction; the only difference was that
the fire-eater actively craved the establishment of a Southern
confederacy while Davis felt that Republican aggression left his
people no alternative. And he would not, could not, emulate
Douglas and stump the country demanding preservation of the
Union when the price, as Davis saw it, was an end to Southern
security and eventual ruin for the complex system of plantation
slavery. Characteristically secure in his conviction that he had
done everything an honorable man could do to avert the coming
tragedy and instruct his countrymen in the ways of justice, the
Senator from Mississippi saw no choice but to await the inevitable
in silence—and be ready for what must follow.

Abraham Lincoln, too, felt that the time for positive action
was temporarily past. From the moment of his nomination, conflicting advice as to what he should do and say in the campaign
began to descend upon him, and after due reflection he concluded that silence was the best policy. He adhered steadfastly to
this decision in the months that followed, even though conservatives within and without his party begged him to make statements
that would reassure the South and the country at large on the
subject of slavery. Lincoln unhesitatingly delivered such reassur-
ances, in person, to the stream of visitors from all parts of the
nation who thronged to his home as the campaign progressed—
callers variously eager to take the measure of this relatively
unknown candidate, find out where he stood on important issues,
or proffer advice. Most of those who saw him, including a few
Southerners, came away satisfied, and many were impressed, but
Lincoln saw no point in further public statements. His record on
the slavery question, he insisted over and over again, was both
clear and consistent; those who wanted to know where he stood
should consult the widely circulated campaign editions of his

past speeches. If he repeated himself now, his enemies would merely find new ways of attacking his position and distorting his views; the harm in becoming thus embroiled in new controversy would far outweigh the good.

As far as it went, his reasoning was sound. Lincoln was right in his desire to avoid the obfuscating hue and cry that anti-Republican editors and politicians would raise against anything he might say during the campaign, and his past record, for those who would take the trouble to consult it, was certainly clear and forthright enough. Furthermore, he was not altogether a free agent in this campaign: he was the party nominee but by no means, as yet, its real leader or major voice, and political tradition—which Douglas unhesitatingly broke—dictated that the candidate avoid the stump and leave the active campaigning to others. There was something to be said, too, for the contention advanced by the less conservative Republican politicians: too much attempt at reassuring the South would smack of appeasement, compromise if not nullify the party's underlying purpose—which was, after all, the containment of slavery—and alienate thousands of free-soil votes in the North. Lincoln and other Republican leaders were convinced that the South was demanding far more than the party could possibly grant, and that the slavery question was moving toward some sort of climax, no longer deferable. The tug was bound to come, as Lincoln would remark a few months later, and one feature of the national mood in 1860 was an intangible, nervous impatience about the whole controversy, an unspoken feeling, almost of relief, that the time for a showdown was at hand.

Almost none of those in the North, including Lincoln, who foresaw and subconsciously welcomed a showdown over slavery had any idea that showdown meant secession and civil war. They thought in terms of a political climax, a new phase in the long debate, an end to drift and uncertainty and a national policy that pampered and indulged the institution, the beginning of the slow process by which the dark unforgivable stain would ultimately be wiped clean. Since Lincoln and other thoughtful Republicans fully intended that this process be gradual and legal, they came close to taking for granted that all parties to the process, including the opposition, would agree to work within its framework.

On this single point Lincoln's grasp of the situation failed completely. His lack of any sense of urgency was based upon the conviction that most Southerners who threatened secession did not really mean it. There were a few extremists, he knew, and others who would be influenced by them, but most of this wild talk was for political effect, an old, wornout maneuver designed to frighten the national majority out of its hostility to slavery. The South, in short, was bluffing, and if enough Northern voters held fast and refused to scare—in contrast to 1856—the Republicans would form the next administration and Southerners, as good Americans, would submit to majority rule.

Basic to this view of the South was Lincoln's faith in Southern Unionism, which he believed far stronger than any impulses toward secession. This faith derived in turn from the depth of his own love of Union, which was of the undiluted Western variety, bred in Kentucky and shaped in Illinois, a potent force indeed in the hearts of those who shared it. Lincoln's customary knack for sensing popular reaction and prevailing sentiment had deserted him here—or rather, he had made the mistake of using the Northwest, which he knew intimately, as a guide to his estimate of the South, which he knew hardly at all. Southern Unionism, weakened or driven underground in recent years by a stronger emotion, was no longer the vital force it had been in the days of Jefferson and Jackson and Polk.

This stronger emotion was fear, poorly understood, if at all, by the confident men of the North, a corrosive fear compounded of provincial isolation, ignorance, an acute sense of minority status, and the deep-rooted insecurities and tensions that must accompany the presence in large numbers of an alien and ill-understood people held forcibly in bondage by a free society. Systematically fed by the incendiary utterances of their own leaders and by the mounting, intemperate chorus of criticism from the free states, this fear had already strayed across the border of hysteria in 1860, clouding every perspective by which less troubled men viewed the national scene. Few Southerners could see beyond an image of the North that was badly distorted and irredeemably hostile, a North whose typical leaders were fanatic Sumners or wily Sewards, whose typical citizens were John Browns, and whose dominant political organization was unalterably dedicated to an all-out war upon slavery—and upon what was already being referred to as the Southern way of life. Contrary to Lincoln's belief, Southern Unionism had become tenuous and conditional. Unless powerfully reinforced, it might not be able to withstand the pressure of Southern fear in the face of a Republican victory, which most Southern leaders genuinely believed would signal the commencement of a sustained assault upon their section. To many in the cotton states, the Union was no longer a refuge but a menace.

Lincoln did not suspect this. Nevertheless, his decision not to speak during the campaign, with all the frankness and eloquence he could muster, remains in part an abdication of responsibility—or, at bottom, a sense of deeper responsibility to something else. Statesmanship would seem to require more of him, in those critical months, than pointing to his past record and reassuring those few Southerners who took the trouble to consult him personally. It may be correct to argue, as Lincoln did, that nothing he said at this time would do any good. He could not be absolutely sure that this was true, and perhaps an obligation to make the attempt rested upon him anyway. Given his devotion to the Union, he might have joined Douglas in going everywhere to plead for it, and this without necessarily compromising the hard core of the Republican position on slavery. It is an attractive picture, and one with epochal possibilities, however faint: Douglas, Lincoln, and Davis momentarily submerging past differences and stumping the country, separately or in combination, on the related themes of a national unity they all believed in and a patient moderation they clearly intended to employ. Posterity would have admired such an attempt, even in failure, and posterity might add that extremism never triumphs over moderation more surely and decisively than when moderates refuse to speak.

Actually, one is tempted to conclude that Lincoln's decision to remain silent in 1860 sprang from more than honest delusion about the true condition of the Southern mind, more even than the equally honest belief that he would accomplish nothing by publicly restating his position at this late date. He had long been convinced that he and his party could never truly satisfy the South without abandoning all they stood for—and this he was not prepared to do, even though secession and war might follow. Lincoln's commitment to the basic Republican principle of containment, as the necessary first step on the long road to final emancipation, had become absolute. Much is made of his essential moderation on the subject of slavery, yet his policy both during and after the campaign—a policy, essentially, of no compromise—indicates that his moderation would not begin to operate until the nation had accepted the containment principle. There was no moderation here: he would neither swerve nor hedge in his drive toward this essential starting-point. Containment represented a value as urgent and compelling in his mind as that of the Union itself, and related to it, all of which helps to explain the readiness with which he expanded a war to save the Union into a war to destroy slavery in the winter of 1862-1863.

As Lincoln viewed the matter in 1860, the South would probably back down from the threat to secede—a belief strongly permeated with wishful thinking—but what the South might do was secondary; containment came first. If this resulted in a war, let the burden be on those who refused to accept the popular will—and, in effect, let the war come. Risk of war was worth taking, if thereby the slavery problem could be pointed toward ultimate solution. It was cold reasoning, almost ruthless. And uppermost in its hierarchy of values was the principle that slavery must begin to die *now*. The Union would be saved on his terms, not at any price.

It is difficult to quarrel with the proposition that the nation could find no real solution to the slavery question without confronting it, but his notion that no Republican appeal short of surrender would have swayed the South is harder to defend. Southern moderates, in whose strength and numbers Lincoln professed such confidence, needed far more encouragement in these troubled times than they were in fact getting. Lincoln's refusal to make an effort in this direction implies, at bottom, that his desire to begin solving the problem immediately, under Republican auspices, was stronger than any desire to solve it peaceably. Given the basic instability of the national temperament in 1860, a peaceable solution was probably impossible, but Lincoln's stature is not increased by his cold-blooded willingness to let this tide run. And the burden of responsibility for all that happened after the election rests not only upon those who refused to abide by its results, but also upon those who refused in advance to provide the South with the slightest tangible ground for believing that any other option was available.

[EIGHT]

AND THE WAR CAME

The national mood displayed an increasing nervousness as election time neared. Apprehension, gloom, and helpless uncertainty shrouded men's thinking in the border states. In the South, where the condition was most acute, nervousness took the form of earnest militia formations, scattered outbreaks of incendiarism and mob violence, an occasional lynching, and above all the wildest imaginable rumors—rumors of abolitionist plots and budding slave revolts and imminent John Brown raids, rumors of what the Republicans would do and were preparing to do in their unholy crusade against slavery, rumors that multiplied and grew as they fed upon each other, thrashing and twisting like agonized serpents across the Southern consciousness. Many of the South's cooler heads, men who had thus far escaped the twin contagions of warlike ardor and blind fear, concluded frankly that their section was in fact desperate enough to go to extremes rather than submit to a Republican president.

Northerners, according to their temperament and political persuasion, were alarmed or exultant, fearful or defiant, overly quiet or loudly assertive, but in each case an undercurrent of tension ran close to the surface; confidence, for all but the most fatuous, was a brittle mask that poorly concealed the haunted face of anxiety beneath. For the most part, however, this anxiety had a noticeable set to its jaw. It was true that timidity and fright tended to rule in commercial circles, where respect for cotton and the Southern market bred dire prophecies of financial panic and economic stagnation in the event of Republican victory. But the most pervasive single feature of the Northern mood was firm resolve, whether silent or vocal, angry or resigned—a determination to put the whole business, including Southern intentions and the very strength of the American political system, to the test. "It is time, high time," Seward warned an appreciative audience in upper New York late in the campaign, "that we know whether this is a constitutional government under which we live. It is high time that we know, since the Union is threatened, who are its friends and who are its enemies." All bets, in short, were going to be called.

The results of the presidential contest surprised almost no one. Its outcome was clearly presaged by sweeping Republican triumphs in the Northern state elections of September and October. On November 6 some 4,700,000 Americans—well over two-thirds of the electorate—marched to the polls and cast their ballots. By the early hours of November 7 it was clear that Lincoln had won, and when the final results were tallied it was clear that he had won rather decisively, with 180 electoral votes against a combined total of 123 for his three opponents: 72 for Breckinridge, 39 for Bell, and 12 for the unfortunate Douglas.

The election of 1860 provided an abundance of grist for the analyst's mill, including much speculative chaff and endless material for irresolvable arguments. A few conclusions stood out almost at once. To begin with, the odd machinery of the electoral college had registered a decisive majority for a man who obtained just under forty per cent of the popular vote, while Douglas, who carried only Missouri and three of New Jersey's seven electors, received nearly thirty per cent of the popular vote, or almost as many as Breckinridge and Bell combined. Sectional politics and Northern preponderance told the story. Aside from the Douglas share in New Jersey, Lincoln captured every electoral vote in the free states. The sectional nature of his victory was further underscored by the fact that he received not a single ballot in ten Southern states, and a bare 26,000 votes—most of these in Missouri—from the other five. Border-state Unionism swung the electoral votes of Virginia, Kentucky, and Tennessee to John Bell; the remaining eleven slave states, including all seven in the deep South, ended up in the Breckinridge column. Almost every statistic confirmed the dominance of sectional voting: the great majority of Douglas ballots, as well as nearly all of Lincoln's, were cast in the Northern states, while both Bell and Breckinridge received the bulk of their support from the South.

One or two other observations are worth noting. Lincoln was a minority President and his triumph was purely sectional, but his title was nevertheless without cloud or flaw. The election had been entirely and indisputably legal, conforming in every aspect to the complex process laid down by the Constitution. Nor did Lincoln owe his triumph to the divided opposition: had all of the Douglas, Bell, and Breckinridge ballots been cast for a single candidate, Lincoln would still have captured fifteen Northern states with 169 electoral votes, 17 more than were necessary. (Only in Oregon, California, and New Jersey, which he split with Douglas, did Lincoln win by a plurality; elsewhere his majorities over the combined opposition were substantial, in some cases overwhelming.) There could not, in short, be the slightest quarrel with the election results on Constitutional grounds—the very grounds, ironically, which those most displeased with the results were in the habit of taking.

The Republicans had done their work well since Fremont's defeat in 1856—broadening the base of their appeal, enlarging and improving their state machines, making the first tentative inroads into the upper tier of border slave states. Lincoln's total popular vote was fully 37 per cent larger than Fremont's had been, an increase that becomes more meaningful when contrasted with the record of the opposition: the combined anti-Republican vote in 1860 showed no perceptible increase over the Buchanan-Fillmore total in 1856. Together, the two Democratic candidates in 1860 polled some 350,000 more votes than Buchanan had received four years earlier, but in the country at large Bell ran nearly 300,000 votes behind Fillmore, his 1856 counterpart—which meant, in effect, that nationwide opposition to Republicanism had barely held its own in four years while the new party continued its vigorous advance. The Republicans had become the majority party in the North. They did not materially increase their Congressional strength, and they would lack control of either House at full membership; but they controlled all save two of the Northern state legislatures, and aside from the relatively insignificant Pacific coast states there would not be a Democratic governor in any Northern capitol in 1861.

Too much about popular sentiment should not be adduced from the returns. Insofar as the election suggested a mandate for anything at all, it would seem to reflect a national vote of confidence (or pious hope) in the continued maintenance of the Union. In varying accents, Lincoln, Douglas, and Bell were devout Unionists, and between them they had polled 82 per cent of the popular vote. The remainder was far from a unit on the other side. As Douglas had remarked early in the campaign, not every Breckinridge man was a secessionist, but every secessionist was a Breckinridge man.

This last, unfortunately, was not as safe an observation as it looked. On the surface, even the Southern vote seemed to give pause to dreamers of the Confederate dream: Unionists Bell and Douglas between them had polled substantially more votes in the fifteen slave states than Breckinridge did. Nor was it entirely a question of moderate border states offsetting the radicalism of the deep South, for Breckinridge failed to achieve a popular majority in either Georgia or Louisiana, and in Alabama his opposition attracted over 45 per cent of the vote.

But there was danger in reading the election figures solely on national terms. As in every election, national questions were muddied or completely overshadowed by local issues, factional rivalries, and in many Southern states by growing opposition to long-entrenched Democratic Party machines. Although these regular organizations supported Breckinridge to a man and included many radical disunionists and others who inclined in this direction, secessionist strength in the lower South was actually greater than the vote for Breckinridge indicates. Many advocates of separation had strong local reasons for opposing the regular state Democratic organizations, and a vote for the Bell ticket in Alabama or Georgia was no sure mark of Union sentiment; it might as easily have been cast by a radical Southern-rights man bent on challenging the local machine. Northerners who interpreted Breckinridge's relatively unimpressive showing in the South as a repudiation of secessionism were compounding the error they had made all along with respect to Southern opinion. This opinion was never monolithic, but it was far less inclined toward the Union at any price than outsiders hoped.

And now a Republican was about to take office as President of the United States. That which leading Southern spokesmen had long insisted they could not accept was in fact going to happen, and all of the dominant impulses in the collective Southern mood acted to propel the citizens of the Gulf states in a single direction, toward what orators were wont to call the "yawning gulf of dissolution." It was not that a clear majority specifically wanted dissolution, but rather that the varying attitudes, emotions, and beliefs of a clear majority, when taken together, made some sort of tacit acceptance of secession almost inevitable; most of those who did not actively desire secession were psychologically unequipped to resist those who did. And secession came, hard on the heels of Mr. Lincoln's victory in November.

Fittingly enough, positive action was taken first in South Carolina, where excitement had been mounting at an unbroken rate since the Democratic convention in Charleston seven months earlier. Federal officeholders in this proudest and most discontented Southern commonwealth, including the district judge, the postmasters, and the marshal, began resigning almost immediately. As luck would have it, the legislature had met in a customary special session just before the election for the purpose of naming the state's presidential electors (only South Carolina denied its voters this function). The lawmakers, after casting the state's vote for Breckinridge, remained in session until the national election results were known. Then, as predicted, they indulged in a flood of secessionist oratory and ordered a statewide election on December 6 in which the voters would choose delegates to a convention, to assemble on December 17 for the purpose of deciding South Carolina's relations to the Union. Few doubted what the convention's decision would be.

Meanwhile several of the cotton states, South Carolina included, appointed commissioners—diplomatic emissaries, in effect —to consult with other Southern governors, exchange views, and discuss alternative courses of action. The goal was a united front, and if response from the border slave states was lukewarm or indifferent, that from the lower South was encouraging. In mid-November the Governor of Alabama, under authority of a state law passed in the excited aftermath of the John Brown raid a year before, set December 24 for the election and January 7 for the assembling of Alabama's convention. Before the end of November the legislatures of Georgia, Arkansas, North Carolina, Florida, and Mississippi had met in special session to consider the crisis, and all save Arkansas and North Carolina duly summoned the voters to hold conventions and decide whether or not to remain in the Union. Louisiana followed suit in early December, and in Texas an irregular convention met in defiance of Governor Houston and called for a statewide election of delegates on January 8. The outlines of the Southern Confederacy had taken distinct shape before the end of the year.

Events moved with dismaying rapidity. While Congress assembled, trying for the last time to compromise its way around the deadlock, while anxious moderates from many parts of the country attended or supported a special peace convention in Washington with an eye to restoring national unity, the political machinery set in motion by the legislatures of the deep South ground fitfully to a climax. On December 20 the enthusiastic South Carolinians passed an ordinance of secession by unanimous vote, withdrawing from the compact of Union which the state had entered seventy-odd years before. By the first of February, 1861, similar ordinances had been passed by conventions in Mississippi, Florida, Alabama, Georgia, Louisiana, and Texas. In some of these states the vote was close and the battle between advocates and opponents of immediate

secession sternly fought, while in others the well-organized secessionist phalanx overrode or outmaneuvered the opposition without
difficulty, but the end result was the same. A belt of seven states
from South Carolina to Texas, embracing nearly one-sixth of the
country's population and nearly one-fifth of the national domain,
had proclaimed its independence and severed its ties with the
Union.

The eight slave states in the upper South yet showed little disposition to do likewise, but the architects of disunion along the
Gulf were more than satisfied with the first fruits of their campaign. The seven seceding states formed a logical and potentially
viable geographic entity, and plans for a confederation took shape
well before the individual states had completed their secessionist
movements. In the first week of February, delegates from the
seven states gathered in Montgomery to frame a constitution and
form a provisional government for the new slaveholding republic
which most Southerners considered essential to the success of their
experiment in disunion. The process had been quick, efficient, and
almost without incident. Most federal property in the seceded
states—arsenals, customs houses, postoffices, dockyards, and
nearly all of the largely unmanned forts along the Southern
coast—were quietly expropriated by the departing commonwealths. Except for two or three coastal forts where the Stars and
Stripes still flew, federal authority had ceased to exist in the
deep South. The Union was broken.

Though swiftly accomplished, the secessionist impulse was
hardly a flood tide sweeping irresistibly toward its goal and shat-
tering or engulfing every obstacle in its path. It was a strong
enough current, to be sure, set in motion and guided by resolute
men who knew exactly what they wanted. But the measure of its
success derives more from the fact that none of the institutions
or groups that might have stemmed it in time—neither Congress,
nor the Buchanan administration, nor the Republican Party, nor
moderate opinion within or without the seceding states—possessed
the strength or the will to act as dikes; all the current really had
to do was flow downhill, and it was downhill all the way. Congress
utterly lacked the capacity to find an acceptable, Union-saving

compromise—none existed, by this time—and the earnest moderates who answered Virginia's earnest call for a peace convention in the early weeks of 1861 were so many voices in the
wilderness. In these final months of his unhappy tenure, James
Buchanan showed more backbone and mettle than his detractors
would have thought possible, but nothing in his temperament or
viewpoint permitted him to act with the sort of Jacksonian firmness that might, just possibly, have kept secessionism at bay. And
the dominant faction within the Republican party, including the
President-elect, were unswerving in their refusal to endorse the
sweeping guarantees of slavery that every compromise proposal
contained. Nor was there anything very substantial in the Southern picture to suggest that Buchanan acting like Andrew Jackson,
or Lincoln acting like Buchanan, would materially have altered
the general swing toward disunion.

There remained the citizens of the cotton states. The out-and-
out or "immediate" secessionists were probably a minority everywhere except in South Carolina, and possibly there as well. The
balance of Southern opinion, however, was badly divided. The un-
conditional Unionists were few and almost totally without influence; the fear-laden, emotional atmosphere of recent years had
cowed into silence all in this camp save the incurably rash or the
socially unassailable. An undoubted majority lay somewhere in
between. If a single label can be said to cover them, it was probably that of "co-operative secessionist," but the term embraced
more than a single position. Some favored secession but dis-
approved of achieving it by individual state action, believing that
Southern independence stood a better chance if the seceding
states co-operated as a unit right from the beginning. A more
moderate group believed that a united Southern front was most
apt to win concessions from the North and permit a quick restoration of the Union on terms the South could accept. A third group,
advocating co-operative secession as a last resort, held that the
South should not withdraw until the North committed some
sort of "overt act"; Lincoln's election by itself did not justify secession. And finally, there were Southern Unionists who espoused

co-operative secession in the frank hope that the resulting delay would blunt the secessionist impulse and keep the Union intact.

There was, in short, plenty of opposition to the drive for immediate secession, but most of it involved little more than disagreement over methods and tactics. A major element in the ultimate success of the disunion campaign was that almost all Southerners believed in secession as a fundamental right, differing only as to how and when the right should be exercised. Southern Unionism could hardly assert itself when the argument was essentially confined to asking the people which sort of secession they preferred.

The immediate secessionists had other advantages, and they exploited every one of them. With the Democratic Party machinery in each of the cotton states almost entirely under their control, they were far better organized than the opposition. This enabled them to hurry the process of electing and assembling convention delegates and forcing a vote before their opponents could close ranks or popular excitement subside. Apportionment tended to favor the districts where secession feeling ran strongest. Besides, the secession movement involved far more than a simple contest between radicals and moderates. It was vastly complicated and furthered by the local power struggles that had played so large a role in Southern politics during the fifties. There were secessionists both inside and outside the regular Democratic organizations, and they were frankly vying for popular support. The state machines did not create the movement, but tried desperately to get in front of it before one or more of the various factions that opposed them—radical factions, thirsting after power and office, hopeful that secession would produce the political turnover they craved—got there first.

The prevailing Southern mood in the fall of 1860—fearful, uncertain, impatient and volatile, eager to adopt the course that best offered hope of deliverance—was ideally suited for the immediacy and urgency of the radical secessionists. They could play upon popular emotion just when it was most susceptible. Thus fanned, mob spirit ran close enough to the surface to intimidate many moderates—the very temperament that inclines men toward moderation is apt to respond timidly when threatened or abused—and to push others closer to the extremist position. The main emphasis of the moderate or "co-operative" secessionist was, after all, upon Southern unity. This made him loath to take the kind of vigorous opposing stand that would divide Southern opinion, weaken Southern resolve, or shatter the eloquent image of a South standing firm and united against the threat from without. The moderate was therefore less inclined to offer strong resistance to the secessionist campaign while it was under way, and more disposed to rally to the secessionist banner once the decision had been made. Moreover, devotion to locality, state, and region was so deep-rooted in the provincial Southland that any argument against secession invited a charge of disloyalty which the radicals were all too quick to hurl.

Psychologically and politically equipped to take the offensive, the immediate secessionists could make all manner of telling points. The primary themes were made to order: the appeal to Southern pride and regional loyalty, the inalienable *right* of secession, the widespread fear and dislike of the North, the unmitigated racial horror that would follow in emancipation's train. There were subtler approaches, as well. The argument for immediate action was bolstered by pointing fearfully to the growing disparity between North and South in population, wealth, and resources: the longer Southern independence was deferred, the less chance it would have to succeed.

On the economic front, long-standing Southern grievances against Northern financial and commercial exploitation, Northern high-tariff policies, Northern monopoly of the coastwise trade, and similar items, were contrasted to the bright future that awaited an independent South, secure and prosperous on a foundation of cotton, free trade, and an inexhaustible European market with no Northern middlemen to siphon off the profits. Playing hard on this lofty vision of a mighty slaveholding republic, secessionist orators went beyond profits and wealth to extol the cultural, artistic, and literary heights that so stable and affluent a society must inevitably attain. These were not new arguments, but they sounded more persuasive than ever in this hour of decision, and by contrast the sober appeal of the moderates—cautioning patience, warning against haste, suggesting that the South await an "overt act"—sounded anemic and unimaginative, almost defeatist. A mood of excitement and urgency demanded programs in kind.

Spokesmen for Southern independence displayed confidence rather than alarm about the possibility of civil war. For one thing, they insisted, the possibility was remote. The North had no desire to coerce the seceding states, and if the abolitionist-Republican element should make the attempt, the great body of moderate Northern opinion would rise to prevent it. Before joining a coercive war the Northwest would probably secede, possibly even join the South, and the border slave states would inevitably do so. The true Yankee, in most Southern eyes, was too crassly materialistic to be warlike; martial ardor and even courage were not in his makeup. And if war should come anyway, it was bound to be short and victorious. England and France would break a Northern blockade and even ally themselves with the South before they accepted a disruption of the vital cotton trade. Resolute Southerners, trained from boyhood in the vigorous outdoor life and the use of weapons and the habits of command, would be more than a match for the sedentary, mongrel population of the free states. Thus the eager secessionists were sure that benefit totally unmixed with peril lay in the course they had charted. (The most important single explanation for the coming of the Civil War is undoubtedly the simplest one: so few, North or South, had the haziest conception of what sort of war it would be.)

Bolstered by every manner of argument and psychological advantage, the secessionists in each of the seven cotton states pushed their campaign to a successful conclusion and co-operated in the rapid formation of a Southern confederacy. Assembling in Montgomery on February 4, 1861, delegates chosen by the seceding states quickly established a provisional government, framed a provisional constitution, and elected Jefferson Davis as provisional president of the new republic. On February 16 Davis arrived in Montgomery for the inauguration ceremonies, responding from a hotel balcony to the cheers of the crowd while the fire-eating

William L. Yancey introduced him with an appropriately dramatic phrase: "The hour and the man have met!" Two days later Davis took the oath of office on the steps of Alabama's prim, whitewashed Capitol, and the Confederate States of America officially assumed their existence. Barely one hundred days had elapsed since the telegraph wires flashed the news of Lincoln's triumph at the polls in November.

For Davis, as for so many Americans, they had been days of trial, uncertainty, and agonized decision. His course, from the closing weeks of the 1860 campaign to the enthusiastic ceremony in Montgomery, had been that of a moderate man driven reluctantly to extremes, but his moderation would admit of no compromise on precisely those issues—the future of slavery and the right of secession—that found the moderate Lincoln equally adamant on the opposing side. Since these two issues underlay the entire controversy, it is difficult to see how "moderates" of this stripe were perceptibly closer to reaching an amicable resolution of the crisis than the extremists on either fringe. Both the inner logic of his own position and his not inaccurate reading of the Northern temper dictated that Jefferson Davis, less precipitously but no less firmly, would stand beside William L. Yancey at the end, even as Abraham Lincoln would ultimately come as close as their disparate characters permitted to a meeting of minds with Charles Sumner. The two war leaders had in fact been pointing in this direction all along.

In the fall of 1860, however, Davis stood with the more cautious and temperate of the Southern leaders. His pre-election advice to the fiery Rhett of South Carolina had discouraged the idea of separate state secession and called for a unity of the "planting states" that looked more toward obtaining concessions from the North than toward final separation. Attending a conference of Mississippi's senators and representatives in November, hastily summoned by the governor as soon as the results of the presidential contest were known, Davis reportedly counseled against immediate state action, "declaring himself," as a colleague recorded it, "opposed to secession as long as the hope of a peaceable remedy remained." At the outset of the crisis, in short, the future president of the Confederacy was at most a "co-operative secessionist," who took this position in the frank hope that delay might avert catastrophe and even, just possibly, preserve the Union on terms acceptable to the South. Appended to his temperate advice at this conference was an important qualifier, thoroughly typical of moderate Southern opinion: he would, he said, loyally and unhesitatingly follow his state in whatever action it chose to take.

Then, somewhat to the relief of Mississippi's less patient and more radically inclined politicians, Davis left for Washington to attend the next session of Congress and confer with the President and other administration leaders. From the moment he reached the capital his moderation began to evaporate. Nothing he saw or heard in this uneasy city gave grounds for his hope that some "peaceable remedy" might be found, and in its absence he saw no choice—the alternative being surrender—but to encourage the secession movement and foster Southern unity.

To do otherwise, as he saw it, would be to sacrifice both his principles and his influence. By early December he learned that the Mississippi legislature, which met in special session on November 26, had taken less than three days to call a state convention for the purpose of deciding whether to remain in the Union, and he knew the temper of his state well enough to realize that a vote for secession was highly probable. Honor-bound to support such a decision, Davis soon concluded that neither Congress nor the President was capable of finding or pursuing those statesmanlike, conciliatory policies which alone might check the secessionist impulse.

He was especially disappointed by the results of his interview with Buchanan, held shortly before the opening of Congress. The harassed President was seeking advice about the contents of his annual message, then in preparation, which he hoped would point the way toward a restoration of national harmony. Buchanan listened attentively to Davis, one or two other Southern senators, and the members of what was still a Southern-oriented cabinet, but the resulting message, though sufficiently weak and pro-

Southern to anger the North, was considerably less than satisfactory to the men from the deep South. To be sure, Buchanan announced that the federal government lacked the legal authority to prevent secession, held the abolitionists and their allies responsible for the sectional conflict, expressed sympathy for the Southern fear, which he considered justified, and advocated a constitutional amendment which would provide the South with every guarantee it had ever sought for the institution of slavery. But the message annoyed Davis on two key points. It stated unequivocally that secession was unconstitutional, and it affirmed, as a corollary, that exclusive authority over forts and other federal properties in any given state belonged to the national government.

Davis not only disagreed with these points on principle; he also feared their practical implications, and with good reason. He foresaw, correctly enough, that if the government adhered to these two principles it would sooner or later find both authority and cause for resisting secession, despite Buchanan's confessions of federal impotence. Weak, timid, and vacillating though James Buchanan undoubtedly was, he had managed to find at the very outset of the secession crisis a line from which at his weakest and most timid he would not retreat—from which, indeed, he would soon draw strength for an advance, bequeathing to Lincoln the firm policy that would ultimately force the South to surrender or make war.

Thereafter, as Davis feared, Buchanan moved hesitantly but irreversibly toward a stronger line. He refused even to consider acknowledging the right of secession. When South Carolina proclaimed her withdrawal from the Union on December 20 and sent commissioners to treat with the President concerning a settlement of all accounts and issues between what were now, in the eyes of South Carolina at least, two separate nations, the question of jurisdiction over federal forts ceased to be academic. South Carolina insisted that all federal properties within her borders had reverted to the state upon her separation from the Union. Buchanan disagreed, and held to his position. He would not, he said, employ these forts in any aggressive action against South Carolina or any other state, since the federal government lacked constitutional authority for such action, but the properties must remain in federal hands—and he would defend them against attack.

The immediate occasion for civil war had now been created, nearly four months ahead of the event. There were other federal forts and properties in the deep South, and in the weeks that followed most were seized without incident while two or three, with small detachments of federal troops, upheld the national authority without provoking attack. But South Carolina had seceded first and raised the question first, and thereafter the argument focused ever more keenly upon the three coastal forts in Charleston harbor: Pinckney, an obsolescent brick structure at the mouth of the Cooper right off the lower end of town, occupied by a lone ordnance sergeant; Moultrie, on the north side of the channel, occupied by a small federal detachment, all its guns pointing seaward, utterly indefensible from the landward side; and Sumter, on a shoal squarely athwart the outer entrance to the harbor, a massive, heavy-walled pile under construction for over thirty years and still not finished, a few of its seventy-eight guns yet unmounted, a tiny squad of regulars on hand to keep the workmen busy. All in all, counting the sergeant at Pinckney and the squad at Sumter, a garrison of fewer than one hundred men constituted the sole challenge to the newly proclaimed independence of South Carolina.

Although Buchanan began by ignoring those Northern advisers who urged him to reinforce the Charleston garrison and secure the position against attack, he was even more adamant in his refusal to withdraw the troops and hand the properties to South Carolina. This refusal, as far as Davis was concerned, virtually ensured that the other cotton states would secede and made civil war highly probable. "Had he [Buchanan] withdrawn the troops from Sumter," Davis later wrote, "it would have been such a conspicuous act of conciliation that the other States would not, I believe, have called conventions to consider the question of secession, or if they had, the ordinances would not have been passed." Dubious reasoning, perhaps, but undoubtedly sincere: Davis never wavered from the belief that conciliation by the North, amounting in effect to complete surrender on matters pertaining to slavery and the right of secession, would alone have kept the Union intact and at peace.

Instead, Buchanan stiffened as time went on. When Major Anderson of Kentucky, the recently appointed commander of the Charleston garrison, transferred his entire command from Moultrie to Sumter in late December, tempers in South Carolina mounted wrathfully and the nation took a long step closer to war. Anderson had taken South Carolina and everyone else completely by surprise. He made the transfer on his own initiative, under cover of night, and on the grounds that the security of his command required it; Sumter was his only defensible position, and the mood of Charleston had become more threatening by the day. While South Carolina troops quickly seized Castle Pinckney, Fort Moultrie, the customs house and the arsenal by way of retaliation, angry Southern leaders confronted Buchanan and insisted that only a prompt disavowal of Anderson's maneuver could avert disaster.

Though horrified by the news, Buchanan held firm. Recent shifts in his cabinet, including the resignation of two Southern members, had given a decidedly Northern tone to this body, and after a few days of agonized consultation, the President upheld Major Anderson and flatly refused to heed South Carolina's demand that he withdraw the troops from Charleston. "This I cannot do; this I will not do," Buchanan replied sharply, giving patriotic Northerners something to applaud for the first time in weeks. Anderson would stay where he was, and the federal government would defend Fort Sumter "against hostile attacks from whatever quarter they may come." The policy inherited by Lincoln on March 4 was now firmly established.

In early January the President half-heartedly attempted to reinforce Sumter. He sent troops in an unarmed merchant ship, the *Star of the West,* and South Carolina batteries opened fire and drove the vessel away before it could reach its goal. By and large, Northern opinion strongly approved the effort and as strongly condemned the refusal to meet force with force; Buchanan could probably have started the Civil War then and there, had he wished. The President, however, preferred to hand the problem of war or peace to Lincoln, and not altogether out of timidity or fear; it was clearly bad strategy for an administration with less than two months of life remaining to make a decision of such import, binding its successor in advance and creating huge problems in the transfer of authority and command. The South, too, was disposed toward caution in January, with the secession process far from complete and the Confederacy not yet formed. Sumter thus passed its second crisis without igniting a major fuse, but hope of compromise was gone. Both sides, in effect, were playing for time; neither would back down on the next occasion. To a saddened Davis, Buchanan's policy toward South Carolina had been "perfidious," stemming not from "wicked purpose" but from "irresolution and an increasing dread of northern excitement." This was unjust to the aging President, whose courage and strength of will had grown steadily since November, but Davis was not writing in calm or objective spirit. His worst fears were being realized, and he was sorely troubled.

Nor did Congress dispel his gloom. As a member of a special Senate Committee of Thirteen, appointed on December 20 to explore the possibility of restoring national unity, Davis saw all his suspicions of Republican intransigence fully confirmed. The Republican members of the Committee steadfastly refused to vote in favor of any meaningful compromise, including what seemed the likeliest program: the earnest, magisterial proposals advanced by Crittenden of Kentucky. The heart of the Crittenden compromise, which also offered a number of specific guarantees for the security of slavery, was a plan to revive and extend the line of 36°30′ all the way to California, slavery to be prohibited in territories above that line and protected in territories below. Davis and Robert Toombs, the two Gulf state members of the Committee, agreed to the Crittenden plan; the border-state senators and the Northern Democrats, Douglas among them, seized upon it willingly. Although it was doubtful that acceptance of the Crittenden formula would arrest the secession movement in the cotton states, there was reason to hope that it offered a basis for eventual reconciliation.

But the five Republican members, including Seward and Wade, refused to budge. From his headquarters in Springfield, Lincoln issued a stern edict against accepting any compromise that permitted the present or future expansion of slavery. The Republican high command, not insensitive to Lincoln's warning that surrender on this point would undo all the party had done, chose to follow his lead. The five Republican senators rejected the Crittenden proposal. Since the Committee of Thirteen had agreed at the outset to recommend nothing that did not command the approval of a majority of each faction, Davis and Toombs voted nay with their Republican adversaries, and the Crittenden compromise went down to defeat. Later efforts to gain Senate endorsement of the measure likewise failed. A House Committee of Thirty-three, in a parallel quest for some workable formula, wrangled itself into deadlock and accomplished nothing whatever. For nearly a decade, under the stress of the sectional controversy, Congress had been tending toward paralysis; at this grim eleventh hour the condition was well-nigh complete.

In mid-December, already sensing the bankruptcy of Congress and the clash that would someday result from Buchanan's firm stand on secession and the federal forts, faintly hoping that Southern unity might persuade Buchanan to give way, Davis joined some thirty other senators and representatives from the cotton states in signing an address to their constituents. The address stated flatly that "the argument is exhausted. All hope of relief in the Union . . . is extinguished. . . . We are satisfied the honor, safety, and independence of the Southern people are to be found in a Southern Confederacy." Since the address specifically urged that this goal be achieved by separate state action, in signing it Davis had swung completely to the radical Southern view a scant month after his cautious advice at the Mississippi conference.

Thereafter, in the few weeks that remained before his resignation from the Senate and final departure from Washington, Davis labored more with an eye to delay, seeking to block hostile action from President or Congress while the Gulf states completed the secession movement, than with any real hope of preserving the Union. On January 5, 1861, he and his fellow Senators from the deep South (all were still present except the two South Carolinians, who had resigned before Congress assembled in anticipation of their state's withdrawal) sent another memorial to their people. They again urged the rapid formation of a Southern Confederacy, this time in specific terms, and asked how long they should remain in Congress for the purpose of defeating hostile legislation. An attempt to coerce the seceded states, Davis strongly believed, would be made by the incoming administration. It was vital for the security of the nascent Confederacy that no such attempt take place under Buchanan and the present Congress. What the South most needed was breathing space, and much of this would be provided if a clash were postponed at least until Lincoln took office on March 4.

From mid-December on, in short, Davis was convinced that the issue was no longer Union or separation but peace or war, and he governed his policy accordingly. In one of his last speeches before the Senate, on January 10, he made an eloquent plea to his Northern colleagues and the nation at large in behalf of peaceful separation. When he spoke, four states—South Carolina, Mississippi, Florida, and Alabama—had already withdrawn or were in the act of doing so, and Georgia, Louisiana, and Texas were almost sure to follow before the month was out. Repeating his contention that withdrawal of the Charleston garrison would have resulted in peace and calm negotiation, he condemned the obstinate and fearful policies of the Buchanan administration and defended the doctrine of state sovereignty with all his customary vigor.

Then followed the warning, delivered more in sorrow than in anger. "The time is near at hand," he said, "when the places which have known us as colleagues labouring together, can know us in that relation no more for ever. I have striven unsuccessfully to avert the catastrophe which now impends over the country ... If you desire at this last moment to avert civil war, so be it; it is better so. If you will but allow us to separate from you peaceably, since we cannot live peaceably together . . . then there are many relations which may still subsist between us ...

If you will not have it thus; if in the pride of power, if in contempt of reason and reliance upon force, you say we shall not go, but shall remain as subjects to you, then, Gentlemen of the North, a war is to be inaugurated the like of which men have not seen."

Davis spent the next few days winding up his affairs and preparing to return to Mississippi. In a parting letter to his old friend Franklin Pierce, Davis again denounced the Sumter policy, predicted that it would result in war, and said that necessity rather than choice had led Mississippi into secession. He also wrote the Governor of South Carolina and cautioned him against demanding the evacuation of Sumter for the present. Delay is preferable, Davis remarked: "if things continue as they are for a month, we shall be in a condition to speak with a voice which all must hear and heed. . . ."

On January 21, having received word from the Governor of Mississippi that his state's relationship with the Union was officially at an end, he addressed the Senate for the last time. Neither anger nor resentment crept into his tone; Jefferson Davis had loved his country, and had taken pride in serving it, and the parting moved him deeply. Secession, he repeated almost wearily, was always a right and had now become a necessity, thoroughly justifiable in view of recent events. In an allusion to the great controversy which underlay the present crisis, he insisted that the equality clause of the Declaration of Independence applied only to the "men of the political community" and not by any conceivable logic to the slaves. Yet the tone remained quiet, and he closed with the assurance that he left without hatred or bitterness. "In the presence of my God," he said solemnly, "I wish you well; and such, I am sure, is the feeling of the people whom I represent toward those whom you represent. It only remains for me to bid you a final farewell." Like Abraham Lincoln, Davis would fight without hating. And like Lincoln, be it noted, he would fight rather than abandon his principles; psychopathic haters would not fight harder.

Less than a month after resigning from the Senate, Davis was addressing a Southern audience in Montgomery as the provisional

President of the Confederate States of America, a whirlwind change of fortune that apparently came to him as a complete and none too welcome surprise. His ambition, as he journeyed southward from Washington in late January, looked to an entirely different and more modest goal. Convinced that he could best serve the South in a military capacity, he readily accepted Mississippi's offer of a major general's commission and command of the state's armed forces, which his newly independent commonwealth was mustering as fast as it could.

He had scarcely been home long enough to put on his new uniform and begin acquainting himself with his task, however, when the unexpected message from Montgomery arrived and summoned him to a larger post. His sense of duty and loyalty to the South made refusal impossible, although he accepted the honor with foreboding rather than joy. The full immensity of what lay ahead was beyond anyone's perception, but Davis had a greater awareness and fewer illusions than most of his countrymen, and the awful responsibility of his new office weighed upon him from the very moment of acceptance. He shared little of the Southern confidence that war would either be avoided or short, and he had none of the Southern contempt for Yankee courage or will to fight. His devotion to the Southern cause was boundless, and in the terrible years ahead he would follow it utterly, hope beyond hope, but his vision of what civil war entailed made him hugely reluctant to accept the office from which the decisions that would mean peace or war, victory or defeat, must be made. Military command seemed so much tidier, so much more congenial and less exacting. His health was poor; fatigue and recurrent neuralgia had taken a heavy toll in recent months, and the eye that had been so damaged by his illness two years before was now totally without sight. Contemporary photographs show a hollow-cheeked, thin-lipped, aloof countenance across which grim lines of endurance, iron will, and pain are clearly etched.

The Gulf state delegates who gathered at Montgomery at the beginning of February to launch the Southern experiment had gone about their work with care. They had met in a mood of earnest dedication, fully conscious of the importance of their task, loftily committed to the goal of creating a government that incorporated the virtues and excluded the vices of the one they had just left. A spirit of enthusiasm, optimism, and exaltation marked the proceedings. The delegates first established a provisional government that would conduct affairs until regular elections could be held. They then labored with painstaking care upon a constitution for their new nation.

This document was strikingly similar to the Constitution of the United States. Not surprisingly, the Confederate instrument laid more emphasis upon state rights, explicitly sanctioned and guaranteed the institution of slavery, omitted the general welfare clause, called for free trade and placed a variety of limitations on federal expenditures. Cabinet members were allowed seats in Congress. Otherwise, except for minor details, the new document followed the old almost word for word—even down to a list of functions denied to the states and a clause affirming that the new constitution was to be the supreme law of the land. The aim was to create a government not weaker but wiser, more virtuous, more frugal, and more efficient than its Washington counterpart. This high-mindedness was genuine, consciously patterned after the noble spirit of America's Revolutionary generation. The Confederate architects at Montgomery saw no incongruity whatever between their lofty vision of a beneficent Southern republic and the ironic, unlovely twist they had given to the principles of 1776: for in its carefully buttressed foundation this was a nation conceived in slavery and dedicated to the proposition that all men were not created equal.

At the outset of their deliberations the delegates constituted themselves the provisional congress for the new republic, and within a few days, voting by states, they unanimously elected Jefferson Davis as provisional president. For vice-president, with like unanimity, they chose Alexander H. Stephens of Georgia. Accounts of the process by which Davis was selected are conflicting and incomplete, although it is fairly evident that in searching for a chief executive the delegates were motivated less by lofty principle than by shrewd practicality, not unmixed with political maneuvering.

Like the Republican strategists in Chicago a few months earlier, the Montgomery convention wanted a man of sufficient prominence and stature to command respect, yet one who would generate the least opposition and give offense to the smallest possible number. Moderation was the keynote of this gathering. These nation builders knew that the Confederacy could not succeed without a broad base of popular support. They knew, too, that even in the deep South public opinion was divided on the wisdom of secession, that many were still resentful or alarmed over the hasty and not always scrupulous manner in which secession had been accomplished, that lingering loyalty to the Union and hope for its eventual restoration existed in many a Southern heart. And finally, they sought a leader who could not only unify sentiment in the cotton kingdom but appeal to the slave states of the upper South, where love of Union and dislike of secession were widespread. The upper South had no taste for extremism; only a respectable moderate could win their support.

The quest for a moderate executive eliminated at least two potential aspirants almost immediately. Pre-eminent among the radical secessionists, and not without full quotas of personal ambition, were William L. Yancey of Alabama and Robert Barnwell Rhett of South Carolina. Both men, Rhett especially, would have welcomed the highest office in a nation they had been trying to create for over a decade, but the Montgomery convention refused to take them seriously. They were agitators, not responsible leaders, their political records barren of accomplishment. In the cotton states as a whole they were without influence, prestige, or a following; even many of his fellow South Carolinians, though often as radical as he, disliked and distrusted Rhett. Over the years the South had listened attentively to its fire-eaters, but it now had need of a statesman, and the fire-eaters simply did not qualify.

The three most prominent and widely discussed candidates at the Montgomery convention were the Georgians: Howell Cobb, Alexander Stephens, and Robert Toombs. All were able, respected men of impressive public record, worthy background, and tried political skill; each was highly receptive. Yet certain political and personal objections weighed against all three.

The massive, moon-faced Cobb, one of the richest slaveowners in the South, had just been named presiding officer of the Montgomery convention by his fellow delegates; his career included five terms in the House of Representatives, one as Governor of Georgia, and the Secretaryship of the Treasury under Buchanan. Cobb was undeniably impressive, but he was unpopular in certain quarters. A lifelong Democrat, his conversion to the idea of secession was fairly recent, and early in the fifties his detestation of the movement had been so strong that he opposed the regular Democratic organization in Georgia to run for governor, successfully, on a Unionist ticket in conjunction with leading Georgia Whigs. Old-line Democrats had never forgiven him this apostasy, and old-line Democrats were too important an element in the deep South to be ignored.

For all his ability, which was considerable, there were too many objections to Alexander Stephens. Admittedly brilliant, this frail, ascetic, emaciated little man was thought to lack the necessary physical vitality and presence demanded by the Confederacy's highest office. Many felt that his brilliance was marred by certain erratic and unpredictable mental qualities. Political objections outweighed the personal: Stephens had not only supported Douglas in the campaign of 1860, but had remained an ardent advocate of Union throughout Georgia's hard-fought secession movement. The Montgomery convention did not want to elect a radical, but they could hardly go to the other extreme and choose a man whose Unionist sympathies had been so pronounced and so recently expressed. Stephens, it was felt, might well use the presidency to bring about a restoration of the Union as quickly as possible. (These suspicions of Stephens's basic loyalty were not misplaced. His subsequent election to the vice-presidency was a blunder, for Alexander Stephens never really believed in the Southern Confederacy, and without resigning his office he would spend most of the next four years in savagely critical and obstructive opposition to the Southern war effort.)

Undoubtedly the most popular of all the Southern leaders was Robert Toombs. An ardent battler and able parliamentarian, good-natured and impetuous and floridly eloquent, highly skilled in the field of public finance, Toombs had served with vigor and distinction in both Houses of Congress. He was a commanding figure, full of vitality and dash, six feet tall and broad-shouldered, with long black hair and compelling dark eyes and lordly manner. There was a frankness about the man that nearly everyone liked; a majority in several of the state delegations at Montgomery were reportedly in favor of his candidacy. But through much of his political career Toombs had been a Whig; in the early fifties, like Cobb, he had been an outspoken Unionist and critic of secession, and in 1861 there were Democrats who continued to hold these things against him. Moreover, rumor had it that Toombs drank too much, and the rumor was so widespread that its factual basis ceased to matter; people believed it, and distrusted him accordingly.

One version of the proceedings at Montgomery, however, suggests that Toombs would have been chosen but for a misunderstanding: Georgia favored him, but four other state delegations who also supported him were led to believe that Georgia preferred Cobb. A unanimous vote for whoever was chosen was deemed essential by all; not wanting Cobb, the other delegations united behind Jefferson Davis, and the surprised Georgians felt obliged to drop Toombs and vote for Davis in the interests of unanimity.

Whether or not this political maneuver, based on dislike of Howell Cobb, played a larger role in the selection of Jefferson Davis than any objective weighing of relative merits, the new nation had ample reason to be content with the choice. Students of the Confederacy will always enjoy speculating as to which of the three strongest candidates—Cobb, Toombs, Davis—would have made the best president. Though each had his failings, all three were highly gifted individuals of proven ability; certainly the South had none better, none even who deserved serious comparison.

On balance, the man from Mississippi seems to have the edge. Davis, alone of the three, combined executive, legislative, and military experience. His grasp of the complex administrative machinery of government, both theoretical and practical, was thoroughly sound—more so, probably, than that of either Cobb or Toombs. The two Georgians were better skilled in the art of politics, a skill which the Confederacy, more shot through with the elements of discord and internal division than was apparent in that hopeful dawn of 1861, would badly need. The suspicion yet lingers that Davis was really better qualified to serve in the capacity he would have preferred anyway, that of commanding general of the Confederate armed forces. But the ingredients that combine to make a successful wartime leader are never precisely measurable, and the parts are less important than the whole. Davis brought to the presidency a strength of character that did much to sustain and ennoble the Southern cause; neither Cobb nor Toombs possessed comparable quotas of patient fortitude, unbending will, single-minded loyalty, or selfless devotion to duty.

The resourceful Cobb may have had ampler funds of practical common sense and quick flexibility, but for all his talents he seems a shallower, softer, and certainly a less commanding figure, cast in less heroic mold. Moreover, Howell Cobb had already demonstrated a knack for making enemies, or at least for inspiring distrust. It was a knack, as the war would show, possessed by nearly all of the South's civilian leaders, Davis included, but Cobb had such a head start in this direction in 1861 that his chances of bringing unity to the war effort appear small.

Toombs stands in a somewhat better light. More attractive personally than Cobb or Davis, with a distinct flair, a refreshing boldness, and a robust good humor that, taken together and properly used, might have fired the Southern imagination and unified its fractious spirit, Robert Toombs would have been a gamble as Confederate president. He lacked Davis's balance and self-control and powers of endurance, and what they said of his instability was apparently true. Sometimes daring to the point of impetuosity, at other times shrewdly cautious (it was Toombs alone who advised against firing on Sumter when Davis consulted his cabinet and made the fateful decision), often erratic despite keen intelligence and common sense, the Georgian had the sort of impulsive, mercurial temperament that could have wrecked the Confederacy within six months or brought it victory within a year, more probably the former. His war record would show more weakness than strength, both as civilian and as military leader, although his patent failure as a subordinate may have stemmed from overweening disappointment at not having gained the highest office; even so, it suggests a spirit that could not adjust to defeat, hence one ill adapted to the demands of war. Davis stands perceptibly taller than the two men from Georgia. Each section was moving into its hour of trial with its ablest leader in command.

Of the two, Lincoln was incomparably the greater man, but Davis's failure over the next four years to keep stride with his counterpart in the Northern White House was a symptom rather than a cause of the collapse of the Southern dream, whose fatal flaw was that it was not one dream but several. Southerners themselves were confused or in disagreement over which dream was the true one. Talent, spirit, courage, and even wisdom were abundant in the Confederacy, but the common principle that might have harnessed them and translated devotion into permanent achievement was utterly lacking. The South truly did not know what it was about. Every idea that motivated these restless folk was a masterpiece of illogic. The vision of a cultured feudal aristocracy based on great landed estates did not coincide with the vision of a pristine Greek democracy based on slavery, and both collided sharply with the spirit of exploitative modern capitalism that had bulldozed the cotton frontier from Carolina to Texas within a single generation and measured its profits in dollars and cents. Most of the would-be aristocrats were self-made entrepreneurs with the instincts of an agrarian Jay Gould; they talked of creating a stable, structured society—and, all too soon, a war government and a disciplined army—out of a people composed of the most fiercely rugged, self-willed individualists on the face of the earth.

They were counterrevolutionaries consciously embarked upon revolution, strict legalists whose every constitutional precept would have to be stretched or broken on the rack of war, defenders of the status quo who had to keep altering it in order to protect it. They were trying to build a modern nation and would soon try to wage something approaching total war on the basis of a devout belief in state sovereignty, local autonomy, and individual liberty. Too provincial to make their new nation the prime recipient of their loyalty, too contentiously democratic to submit to wartime discipline or arbitrary leadership or a strong central government when these alone might have saved them, too full of legal scruple to stretch the rules far enough or fast enough, this ill-coordinated people was united only in possessing (so fully that it nearly saw them through in spite of themselves) the will to fight. And at bottom, they were fighting for their freedom in order to preserve slavery. The wonder is not that Jefferson Davis failed to lead this Hydra-headed dream to victory, but that he kept it alive and more or less functioning for four incredible years.

Precisely two weeks after Davis took the Confederate oath of office in Montgomery, Abraham Lincoln read his inaugural address from the steps of the unfinished Capitol in Washington, and the two men who had been born so close together in the Kentucky backwoods half a century ago were now the rival chief executives of a divided nation. Fifteen years of sectional conflict had resulted in secession; it now remained to determine whether secession would result in civil war. Both sides, as Lincoln was to remark four years hence, deprecated war. But neither side, and neither president, could envision an honorable way of retreating from an impasse that seemed to make war or retreat the only alternatives.

The symbol of this impasse loomed up before the eyes of the people of Charleston with every dawn. A palpable tension hovered ever more closely about the fort and the city on the Carolina coast, and amid all their other duties the executive in Washington and the executive in Montgomery could never forget that a decision about this fort must sooner or later be made by both. Decision could not be deferred indefinitely; even deferment, even inaction, were decisions as laden with consequences as any positive order to advance or fall back. On Sumter lay the issue of peace or war; on Davis and Lincoln lay the issue of Sumter. It was as simple, and as complicated, as that.

The right of slavery and the right of secession: the entire controversy hinged upon these, and the debate was very nearly over. Disagreement over the first, centering in particular on the right of slavery to expand into new areas, had sectionalized American politics until the deep South, unwilling to accept a denial of the first right by a national majority, chose to exercise the second. The argument shifted ground immediately, and disagreement over the second, unless speedily reconciled in favor of one side or the other, would produce war.

Lincoln's major task in his inaugural address was to make explicit his views on this second question. His views on the first had always been consistent, forthright, and unwavering. He had opposed the expansion of slavery without letup since his re-entry into politics in 1854, and on this single item he positively refused to negotiate or compromise during and after the presidential campaign. Shortly after the election he let it be known, as he had in the past, that he and his party had neither the authority nor the intent to molest slavery where it already existed or to interfere in any way with the domestic institutions of the states. When this produced no favorable response, he resumed his policy of avoiding public statements, more convinced than ever that his opponents would twist or ignore anything he might say. In letters and private conversations, however, he repeatedly made clear his determination to do no harm to slavery in the South.

During the Senate debate on the Crittenden compromise he went over the ground once more. On all save the one key item he readily acquiesced. He was willing to enforce the fugitive slave law, uphold the domestic slave trade, and support a constitutional amendment guaranteeing no federal interference with slavery in the states or in the District of Columbia. But he flatly rejected the key Crittenden proposal to permit slavery south of 36°30′ in all federal territories both present and "hereafter acquired." The latter could mean Cuba, or Mexico, or Central America, or Hawaii, all regions that had come within the covetous gaze of Manifest Destiny in recent years. The territorial battle would begin all over again, and within a year the South would start a new agitation "till we shall have to take Cuba as a condition upon which they will stay in the Union." He would consider no project that made room for the expansion of slavery; on this point, he wrote, "hold firm, as with a chain of steel." The party did so, and the Crittenden plan went down to defeat.

By the first of the year the slavery argument had pretty well run its course, and secession became the question of the hour. Absorbed though he was with the task of putting together a cabinet, harassed to the point of exhaustion by the swarm of office seekers that buzzed about his Springfield headquarters, Lincoln kept a careful eye on the course of national politics in those early weeks of 1861. He was sobered but not unduly alarmed by the rapid secession of the Gulf states. Union sentiment in the deep South, he felt, had been submerged but not extinguished, and if given time it would reassert itself. He was much heartened by the strong manifestations of loyalty from the upper South. Secessionist sentiment in those eight states, though present, was clearly in the minority, and under proper handling would remain so. If the national government could avoid both weakness and belligerence, he thought, maintaining its authority without taking aggressive action, the border slave states would adhere to the Union, and the Gulf states, thus isolated, would soon return. He continued, as before, to overestimate the latent strength of unionism in the deep South, and his refusal to compromise on slavery expansion was partly based on his confidence that national ties would prove stronger than sectional, even along the Gulf.

But if worse came to worst—and Lincoln was never so fatuous in his optimism as to overlook this contingency—he was prepared to see the thing through. This did not mean attempting to coerce the seceded states, for any such aggression on the part of the national government would be thrice disastrous: many Northerners would refuse to support it, secession feeling in the Gulf states would be greatly strengthened, and the border states would leave the Union. Instead, seeing it through meant holding firm. It meant enforcing the laws where this could be done without aggressive action, and refusing to recognize secession or the independence of the Confederacy, and retaining those few federal properties in the South that had not already been lost, and defending them if attacked. In other words, Lincoln would fight before he retreated, and the next move, in effect, was up to what Britain's Lord John Russell would sardonically refer to as the self-styled Confederate states.

Lincoln had fully decided upon this policy before he took office, but he did not have to initiate it. He inherited it, full blown, from his predecessor, for after much fumbling and inner agony James Buchanan too had decided that the federal government must never give way to secession, and once committed he had clung to this line with what amounted to Lincolnian firmness. And now on this brisk March afternoon in the nation's capital, morning clouds having given way to sunshine, while flags whipped from their staffs and cavalry patrolled the streets and infantry sharpshooters watched from the roof tops to guard against trouble in this hyperemotional, Southern-oriented town, while a curious throng clustered about the east front of the Capitol, the cranes and scaffolding that festooned its unfinished dome pointing like stiff symbolic fingers at the unfinished nature of the national experiment, Lincoln stood tall on the Capitol steps and read the message that would make his position clear.

Close behind and beside him in the privileged seats were the notables, conspicuous and solemn and thoughtful, their ranks thinned, for the first time in the nation's history, by the absence of leaders from the lower South. At his elbow, nevertheless, were many who had contributed much to the present state of affairs: alert, beetle-browed Seward and pompously handsome Chase, ranking members of Lincoln's new cabinet, each doubtless pondering, ruefully, the turn of events that had made Lincoln the central figure in this program instead of himself; aging, careworn Buchanan; the stooped, wrinkled figure of Chief Justice Taney; Stephen A. Douglas, his body so worn by exertion that it would sustain him but three more months, his spirit indomitable as ever, still tenaciously devoted to Union and compromise.

Lincoln's message was a precise compound of reassurance, determination, and appeal. He repeated all of his promises to the South: the administration would not disturb slavery in the states, it would faithfully enforce the fugitive slave law, it would impose no hindrance to the domestic slave trade. He endorsed the recent proposal of a constitutional amendment forever guaranteeing slavery in the states. (Ironically, the departing Congress in one of its last acts had, with Republican support, passed such a measure and submitted it to the states for ratification. The war intervened, and rewrote this Thirteenth Amendment rather drastically.) The government would not assail the seceded states, Lincoln went on. He would try to enforce the laws, collect the customs, deliver the mails, and maintain the national authority, but never by force. There would be no invasion; no "obnoxious strangers" would be appointed to federal office in districts where hostility to the government made this impractical. He assured the South that all of its rights would be fully protected within the Union, and expressed the hope that time and patience and friendly atmosphere would make possible an adjustment of all points in dispute. His closing appeal to national unity and a restoration of harmony was eloquent and moving, and the tone of the message was, for the most part, conciliatory and mild.

Yet there was, as one observer noted, "a clank of metal in it." On secession Lincoln minced no words. "I hold, that in contemplation of universal law, and of the Constitution, the Union of these states is perpetual. . . . No state, upon its own mere motion, can lawfully get out of the Union, . . . ordinances to that effect are legally void, and . . . acts of violence, within any State or States, against the authority of the United States, are insurrectionary or revolutionary, according to circumstances." By this view, Lincoln continued firmly, "the Union is unbroken; and, to the extent of my ability, I shall take care, as the Constitution itself expressly enjoins upon me, that the laws of the Union shall be faithfully executed in all the States." There followed the modifier to the effect that force and violence would not be used in pursuit of this goal. Nor, on the other hand, would force and violence from another quarter lead to its abandonment: whatever happened, "the power confided to me will be used to hold, occupy and possess the property and places belonging to the government . . ." There would be no invasion, he said, "beyond what may be necessary for these objects"—a clause which, as critics were quick to point out, left the door to this contingency sufficiently ajar. For all its clarity, the address left the future in doubt. The government would respond to events rather than force them, and the "momentous issue of civil war" was explicitly placed in Southern hands, but Lincoln more or less frankly reserved the right to interpret the situation as he saw fit. The South had been told, in no uncertain terms, that secession was wrong, the union perpetual, and the government firmly committed to upholding the national authority. The clank of this metal could be heard all too clearly by the leaders in Montgomery.

The address, read with care in all parts of the country, ranged broadly enough to make any number of interpretations possible, and nearly everyone read into it what his own view of the situation encouraged him to see. Observers in the deep South naturally condemned it as warlike and provocative, one more manifestation of Republican hostility. Response from the border states reflected the divided opinion in that unhappy region, Unionists professing to see hope for peace and restoration while Southern-rights men and secessionists felt that the address looked toward coercion and war. Northern confusion, rampant and growing since the election, was faithfully echoed by the discordant babel that greeted Lincoln's words. Northerners who favored peaceful separation recoiled from his firmness; those who favored making war upon the South despaired at his softness. The majority between these extremes was not of one mind: some hailed the address as a proper mixture of firmness and conciliation, while others thought that it leaned too far in one direction or the other, or that it was too ambiguous to provide the country with a much-needed statement of clear intent.

Lincoln's intent was clear enough; the ambiguity lay in the situation. In principle, the two Presidents were unalterably and outspokenly opposed. One believed in secession and would fight, if necessary, to uphold it; the other refused to recognize secession and would fight, if necessary, to maintain federal authority. But in practice there was room for maneuver, and neither man had fully made up his mind about how his principles might apply to a specific test case—above all to the test case that lay so irre-movably astride the entrance to Charleston harbor. Neither man wanted war, if peace could be had on terms that could be made to fit his definition of the North-South relationship. More im-portant, neither man wanted to be responsible for appearing to *start* a war, since the aggressor would forfeit sympathy and sup-port in all parts of the country.

Urgency was added by the fact that an indefinite continuation of the present stalemate was politically impossible. Sumter was a "point of pride," as Jefferson Davis himself had called it a few weeks before. (The nation had made symbols and points of pride out of every episode in recent years: Kansas had been a symbol, likewise Brooks and Sumner, and Lecompton, and Dred Scott, and John Brown.) So long as Major Anderson and his small band of regulars kept the American flag in view above Fort Sumter, they constituted a visible denial of the Confederacy's vaunted claims to independence. Southern pride would not permit this symbol of Union to remain on their doorstep much longer, and Northern pride would suffer irreparable damage if it were with-drawn without resistance. Lincoln and Davis knew this perfectly. They also knew that Virginia and the other border states would set their policy by the way in which the two governments dealt with Sumter. Both men therefore moved cautiously, even uncer-tainly, but each step led them closer to the denouement which the logic of their respective positions had long since rendered unavoidable.

Lincoln had not been in office twenty-four hours before learn-ing how quickly his inaugural policy must be put to the test. On March 5 he heard that Major Anderson had enough provisions to last for perhaps six more weeks; if additional supplies were not obtained in the interim, he would have to evacuate the fort. Ander-son's message touched off more than three weeks of agonized in-decision, heated debate, and intricate maneuver.

They were trying days for the new President. Besieged by office seekers, totally unfamiliar with the details of his office, surrounded by an ill-assorted cabinet whose members, deliberately chosen to mollify diverse political factions, had little trust for one another and little respect for their chief, too unknown and untried to possess the confidence of the public, Lincoln grasped the controls with a hesitant and uncertain hand. Eager to avoid rash action or hasty judgment, he listened carefully, sought advice, sifted the evidence, and pondered deeply before reaching firm decisions. The sure touch that would steer the nation so handily through the next four years was understandably lacking at first. All men must grow into the presidency. Lincoln always believed in thought before action, and nothing in the nation's experience, or in his own, offered any sort of guide to the present crisis.

Near the end of March, after much wavering, Lincoln decided to send a relief expedition to Fort Sumter. Both Major Anderson and Winfield Scott, the ponderous, rheumatic commanding general of the United States Army, had made prohibitive estimates of the military force required to storm the Confederate batteries and relieve the fort. Incredulous, Lincoln sought other professional opinion and agreed that a supply ship with armed naval escort could probably run the batteries successfully. A majority of the cabinet, though at first opposed to sending an expedition, gradually swung to the view that relief was necessary; the only alternative was evacuation, and the effects of such a move on Northern public opinion would be disastrous.

Seward, the new Secretary of State, was acting on two assumptions which added materially to Lincoln's burden in these agonized first weeks. Seward believed, first, that Fort Sumter should be evacuated at once, on the theory that Southern Unionism would reassert itself if the North showed its lack of hostile intent by avoiding any appearance of force or coercion. He pulled every wire he could to persuade Lincoln of the need to abandon the fort, and at the same time he managed to convince the three Confederate commissioners, whom Davis had sent to Washington by way of establishing diplomatic relations between the two countries, that the administration would in fact withdraw Major Anderson very soon. Seward's other assumption, based on the conviction that leadership and responsibility in the new administration should be taken by the best qualified person, was that he and not Lincoln ought to be in charge of policy. It took the President a few weeks to disabuse Seward of this notion and curb the Secretary's tendency to act as if it were true. (Once persuaded, Seward became a loyal subordinate. "Lincoln is the best of us," he confided admiringly to his wife a short time later.) But on the Sumter question, he worked at cross-purposes with Lincoln right up to the moment of decision.

Before making up his mind Lincoln consulted with spokesmen from Virginia, whose convention had deliberately remained in session until the administration's policy toward the South became known. The large Unionist majority in this convention would not hold together if the national government attempted to coerce the seceded states, and Lincoln, eager to retain the loyalty of the upper South, explored the possibility of a *quid pro quo*: he would evacuate Sumter if the Virginia convention would adjourn, thus cementing the state's loyalty to the Union. (Most of the border states, he knew, would follow Virginia's lead.) But the convention chose to stay assembled, pointedly leaving the door to secession open.

Meanwhile, leading Republicans in the Senate began to threaten impeachment—they particularly had Seward in mind—if federal authority were not maintained. As time passed without positive action, rumblings of dissatisfaction and impatience with the government's lack of policy sounded across the North. Momentarily prostrated with anguish and strain, Lincoln went over the matter once more and directed that a relief expedition be made ready to sail on order. Once persuaded that relief of Sumter was militarily feasible, he could not honor his commitment to "hold, occupy and possess" federal properties without making the attempt.

On April 6, Anderson having written that he had about one week's supply of provisions remaining, the President ordered the relief ships to sail. He so informed Anderson, also notifying Governor Pickens of South Carolina and General Beauregard, commander of the Confederate forces in Charleston, that a relief expedition was on its way to Sumter. In these latter messages Lincoln took pains to make it clear that only food and supplies would be landed and no force used unless the South offered resistance to the expedition. It was adroitly done: Lincoln could argue that his intent was not aggressive, and that his sole purpose was to enable the existing garrison to maintain itself.

Receiving Lincoln's messages on April 8, Pickens and Beauregard promptly relayed the news to Montgomery, and the agony of decision passed to Davis and his advisers. The Southern leaders were surprised and resentful. Thanks to Seward, who for weeks had been privately assuring the Confederate commissioners in Washington that Sumter would be evacuated and no relief sent, the Confederate government felt that Lincoln was acting in bad faith. Davis saw little choice in the matter. To take no action now would be to admit the permanence of federal authority in Charleston harbor, virtually confessing to the world that the Confederacy was not truly independent. All the members of his cabinet save Toombs urged Davis to order an attack on Sumter before the expedition arrived. Southern ardor was chafing at the bit anyway, and failure to meet this challenge threatened to undermine public confidence in the government and weaken Southern resolve. There was always the danger, too, that hotheads in South Carolina would act on their own if no order came from Montgomery.

In Davis's legalistic view, the North was the aggressor—as it always had been. "The order for the sailing of the fleet," he announced, "was a declaration of war. The responsibility is on their shoulders, not ours. . . . A deadly weapon has been aimed at our heart. Only a fool would wait until the shot has been fired. The assault has been made. It is of no importance who shall strike the first blow or fire the first gun." Lincoln's claim that replenishing Sumter's food supply was not an aggressive act was unacceptable to the Confederacy. To Davis, refusal to withdraw the Sumter garrison was itself an aggressive act, and the South was justified in taking defensive measures. Beauregard was duly instructed to demand the surrender of Sumter, and to open fire and reduce the fort if the demand were not met.

Beauregard delivered this ultimatum to Anderson on April 11. The unhappy Kentuckian refused to surrender, adding, however, that if the South would postpone the bombardment a few days his food would be gone, and evacuation could take place without a shot being fired. This was relayed to Montgomery. Davis, through his Secretary of War, directed Beauregard to get a definite commitment from Anderson. "Do not desire needlessly to bombard Fort Sumter," the message ran. "If Major Anderson will state the time at which . . . he will evacuate . . . you are authorized thus to avoid the effusion of blood. If this, or its equivalent, is refused, reduce the fort."

Anderson received the second Confederate message shortly after midnight on April 12. He replied three hours later, after consulting with his officers, that he would evacuate Sumter by noon of the 15th. In the meantime, Anderson said, he would not open fire unless attacked, but he added an ominous proviso that made his promise dependent upon not receiving "controlling instructions . . . or additional supplies." Since everyone, including Anderson, knew that the relief expedition would arrive well before the fifteenth—was due, in fact, later that very morning—this sounded like equivocation; additional supplies and controlling instructions were so imminent as to make the evacuation promise meaningless. The Confederate emissaries consulted among themselves, concluded that Anderson's reply was unsatisfactory, told him so, and on their own discretion informed him that the Southern batteries would open fire in an hour. The Confederate government would assuredly have agreed with this decision; they were committed to attack Sumter before permitting the relief expedition to get through.

When the Confederate emissaries returned from Sumter they issued orders for the bombardment. For days the troops and artillerists in Beauregard's command had been ready at their posts. At 4:30 in the morning of April 12, the signal gun—a ten-inch mortar in one of the Confederate emplacements along the harbor shore—flashed and roared. Fuse sputtering, the shell described a high arc, curved downward, and exploded in flame above Fort Sumter. A few seconds later the primed batteries about the lower harbor opened fire in crash after crash. Some time later the guns of Sumter thundered in response. Watchers on the Charleston rooftops stared transfixed at the bright flashes that sparked and stabbed in the dawn about the harbor entrance.

It all came back to the two Presidents, neither of whom could have avoided some such violent resolution of the deadlock without sacrificing a vital principle. The South could not afford to let the American flag remain over Charleston harbor ; the North could not afford to haul it down. Both men had felt this way from the beginning of the secession crisis, even as their views on slavery expansion had destroyed the basis for compromise and brought the secession crisis to a head. Lincoln and Davis had never retreated from principle. War was genuinely distasteful to both, but abandonment of their profoundest convictions was more so. Notwithstanding that each section of the country betrayed confusion and lack of consensus, millions of Americans in the South accepted Davis's principles—the good of slavery and the right of secession—and millions in the North accepted Lincoln's—the evil of slavery and the wrong of secession—with sufficient enthusiasm to explain the course and outcome of the sectional controversy. They were led by men who embodied these principles perfectly, whose rise to leadership was based upon commitments which a majority of Americans were willing to endorse. Now they had their war, and the true meaning of the American experiment, viewed so differently on two vital points by these two men, would be tested, as their unbending refusal to give way had in effect required that it be tested, by force of arms.

[I N D E X]

[A B O U T   T H E   A U T H O R S]

Bruce Catton, our most widely read Civil War historian, was born in 1899 in a small town on Lake Michigan. After serving in the Navy during World War I he graduated from Oberlin College. From 1920 to 1929 he worked for a variety of newspapers around the country, after which he had a syndicated column until the war intervened. During the war Mr. Catton served as Director of Information for the War Production Board, and after the war stayed with the Federal Government for about a year and a half as Director of Information for the Department of Commerce. It was while he was in Washington that he began his series of Civil War books, the first being *Mr. Lincoln's Army*. Mr. Catton is now senior editor of *American Heritage Magazine*.

William Catton was born in Cleveland, Ohio and raised there and in Washington, D.C. He served in the Army in World War II, winding up with our occupation troops in Tokyo. After leaving the Army, he attended the University of Maryland where he received his A.B. and M.A., from there going to Northwestern to take a Ph.D. in history. He has been an instructor of history at the University of Maryland, at Princeton, and at Middlebury, where he is now Professor. This is his first published book.